FEAR
UP
HARSH

FEAR UP HARSH

AN ARMY INTERROGATOR'S DARK JOURNEY THROUGH IRAQ

TONY LAGOURANIS
and ALLEN MIKAELIAN

NAL
CALIBER

NAL Caliber
Published by New American Library, a division of
Penguin Group (USA) Inc., 375 Hudson Street,
New York, New York 10014, USA
Penguin Group (Canada), 90 Eglinton Avenue East, Suite 700, Toronto,
Ontario M4P 2Y3, Canada (a division of Pearson Penguin Canada Inc.)
Penguin Books Ltd., 80 Strand, London WC2R 0RL, England
Penguin Ireland, 25 St. Stephen's Green, Dublin 2,
Ireland (a division of Penguin Books Ltd.)
Penguin Group (Australia), 250 Camberwell Road, Camberwell, Victoria 3124,
Australia (a division of Pearson Australia Group Pty. Ltd.)
Penguin Books India Pvt. Ltd., 11 Community Centre, Panchsheel Park,
New Delhi - 110 017, India
Penguin Group (NZ), 67 Apollo Drive, Rosedale, North Shore,
Auckland 1311, New Zealand (a division of Pearson New Zealand Ltd.)
Penguin Books (South Africa) (Pty.) Ltd., 24 Sturdee Avenue,
Rosebank, Johannesburg 2196, South Africa

Penguin Books Ltd., Registered Offices:
80 Strand, London WC2R 0RL, England

First published by NAL Caliber, an imprint of New American Library,
a division of Penguin Group (USA) Inc.

First Printing, June 2007
10 9 8 7 6 5 4 3 2 1

NAL CALIBER and the "C" logo are trademarks of Penguin Group (USA) Inc.

LIBRARY OF CONGRESS CATALOGING-IN-PUBLICATION DATA

Lagouranis, Tony.
    Fear up harsh: an Army interrogator's dark journey through Iraq/Tony Lagouranis and Allen Mikaelian.
      p.   cm.
    ISBN: 978-0-451-22112-4
    1. Lagouranis, Tony.   2. Abu Ghraib Prison.   3. Iraq War. 2003—Personal narratives, American.
4. Military interrogation—United States.   5. Military interrogation—Iraq.   6. Iraq War, 2003—Prisoners
and prisons, American.   7. Iraq War, 2003—Atrocities.   8. Torture—Iraq.   I. Mikaelian, Allen.
II. Title.

    DS79.76.L34A3   2007
    956.7044'37—dc22   2006101929

Set in Electra LH
Designed by Ginger Legato

Printed in the United States of America

This book is dedicated to my uncle Jay Mominee,
the greatest American I ever met.

CONTENTS

Remember those who are in prison,
as though you were in prison with them;
those who are being tortured,
as though you yourselves were being tortured.

—Hebrews 13:3

A NOTE ON THE TEXT

Great care has been taken to protect the identities of persons in this book. Real names are used only for those who are already well known to the public, and identifying information of all nonpublic figures has been altered.

This has been done to preserve the privacy of people I served with, to protect the lives and security of Iraqis I interrogated, and to avoid revealing classified information.

The manuscript of this book was voluntarily submitted to the Department of Defense to ensure that no classified information was inadvertently revealed. The views in this manuscript are solely those of Tony Lagouranis, however, and do not necessarily reflect the views of the United States Army or Department of Defense.

FEAR
UP
HARSH

INTRODUCTION

should never be mistaken for a hero. But as my unit completed a year in Iraq, as we waited in Kuwait to deploy back to the United States, our officers and leaders called us heroes all the time. "You did a great job. You saved lives. You should be proud." The disgrace of Abu Ghraib was hanging over all of our heads, and the entire U.S. project in Iraq was starting to look like an utter failure. Our leaders were trying to keep morale from sliding into a pit. They really overdid it with their praise and didn't do much to change how we felt about the mission. Finally, one of our senior NCOs went completely over the top and, in an honest moment, broke some of the tension by making fun of himself and those who called us heroes. As he led us on a ruck march, he shouted, "You are the lions of the desert! You are the scorpions of Abu Ghraib!"

I was an interrogator with a military intelligence battalion. When they said we saved lives, they meant it was through gathering intelligence. When they said I did a great job, they meant in the interrogation booth, breaking prisoners. When they said those things, I didn't know what they were talking about.

Leaving Iraq, I couldn't get over the feeling that I had accomplished almost nothing; I had not helped advance our goal of rebuilding the country, and, in fact, I had done horrible things that probably turned Iraqis against us. When they called me a hero, I bristled.

We landed at JFK on our way back to Fort Gordon, Georgia. We had a long layover, but were given very specific reminders that we were still on duty and still under the prevailing orders of a combat zone—namely, no booze.

A buddy and I didn't even think about obeying that order. We went to the bar farthest from our gate, asked the bartender to put some whisky in coffee cups, and sat in a booth, trying to fade into a corner despite the fact that our uniforms screamed at everyone who walked by. Most tried to avert their eyes. We were obviously back from Iraq and they didn't know what to say. A few of them approached and thanked us awkwardly for our service.

Soon, a very happy but somewhat confused man joined us. He said he was dropping off his wife and heard that a plane loaded with soldiers back from Iraq had landed here. He expected the bar to be full of uniforms, but there was only us. He insisted on buying us drinks—that's why he came. He was dying to buy a soldier a drink. He called us heroes.

I wanted to change the topic before he started asking me uncomfortable questions about Iraq. "So, what do you do?" I asked. Turns out he was a firefighter, and yes, he'd been there, Ground Zero. He said that most of the guys in his Brooklyn fire station were killed in the collapse of the towers.

Here was an actual hero, someone who regularly made a difference and undoubtedly saved lives. I almost couldn't bear to sit in his presence, let alone allow him to buy me whisky, and it wasn't just the comparison between him and me that I couldn't stand. It was a reminder that some folks in Washington had taken 9/11—which to this man was a very personal tragedy—and used it to justify sending me, and others like me, to Iraq. This man's government had betrayed him immensely.

It was hard for me to think of myself as a hero when I remembered Iraqis like Alim, a fifteen-year-old boy who cooperated with us, gave us information we could use, and then was rewarded with a trip to Abu Ghraib and an indefinite detention. Or another fifteen-year-old who came to me with his face battered and bruised, and had no idea why we were holding him captive. Or the old, feeble men who could barely move after I was done with them.

It's hard to be a hero when your job is to deal with prisoners whom you hold absolute power over. Still, when people hear I was an interrogator, they get very interested. It seems like many of them think of my job as a kind of duel, a face-to-face match, a test of power and a test of wills. When I was in training, I thought of interrogation like that, and I thought I'd have a chance to save lives, even if I never rose to the level of "hero."

So I went into my first interrogations with gusto, and this enthusiasm came out in the form of Fear Up Harsh, a specific "approach" to a prisoner that attempts to raise his level of fear, and does so in a harsh manner—lots of yelling, maybe some physical intimidation, like slamming a fist on the table or flinging furniture around. It established me as the powerful one in the room; if it was a duel, I won. But did I get intelligence? Save lives? Protect America? I don't believe I did any of those things.

PART I

ABU GHRAIB
JANUARY TO FEBRUARY 2004

*In prison, of course, there was a great deal he did not see
and did not want to see; he lived as it were with downcast eyes.
It was loathsome and unbearable for him to look.*

—Fyodor Dostoyevsky, *Crime and Punishment*

CHAPTER 1

Crossing Over

We'd been at our jumping-off point in Kuwait for three weeks, waiting and stewing in unbearable anticipation while the desert rain poured into our tents, gear, and boots, turning dust into mud and leaving a stench of mildew on everything else. A thick orange mold was growing on the plywood floors of our tents. We could take a running start and slide across it. On top of that, we were freezing. Sitting on this particular starting block for so long was agonizing, but there was only one way out of this extended, uncomfortable crouch, and that was over the berm, into Iraq.

When we finally left, we moved fast and the relief was tangible. Several convoys of Humvees carrying our entire battalion rushed toward the border. I was five vehicles back from the lead, riding as a passenger while holding a Vietnam-era, but dependable, M60 machine gun and carrying a 9mm pistol. We weren't in armored vehicles, but we had makeshift quarter-inch steel plates for doors and sandbags lining the floors to protect against improvised explosive devices (or IEDs, as I think most readers know by now). The driver, a counterintelligence agent, was noticeably wound up and very, very intense, his eyes wide and his knuckles white. The group of convoys pushed forward, and very suddenly we crossed into Iraq.

Everyone experienced this differently, but it was a huge event for all; a yearlong chapter of our lives that we would remember forever started *now*. I felt a mix of fear, relief, excitement, and power, but above all, a kind of awe. I remember once, years before, on a flight to Tunis, looking out the window and seeing Africa for the first time. This place that I had imagined, had heard and read about, but for me existed only as a kind of legend, was *there*. Actually before me. Now I was in a combat zone. For three years, I had done little else but prepare for being here. *Wow, okay, this is it. Now it's real.*

To be honest, this was why I'd joined the army back in June 2001. I hadn't exactly hoped that we'd go to war, but I was looking for that feeling I had while crossing the border. I'd always been looking for that feeling, in one form or another. After growing up in Ohio and then in midtown Manhattan, I left New York after high school graduation and found that feeling by shedding my belongings and hitchhiking cross-country. Later, I found it by giving up everything and moving to Tunisia with nothing but $500 in my pocket. I was looking for situations where I was not in control, and where I had no way of knowing what to expect. I'd be moving through life at a regular pace on familiar paths, and suddenly encounter a wall protecting me from a swirling unknown. I could peer over that wall, and see what was on the other side, or I could throw myself over, cede control to fate, and totally immerse myself in that abyss. That's what I usually did. It was impulsive and maybe irresponsible, but my times in the abyss are those when I have felt most alive.

So in this way, the army and I were a perfect match. What other institution, religious cults aside, allows you to totally cede control? How many other situations offer fewer opportunities for control over your fate than a war zone? In other ways, however, the army and I were totally incompatible, and that's probably why it took us so long to find each other. I didn't enlist until I was thirty-one.

When explaining this decision to fearful family members and confused friends, I focused on the fringe benefits, the most important being the army's promise to teach me Arabic. This was no small part of my desire to enlist. For years, I had wanted to learn this language; for years, each attempt had been frustrated.

I had harbored a long-standing love of ancient languages, dating back to my study of ancient Greek in college. Strangely, it was a required course at the idiosyncratic school I attended, and I was surprised to find that I loved it. Maybe being Greek-American was the first thing that drew me in, but later I found as much pleasure translating the New Testament as I did translating Plato. I wanted more, and turned to Hebrew—which was not a credited course at this college. I had to do this in my spare time. It only worked because I was determined and because I was good at it.

Whether translating Greek or Hebrew, I felt a direct connection to the text—and even to the author. There is no comparison between reading a translation and reading the original. In one case you have to deal with an intermediary who guides you through the book's events and ideas according to his own interpretations. In the other, the text opens up to you directly and profoundly. In time, what comes through the words and symbols is more than the text itself. I started to glimpse the very roots of ancient cultures and religions.

Biblical Hebrew was easy, especially compared to ancient Greek. Now, in my last year of college, in 1997, I wanted to learn Arabic, the language of the third and newest great Western monotheistic religion. I wanted to read the Koran, but I didn't want to stop there. Anyone could see that the Middle East and Islam were increasingly driving world events. I could see this on TV and read about it in the papers, but this amounted to taking the word of an intermediary. I was tired of having complex issues explained to me by cultural translators. I wanted the same thing I had with the Bible and the Torah— direct access.

I didn't fully understand what I was getting myself into. Arabic was also not a course at this particular college, and proved impossible to learn on my own, even with the help of a Lebanese friend. Arabic has a unique structure, an unfamiliar internal logic, and an expansive vocabulary. I needed prolonged, intensive study under real experts. The army offered the courses I wanted, and all I had to do was work for them for a few years.

Time seemed to slow down as the convoy crossed the border, but then we suddenly lurched ahead, skipping along much faster than before. We were moving at a barely safe speed. My partner strained to focus on his driving while I constantly scanned the landscape for any potential threats. I kept my ear on the radio handset, which was always alive with chatter. Several soldiers had heard that one could detonate a radio-controlled roadside bomb before the convoy was dangerously close to it by clicking the handset's "talk" switch off and on. So the snapping sound that resulted was constant, interrupted only by warnings of people on the bridge ahead, farmers working in the fields, kids playing, or especially someone carrying a propane tank. We got so many panicked warnings about propane tanks that our commander came on the radio to explain to us that people actually used them for fuel.

I didn't know the driver well. He was a sergeant named Chuck from another company in the battalion. He was always extremely serious, to the point of being annoying. He was one of those guys who seemed to have absorbed every media cliché about the military and made it his own. Nothing ever cracked his jaw-clenching intensity. There was never any hint of any internal feelings, thoughts, or doubts. I found him sadly predictable.

But now, with every movement or irregular bump on the road a potential threat, and with my life in his hands, I appreciated his intensity more than I thought possible. It didn't matter to me now who he was, what he was thinking, or if he even had a soul, so long as he stayed focused, intense, and on the road. Much later, Chuck was sent home after being blasted by shrapnel from a mortar in Baghdad.

The general emptiness of the desert only served to highlight the potential threats, which increased the radio chatter. Whatever it was they were talking about, I'd try to get a glimpse myself, and maybe raise the barrel of my M60 a little higher when it came into view. We were all scared, tense, and feeling extremely vulnerable. Then we passed an IED and our tension increased considerably. Our entire convoy unknowingly passed this bomb, but for some reason, which I will never know, it did not detonate. A soldier in a convoy behind ours finally noticed it, his convoy stopped, and they safely blew it up. Even though we were far up the road, I could hear it—the first explosion I heard in Iraq. The radio crackled even more, issuing repeated warnings about one mundane roadside object after another.

My army recruiter, Sergeant Marquez, had told me that life in army intelligence would be no different from getting up and going to work in an office. I didn't believe him, and I didn't want to. I was sick of reporting daily to a white-collar job. Why join the army if there wasn't at least a little adventure?

I was a drifter before college. When I was nineteen years old, I hitch-hiked to Santa Fe, New Mexico, to visit a friend, and discovered an odd school where, as I mentioned before, ancient Greek was a required course. In Greek and in other classes, this school's approach was to allow us direct access to the classics. No textbooks, no lectures, and therefore no intermediaries. It seemed just right for me, but it wasn't something my parents were able to pay for. It took me several years to save up and become old enough to be considered an "independent student," eligible for increased financial aid. So I was an old man compared to my classmates, but that didn't necessarily translate into being more responsible. Many of my classmates figured out ways to turn their esoteric education into paying jobs. After graduation, I went back to drifting.

Still wanting to learn Arabic (and still looking for a defining experience), I bought a ticket to Tunisia in 1999 and left with $500 in my pocket. My plan was to live there, learn Arabic, try to earn a little money, and then travel in the Middle East. Tunisia was totally unfamiliar to me, which made me even more eager to dive in. I loved the people, the French-influenced architecture, and the landscape that reminded me of the desert outside Santa Fe. But my plans failed totally. Most Tunisians spoke French to foreigners, giving me little chance to learn Arabic. My money ran out, and I came back after four months with little gained but a bit more life experience.

My lesson unlearned, a year later I roped a friend into going back with me to try to start a business importing olive oil. This was a crazy idea, but it might have worked if not for a lack of capital. The little money I'd saved in my time back in the United States evaporated in the North African desert. I came home broke again. I started substitute teaching and waiting tables in suburban Chicago.

This entire time, I was avoiding student loan payments or paying the minimum, but this was untenable. Since I had so few resources when I went to college, my debt was monumental. I had no chance of even keeping up with the interest on my meager earnings. I ultimately got a job in a customs brokerage firm through a friend. The work was mind-numbing and the environment was Dilbertesque. It pained me to be there, but it was hard to imagine how I could get a better-paying job. I hated this, because the only reason money was important to me was because of those loans. I really wanted to be back in school.

My army recruiter had no trouble selling me his goods. He really didn't have to lie as much as he did. All he had to tell me was what I already had figured out on my own: in the army, I could learn Arabic and erase my loans at the same time. It was perfect. Plus, that short stint in the white-collar world had triggered the early onset of a midlife crisis. I was looking forward to running around in boot camp, getting in shape, shooting at targets, acting young. My recruiter didn't have to point out that we weren't at war, and we were unlikely to go to war—I read the papers. I couldn't see any real threats on the horizon. In early 2001, who could? It was such a hazy, peaceful world. It was just a little over a decade after we stood down from the Cold War, and already war itself, on any scale that made a difference, seemed like such an abstraction.

That was a little disappointing. To be uncomfortably honest, there was something attractive about going to war. I didn't admit that to anyone, and tried not to think about it. The big question of how I would do in combat was the same that must occur to everyone who joins the military. But I also recognized that war was something I longed to see. If I wanted to be in places where I was not in control, what more could I ask for? The swirling chaos of a combat zone was a place stripped of all rationality. The famous first word of the war poem the *Iliad*—μηνιν (*menin*)—is almost always translated as "rage" or "wrath." But it could just as easily be translated as "madness."

Morally, I was disturbed by war, even as I signed the paperwork that would ultimately put me in the middle of one. But at the same time, I felt drawn to war, despite its promise of horror and inevitable brutality. In this instinct, I wasn't alone. Many took it much further than I did. Before we crossed over the berm that separates Iraq from Kuwait, I talked to other soldiers who were looking forward to combat. Even though President Bush had declared the end of major combat operations a full nine months before, we had a strong contingent of bloodthirsty eighteen- to twenty-year-olds who wanted nothing more than to get into a firefight and finally "kill some terrorists." I found this very creepy, but I could understand where it was coming from.

I was also excited about the mission. I would finally get a chance to use the skills I'd been developing for three years. That included combat skills, but also interrogation, and, most important, my hard-won Arabic language abilities. Finally, I was in an Arabic-speaking Middle Eastern country, with the chance to fully communicate with the people who lived there, no intermediary necessary.

My first contact with Iraqis was on the second day of our convoy, as we pulled security while a squad changed a tire on a disabled Humvee. I didn't get a chance to use my language skills because I was too busy training my machine gun barrel on anyone who came close.

We were near our final destination when the tire blew. We knew—or thought we knew—this area through our research. As a military intelligence battalion, we paid a little more attention than other units to reports from the army and media, and what we read put us on edge. Two helicopters shot down in November, a hundred thousand protesters in Baghdad days before, suicide car bombs across the country, a rocket attack that nearly killed Paul Wolfowitz, a mounting U.S. death toll that had just crossed the five hundred mark, and a CIA warning that Iraq was heading for civil war.

We were on a small overpass with farms on both sides of us. Pickups and cars moved past us and below us and children played close by. The kids approached to give us the thumbs-up and see if we would give them candy or an MRE (Meals Ready to Eat).

It took us way too long to change that tire. We didn't carry a spare and had to wait for another element of our battalion to bring one to us. We were completely exposed and the minutes dragged. The radio, which had felt like my lifeline for the last two days, seemed to have taken on a personality of its own—that of an overwrought Cassandra. Nothing moved outside of our perimeter without being reported on the radio.

Iraqis passed us on the road slowly and patiently. We kept our guns trained on them as they moved through. This was our first close-up look at these people, and it was not a friendly exchange. Their stares were full of wonder at why they were under our guns, mixed in with a bit of disgust at our overreactions. Soon, adults pulled their children inside their houses, with backward glances at us that spoke volumes. But their actions just made us more worried—were the kids being called in because we were about to be attacked? Another ratcheting of tension moved in a wave down the convoy.

We were terribly green, and I would laugh now at our intensity if we hadn't put such fear into this little corner of Iraq. We didn't know that we had little cause to be so aggressively defensive. The guerrillas don't attack you when you're standing guard, out of the vehicles, ready for them. They attack when you aren't ready. It wasn't necessary, looking back, to point a gun at every Iraqi who came close. A normal level of vigilance would have gotten us through.

In this moment, and almost all others that followed, force protection was our number-one priority. Everywhere I went, Americans were hunkered down and on alert, quick to point a gun at an Iraqi, quick to use it. Our primary preoccupation was not with rebuilding the country, but with keeping danger at bay; not with providing security for Iraqis, but with making sure that we were safe inside our bubble. I saw this with my own eyes, heard other soldiers either admit it or complain about it, and got clear messages from commanders that creating a tight and safe little perimeter, as opposed to creating a safe Iraq, was paramount. This was our de facto mission and it was absolutely ridiculous. Why go into a dangerous neighborhood when the only thing you intend to fight for is your own safety? What, really, could be more absurd?

I was against the invasion from the start. I'm sure we went in for the wrong reasons and probably did it in the wrong way. I think the reader should know that. Certainly everyone I served with in the army knew that, yet I caught hell from some of my fellow soldiers every time I opened my mouth in protest. But sitting on the border, ready to cross into Iraq, or sitting in my Humvee on the drive up, I had nothing to be against. The invasion was over. There were no more arguments about WMD or about a connection between Saddam Hussein and al-Qaeda. The only possible reason for us to be in this desert was to protect Iraqis from a growing insurgency. To this mission—rooting out the bad guys, building democracy—I was totally committed. I wanted us to succeed in the best way possible, which meant creating a safe and democratic Iraq for Iraqis, and then getting the hell out.

※　※　※

The tire back on the Humvee, we snaked north and made our way west of Baghdad, to our final destination. We'd researched this place heavily. The base that was to be our new home was in the middle of a town full of Sunnis and got hit by mortar fire almost every day. Yet, our battalion commander told us, the road between Baghdad International Airport and the base that would be our new home was wide and safe. Not so. It turned out to be, for American military, one of the most dangerous places in the country.

There would be little to no contact with the people of this town while we lived here, except for the mortars they lobbed, the rockets they fired, and the potshots they took at us. We gingerly made our way to our base, which was blissfully surrounded by a very high wall. It was a place that none of us had ever heard of before, but it was a place that all Iraqis knew, at least by reputation. The soldiers at the gates waved us through quickly, and we disappeared behind the walls of Abu Ghraib.

CHAPTER 2

The Arab Mind

"Something very bad happened here," the colonel standing before us said. This, the opening statement of our first briefing at Abu Ghraib, got my attention. We were assembled in a cinder-block building, still recovering from the mad rush from the border. It had recently rained. There was mud everywhere. I never thought I would see so much mud in the desert.

"I can't tell you what happened, but you will hear about it in the news. Don't ask anyone about it. Don't talk about it with anyone here." Now I was very curious. He hinted that it involved guards. Had someone killed a prisoner? Another guard? This seemed *very* serious. I waited for the next shoe to drop—for the order to report anything suspicious or out of place. Instead, he said, somewhat defensively, "We're not doing anything wrong." I thought, *That's it?* And in fact that was it.

This is what we didn't know: just days before we arrived, a young specialist handed over a CD of photos to the army's Criminal Investigation Division (CID), setting off an investigation that would, months later, leak into public view. The photos were of guards beating prisoners, sexually humiliating them, and forcing one to stand, sandbag over his head, or face electrocution. We were standing on the edge of a historical moment and one of the biggest shit storms to hit Americans in Iraq, and none of us had any idea.

The colonel moved quickly to discuss the prison's layout, population, and rules as my mind drifted, preoccupied with thoughts of what might have happened and how I could find out. I didn't start paying attention again until the colonel introduced a young and eager major, an army psychiatrist who'd take us through the next topic: "The Arab Mind." Perfect. What could be more useful to an interrogator than a map of the minds we would soon try to penetrate? *This,* I thought, *should be interesting.*

Major Morgan started his lecture by admitting that he didn't know any Arabs, and had little contact with them. He assured us, however, that he had read a few books on the subject. This was unsurprising. The army often gave us trainers who had no experience in the topic they were covering. Most of our interrogation instructors had never interrogated a prisoner, just as our combat trainers had no experience in combat. There was still a chance to learn something here, I told myself, though it was odd that someone stationed in the middle of Iraq and charged with lecturing on the Arab mind had not taken the time to get to know a few Arabs.

We kicked things off with a few items of cultural sensitivity. *Don't show an Arab the sole of your foot, or point with your foot, or touch them with your foot. Don't humiliate a man in public. Men should not touch Arab women—and female soldiers should avoid touching Arab men. Arabs like to exchange pleasantries before getting down to business—ask about their families.* I considered the absurdity of doing this in an interrogation, as our lecturer moved ever more deeply into the Arab mind.

Arabs, apparently, *can't create a timeline. They don't think linearly or rationally. They have a different relationship with truth than we do. They prefer the beautiful to the true. They rely on metaphor instead of facts. They think through association, not logic or reason.* Okay, so the people who invented algebra can't think logically? That was news to me.

I started to fade out again, but there were some things that directly pertained to my future interrogations: *Lying is not taboo or dishonorable to Arabs.* This seemed to relate to that different relationship with truth they have. *So you can't trap them in a contradiction or force them to admit they're lying. They'll consider you impolite and uncultured.* I rolled my eyes and looked around the room to share my dismay with others. But most were nodding in understanding and agreement. Very few of us recognized this as racist bullshit.

Our instructor wasn't relying on a very large body of research to produce these "facts." He essentially borrowed everything he said from a single book, *The Arab Mind* by Raphael Patai, a fascinating example of how romanticism and racism can coexist in a single psyche. Published in 1973, the book is, despite whatever faults it may have, remarkably straightforward. While Patai claims to love the Arabs, he does not shy away from pointing out their supposed cultural failings—on almost every single page.

Perhaps there are many subtle and important messages in this book that deserve to be debated, but these are by and large lost on its current readership. Patai was ultimately savaged in academic circles, and especially by Edward Said, but was embraced with wide arms by the U.S. military and policy-makers struggling to understand the Middle East.[1] I saw multiple examples of officers and interrogators reading or referring to this book as a definitive guide, and interpreting its sweeping statements as practical advice.

The central problem with *The Arab Mind*, and with the lecture we got, was with the way they both set up the Arabs as distant from and alien to the "Western mind." Nothing about the Arab mind, it seems, can be understood unless it is compared to the Western mind. We reason—they tell stories. We use facts—they use metaphors. And so on. There was no attempt to understand Arabs on their own terms. It was strictly us versus them. And so, while the intention of the lecture was to help us appreciate this alien culture and work with it, the effect it had was to reinforce prejudice and give many soldiers an excuse to give up on ever understanding or improving Iraqi society. *That's just the way they are. Nothing we can do about it.*

Patai and the lecturer both dwelled quite a bit on the Arabs' supposed fatalism. Soldiers everywhere believed they saw this summed up by Iraqis' constant use of *inshallah*—usually translated as "God willing" but literally meaning "may God establish it." Even Americans who spoke no Arabic were well familiar with *inshallah*. We heard it as a stock response to anything that might happen in the future. Will you do as you promised? *Inshallah.* Will

---

[1] Besides my own experience with this, others have noted the military's obsession with this book. See Seymour M. Hersh, *Chain of Command: The Road from 9/11 to Abu Ghraib*, 1st ed. (New York: HarperCollins, 2004), pp. 38–39.

you be here tomorrow? *Inshallah*. Will a free and democratic Iraq arise from the ashes of this invasion and insurgency? *Inshallah*.

This became a running joke among soldiers—a joke with a sharp edge, vocalized repeatedly to me as: *These people can't do anything for themselves. They just wait for God to do it for them.* The American mind, with its built-in bootstrapism, rebelled against the notion of such indefinite answers and the inclusion of a higher authority in the course of the future. I had a hard time explaining that there was more to it than pure fatalism. Sure, submitting to God is a central part of Islam (even a legitimate translation of the word "Islam" itself), but there were other reasons for the use of *inshallah*. It is an actual substitute for the future tense in some dialects. In Iraq, even very secular Iraqis always used it with the future tense. It was just the way to talk about something that hasn't happened yet. Often, it was a way to express hope for something that seemed unlikely. For secular Iraqis, it was no more an indication of fatalism than Americans' use of "bless you" after a sneeze is an indication of deep religious belief.

It was also a way to be polite. I found this out the hard way in Tunisia. After making a plan with someone, I asked if this plan was set. His response, *Inshallah*, was, in that case, just a polite way of saying no. I showed up at the designated hour; he didn't.

Now, listening to the trainer's diatribe, I just couldn't believe that the Iraqis were that fatalistic. Most of the Iraqis I met—religious or secular, cosmopolitan or rural—were getting up and hustling daily for their families, and trying to make a difference in their own lives. I didn't see them waiting for God to do it for them.

The prejudice-laden lecture that introduced us to Iraqi culture wasn't, amazingly enough, as bad as the hate-filled rants and bombast we got from our instructors at the Defense Language Institute (DLI) in Monterey, where I learned to speak Arabic.

There was the time I was waiting for class to start and was attempting to read the Koran in Arabic. (I later gave up. It's nearly impossible using the modern Arabic I studied.) The head of the department paused as she walked by. "Do you know what the difference is between this book and the Bible?"

she asked me, barely pausing as she answered her own question while tapping the Koran's open pages: "There's no love in this book. At all." Then there was the other day I'll never forget, as we sat in class and watched the "Shock and Awe" bombing of Baghdad on Al Jazeera. Our teacher, a small, stout woman with a huge wooden cross around her neck, was beside herself. "Kill them! Kill them all!" She hated Muslims.

Our instructors in Monterey were almost exclusively Egyptian Copts, members of an early Christian church that suffered heavy persecution under the Romans and the Arab empire (after a period of tolerance and acceptance, which was more in keeping with Islamic Sharia law). Targeted killings of Copts by Islamic fundamentalists during the first intifada fanned a lot of very old hatred. Unfortunately, this group of instructors spread their hatred evenly across the Arab world. They had an opinion on every single kind of Arab. Iraqis, for example, were loud, brash, macho, and very stupid. The most positive thing I ever heard them say about an Arab was that the Yemeni speak very beautiful Arabic, despite their low intelligence.

I resented the prejudices of my instructors, but they knew Arabic and could teach it well. I loved learning Arabic. It was something I had wanted for so long, and it fully met my expectations. The frustrations and mysteries I faced when I tried to learn it on my own fell away, and I could see, finally, the poetry of this ancient language.

Arabic is like one of those intricate patterns you will see in Middle Eastern mosaics, weavings, art, and architecture. Beautiful and logical, ornate and self-contained, it is fascinating from a distance and fascinating from up close. Its grammar is mathematical and its flourishes are musical. Arabs talk and write like no other people on earth, and they know this. They are very aware of and extremely proud of their language. It's much more than a tool, much more than a way of getting what you want from people. If it's true that Arabs are inclined to long conferences or an exchange of pleasantries before business, as the stereotypes tell us, I'd venture that it's not laziness or procrastination—it happens that way because Arabic is just so nice to listen to.

During my sixteen months at DLI, I spent eight hours a day in class, followed by hours of homework each night. I'd never studied so hard, felt so constantly challenged, or had so many occasions to feel so stupid. I was surrounded by young, smart men and women from different branches of military service and trained in different disciplines who were competitive in the extreme, adding another layer of pressure. The intensity didn't let up, it never got easier, and a third of those who started didn't finish. Those who did finish did so because, like me, they wanted this very badly. Many, like me, wanted it because they just loved the language. These were the people I gravitated toward.

The guy at DLI who seemed least likely to harbor a love of Arabic became my best friend in Monterey. Specialist Tomas L., then not even old enough to order a drink, tells me he is still uncertain why he was drawn to the army, and to Arabic. If I had to guess, it probably had something to do with his restless, probing mind. It was unstoppable and insatiable, actively seeking challenges and new ideas.

Tomas had been a world-class athletic prodigy in his former life. With two major championship titles in his chosen sport and a list of corporate sponsors under his belt, he was looking at settling into a very comfortable life at a very early age. Instead, he cut short his own steady rise and put himself on a new course by joining the army. He told me he did it to get an education—that learning was something he couldn't do without, and he couldn't get it while playing sports.

When I knew him at DLI, he was a right-wing reactionary. He was raised in an evangelical Christian household and held a fairly predictable set of views about religion, society, American politics, and the world. This would have bothered me, a lot, if he was closed and bigoted, but he was exceptionally smart and willing to think through every corner of his belief system. I reciprocated by taking his views seriously—as far as I was able. His love of Ann Coulter was a bit much, but I managed to slog through one of her screeds on his recommendation. That, I thought, was a true test of friendship if there ever was one.

Our ongoing conversation during that year ranged across such issues as abortion, evolution, the 2000 presidential election, and taxation. "I didn't know you were an envious person," he told me when I argued against Bush's tax cuts for the wealthy. He continued. "I didn't know you hated rich people because they're wealthy." This was one of those times when I was taken aback by how openly he would speak, not afraid of risking offense. When I explained to him that my sympathies were with the poor—not against the rich—I could see that he considered what I told him. I might not have convinced him, but he gave me the respect of thinking about what I'd said.

Tomas surprised me again as we watched Bush and his team argue for an invasion of Iraq. So many pieces of Tomas's belief system pointed him to a single conclusion—to believe the president when he said this war on Iraq was part of the global war on terror and fighting the terrorists means fighting Iraq. We were in an environment where most people, especially our superiors, took this as a truism. And yet, Tomas never saw the connection. He might have wanted to be convinced (that would have been a lot more convenient), but he couldn't avoid noticing the signs that said Iraq was a diversion from the real war on terror.

Tomas was one of a small group of us who came through DLI and/or interrogation school together and ended up in Iraq. We had little in common but a love for Arabic. Matt S. was about my age, but had a wife and a kid. He got into the army because he couldn't decide what else to do. I could relate to that. He was whip-smart and very funny, but came across as a little spaced-out and without focus. I knew he had political beliefs, but they seemed abstract. For some reason, he repeatedly wanted to tell me about his idea of building homes out of old tires. It so happened that I knew a guy in Santa Fe who was doing just that, so I'd tell him. This seemed to cause him to lose interest, and he'd drop it. The next time I'd see him, he'd tell me about it again. This happened at least a dozen times.

In every group of Americans who are serious about learning a language, there has to be one who fully intends to go native. In our little group, Fred T., who was always quoting Edward Said and even preferred to be called Fareed, filled that role. We teased him steadily. He loved Arabic pop, which really must be an acquired taste. It drove us nuts. Fred would develop a very unique interrogation style and had a radically different experience than the rest of us, for which I'm glad.

*   *   *

Because the army sent me to DLI to learn Arabic, I missed the major actions in Afghanistan and the invasion of Iraq. I think that if I hadn't chosen Arabic, and filled the language requirement for the job with French, for which I had passed the exam already, I'd have seen Kabul or Bagram Air Base right after training as an interrogator, and maybe I would have been sent into Iraq with the invading force. But my timeline put me in Iraq well after the invasion, well after "Mission Accomplished," and not long after the attacks on the UN and Red Cross that would, in retrospect, signal the start of a long, dark journey for Iraq. As I finished DLI and prepared to leave the beautiful Monterey Bay, I had only the vaguest idea of what I was getting into.

I should have researched my possible assignments more closely. That would have been the responsible thing to do. I had a hazy idea that I wanted an intelligence assignment that was strategic rather than tactical. I wanted to look at the bigger picture rather than the small tactical details. But I didn't know where to go for this. I ended up with an assignment that was very tactical, with a unit that specialized in air assault, and which sounded to me like a job for the younger, shinier pennies. One of my classmates had an assignment I wanted at Fort Gordon in Georgia. Traditionally, this battalion did counterintelligence work or strategic work in active conflicts. She had the assignment I wanted, and I had the assignment she wanted. We knew either way we'd both end up in Iraq; neither of us was trying to avoid the war.

We switched assignments. Shortly after arriving in Iraq, she was killed trying to disarm an IED.

If we hadn't switched assignments, she wouldn't have died. Rationally, I know that nothing was predictable when we made the swap. We were looking into a murky future with little information. But I can't help it; when I look back on this decision, I wish we had left things as they were. And I wish I could tell that young woman that I am so sorry.

CHAPTER 3
Prisoners

I did very well at the Defense Language Institute. On the final exams, which test reading, listening, and speaking ability, I got the highest possible marks in reading and listening. I did fine in speaking. Still, I was worried about how well I'd actually be able to communicate in Iraq, especially in a high-pressure situation like an interrogation.

For one thing, we studied Modern Standard Arabic, which is perhaps the most universal version of Arabic, but no one really speaks it on the street. Using this version of Arabic in Iraq would be like walking up to someone in Cincinnati and speaking to him in King James English with a Chinese accent. That concern aside, most of our conversational lessons were designed with officers and attachés in mind. I was confident I could do things like open a bank account or make a hotel reservation in Baghdad, if the opportunity ever arose, but not so sure I could demand to know where an insurgent cell was holed up or where the weapons were hidden.

Finally, after I got to Abu Ghraib, I had a chance to test my Arabic. Ordering an ice cream from the chow hall shouldn't be a problem, I thought, even for a novice like myself, so I confidently looked the Iraqi behind the counter in the eye and politely said, *"Ooreed shocolat, min fudhlik."* He barely moved and said nothing. My heart sank. Sixteen months of intensive study, near perfect test scores, and I couldn't even make a simple food order? I muttered some simple English and pointed out what I wanted.

The guys in the chow hall weren't, as it turned out, Iraqi or even Arabic. The well-connected international contracting company that prepared and served our food had recruited them as dirt-cheap labor from Tibet, Bangladesh, and East India. When I found this out, much later, I was completely flummoxed. Our army cooks had nothing to do, there were countless Iraqis looking for jobs, and this contractor was pulling in people from thousands of miles away because they would work for pennies a day. Once they were set up in Iraq, of course, they needed to be protected—by us. I can't count how many times I stood guard over some element of American private enterprise that had no business being there, risking my own life and threatening the lives of Iraqis who got too close, marveling at the absurdity of the system we'd set up, one that increasingly looked like a viper eating its own tail.

I got a chance to talk to some of these Asian workers, ones who had signed up with an American-owned corporation, later in my tour. They explained, in an offhanded way that suggested they'd come to terms with it, how they were promised work in Kuwait. They left their villages for a relatively safe enclave in the Persian Gulf for what seemed like great pay. Then, one day, their boss told them to pack up, and suddenly they were, without fully understanding what was happening, in a place where insurgents were trying to kill them. They told me they had no choice in this terrible bait and switch. What could they do? Quit and catch a bus home?

The Asian workers, whose cheap labor helped line the pockets of an American contractor, were near the bottom of the little isolated society we'd built at Abu Ghraib. Just a few notches above them were the Iraqi laborers. These men gathered outside the gates every morning to be frisked and sent inside to deliver goods, clean toilets, rewire air conditioners, and lay gravel. Some of them served as translators, but never in any interrogations or sensitive areas. Everyone suspected them of being spies. There was no doubt in our minds that some of them got a little money in exchange for information on the layout of our positions. The mortars consistently fell too close to places soldiers gathered, like the chow hall or Internet tent, to be random. Since these Iraqis were all suspected spies, we generally avoided them.

We also had a number of Iraqi police, trusted even less than the Iraqi civilians. At Abu Ghraib they occupied part of the hard site and maintained their prisoners there. We didn't have much contact with them, except to ask them for their bread (*zamoon*), which they had delivered every morning. It was the best food at Abu Ghraib.

Serving more closely with the Americans were the contract interpreters, who were provided to fill the gap between our immense need for Arabic speakers and our sparse actual numbers. These folks fell into two classes. There were native speakers who were American citizens and had security clearances. They worked with military intelligence. Then there were local Iraqis who translated for MPs and infantry. Both groups were treated with mistrust. The mistrust, of course, fostered understandable resentment from the American translators.

We soldiers presided over this dyspeptic global village with suspicion and unease. I was shocked to see so many prisoners. Someone told me there were upwards of nine thousand, but I don't recall for certain. I read later that the prisoner population had been thirty-five hundred in September 2003, then seven thousand in October. To these thousands, there were only about one thousand nonprisoners, including all the contract workers and day laborers. Of that thousand, only about two-thirds were armed and could be counted on in a crisis, like if the prisoners decided to revolt. Behind the makeshift outdoor prisons and the original Saddam-era prison buildings, where the captives wiled away the hours and firearms were not allowed, the mismatch between guards and guarded was stark and visible. I read later that the ratio of captive to captor was seventy-five to one. We were truly a colonial cautionary tale waiting to happen. My buddy Fred and I discussed the possibility that we'd witness a major prison uprising during our year there. We thought the odds were high.

It would have been easy to be haunted and preoccupied by the threats from within, but we were also being bombarded from without on an almost daily basis. I think you always remember your first mortar; mine was on day two. I heard an explosion and turned to ask a sergeant: "Incoming?" He shook his head no. Outgoing—the sound of a launch. Being able to tell the difference is a very useful combat skill, one I hadn't graduated to yet, so I was glad I asked. I didn't want to look like an idiot, hitting the deck at every pop, crack, or boom. I turned and walked confidently forward across an open area toward our living quarters, but there was an incoming round after all. A blast formed ahead of me in the path I'd planned to take. I flattened myself on the muddy ground.

I was totally unprepared for how *big* the sound was—the loudest thunder times twelve, accompanied by a shock wave that didn't hurt but moved through every cell in my body. The adrenaline started moving at the same time. It was exhilarating, and over too quickly. So that was the first one. Over the course of the year, hundreds more would follow.

As I looked around during my first days, I tried to adjust to the fact that I would be spending a full year in this hellscape. The buildings were as oppressive and decrepit as any prison the developing world could offer. The hard site—the actual cell blocks where the worst of the scandal took place— was overfull with prisoners. So the vast majority of prisoners actually lived outside the cell blocks in compounds of tents in open areas surrounded by concertina wire, where they were always visible, their jumpsuits forming an orange mass that moved slowly, shifting back and forth in a manner both pathetic and menacing.

We soldiers lived in hard buildings that would protect us from mortars. The chow hall, the Internet room, and our living quarters were all protected. My first cot was surrounded on all sides by other cots, with a clearance of about six inches. This large open space, which was probably a former warehouse, was filled with noise: bleeps from the Game Boys, rap or death metal from the boom boxes, bad dialogue from the portable DVD players. It was more of a rec room than a barracks, except for the rifles.

"So there I was. Abu Ghraib. Mortars falling all around me." An analyst in the Joint Interrogation and Debriefing Center (JIDC) loved to ironically narrate the action as it happened. Here, mortars actually were falling, and he had already incorporated it into the war stories he knew he would tell back home to the girls in bars. He had been there almost a year, and loved talking to the new guys. He was the first to sit me down and tell me how he had failed to accomplish anything in his year at Abu Ghraib. The intelligence sucked. Either the prisoners had nothing to tell or the interrogators were really bad. The Tactical Human Intelligence Teams, the ones who actually went out into towns looking for intelligence and even running agents, had all been rolled up and not allowed out of the gate because the town was deemed too hostile for that kind of work. With nothing to analyze, he spent his time playing video games while the insurgency boiled on just outside the prison walls. I didn't believe it could be as bad as he said, but I remembered the conversation well.

I soon ran into William H., who'd also done nearly a year in-country. We'd gone through basic, DLI, and interrogator school together, but because he chose French, he completed language training in only six months and got to Iraq much sooner. Will is a big man with a wrestler's build and the disposition of a day-care teacher, someone who would wrap anyone in his bear hugs. I even saw him do it to people he was supposed to interrogate. I was shocked to hear that someone so optimistic had become totally disillusioned. When he first got to Iraq, he ran around the country with an infantry unit, slept under the stars, and had good relations with the Iraqis. But as the insurgency heated up, he and his team were reeled back to safety. Now he just got through his interrogations as fast as he could.

I was finding morale at its depths, and this didn't even seem to have anything to do with the "something bad" that had happened here—the bad thing that no one seemed to know about and that stayed secret. But people openly discussed an episode where a prisoner got ahold of a gun, tossed into a window by an Iraqi policeman, and shot at a guard. But still, no one with real knowledge would go near discussing the "bad thing."

All I got were second- or thirdhand rumors, talk of guards dressing prisoners in Santa Claus outfits or doing crazy, sick, and degrading things involving midgets, but no one seemed to actually know. From the day I first arrived in Abu Ghraib to the time the scandal broke in the media—a space of four months—I knew only of "something bad." I clearly wasn't supposed to find out about it unless the media did.

Was morale really bottoming out, or was it just soldiers bitching? Either way, I was facing a year in this place, and it was too soon to let these bitter veterans dampen the excitement I felt over getting a chance to use my training, interrogate bad guys, twist their minds into knots, and get (I was certain) the big piece of intel that would save American and Iraqi lives. This was the biggest prison facility in the country. It had to be an intelligence-rich environment. I just had to go into the booth and get it.

I knew, almost immediately, that I would first have to deal with the totally unexpected reaction I had to seeing, for the first time, human beings in cages. This was shocking to me: a totally alien social situation with new and unwritten rules. I'd never had anyone dependent on me, and here there were thousands of them. I'd never been so separate from another person, and here I was separated by bars, wires, and the fact that I was free and they were not. I'd never interacted with someone on such unequal footing, and here I held pretty much absolute sovereign power over them.

To make it all more confusing, they didn't cower in their cells. As I walked by, they reached hands out through the bars, or fingers through the chain-link fence, and pleaded desperately with me, "Mister, mister, mister." When I stopped to check, I'd find that they wanted something: an extra blanket, soap, or some other fairly reasonable item that had no chance of being provided. They also wanted to know about their cases. *Did you check on my case? When will I be released? Has anyone notified my family? Why am I here?*

Things only got worse once they established that I knew Arabic and they didn't have to go through one of the translators. (Most of whom had absolutely no love for the prisoners.) If I stopped to listen to someone's problem, soon I had a dozen different problems to handle as the prisoners crowded up to the barrier. I didn't want to face them, I didn't want to look in their eyes, and I didn't want them looking at me. I was completely disoriented and had no idea how to behave.

It was similar to having a homeless person, visibly destitute, walk up to you and ask for change. You have something he needs. You can afford to give it to him, but probably won't. Don't look this person in the eye, because you might see his humanity. Instead, mutter something like an apology under your breath and shuffle away. In walking past these cells, I felt the same way. Embarrassed.

Only it was worse. Prisons are places where you put people when you want them to be observed. If you are a captor, you *have* to look at them. As an interrogator, I was supposed to look at them deeply. And while a homeless person might want money, these people wanted their freedom, which was not in my power to give.

Prison has, like the army, its own culture, structure, and mores. The army gives you all of its rules up front. Prison only gives you part of them. The rest you learn by watching. I picked up everything I needed to know about how to act in a couple days. I watched other guards and interrogators, followed their cues, and retained a little envy over how easily they seemed to accept that some men are free while others are in cages. I learned how to act, but I continued to struggle with embarrassment and discomfort over being a captor and having so much power.

Of course it helped knowing that these men, all nine thousand of them, were bad guys. If not killers, then potential killers. If not potential killers, then thieves. Enemies of the U.S. Army and the nascent Iraqi democracy. While my instincts wanted to grant them humanity, I could keep this in check knowing that they were on the wrong side. The free were free because they were innocent; the caged because they were guilty. There was justice here, not just raw power. It became easier, though never perfectly easy, to ignore them or simply tell them to shut up.

Besides learning to suppress my compassionate instincts, the other thing I felt I had to learn was what to do when someone wouldn't talk. I felt that the surprisingly short time we spent on approaches in interrogation school left me very unprepared for this. So what do you do? I asked several interrogators who had much more experience. *Take away his blanket. Change his meals—give him MREs instead of food from the chow hall. Put him in isolation, march him around barefoot in the cold mud.* Considering that we were dealing with vicious insurgents who were sending mortars over our walls on a daily basis, these approaches seemed totally reasonable at the time. As harmless as they seemed, however, they definitely pushed the limits of, if not flatly contradicted, what we had learned in school.

When the United States of America signed the Geneva Convention relative to the Treatment of Prisoners of War, it agreed to never commit "acts of violence or intimidation" against prisoners.[1] In school, we learned that not only could we not threaten someone with violence, we could not imply a threat. No American soldier may place a "knife on the table"—literally or figuratively—for purposes of intimidation. I would find out later that the top brass at this prison had openly approved several techniques, like the use of military working dogs, that clearly crossed the line. But by the time I got there, while the lines were being pushed, one could possibly argue they were not crossed.

The Abu Ghraib I knew looked nothing like the pictures we all later saw of MPs turned sadists. I saw no nudity, sexual humiliation, or use of dogs. The hard site stank and was a terrible place to be, but it seemed well run and humane. Only after I read the Taguba Report, which was leaked to the press in April 2004, did I see that the humane treatment and by-the-book approaches to interrogation had arrived at Abu Ghraib at about the same time I did. I was lucky. I know now that if I had been there during the worst of the scandal, I would have been disgusted with most of these sadistic acts. I might have reported them. But I also know that when it came to other interrogation "enhancements," I would have joined right in.

---

[1] Geneva Convention relative to the Treatment of Prisoners of War, Part II, Article 13.

CHAPTER 4
The Booth

When the prisoner's voice cracked, when he started to blubber, and when he finally gave up on holding back his tears, I barely suppressed a satisfied smile. This wasn't easy, because it was exciting watching his uncontrolled sobs. We had broken this man. We'd matched wits and we had won.

This was the first real interrogation I witnessed. I was there as an observer, taking a "right-seat ride." The interrogator, Specialist H. Davis, was a fresh-faced twenty-five-year-old with boundless self-confidence. Yaqud, the prisoner, had served on the personal security detail of a very high-ranking Baathist. He was a huge stone wall of a man and a reportedly vicious sadist. The monster he served may have given the orders, but countless Iraqis had suffered at Yaqud's hands. It was right that he was now in prison and right that he should be made to cry.

Before the interrogation, I was incredibly nervous going into the booth. Even though I was only supposed to watch, I worried that the prisoner would see right through me and would know that I was terribly green and still unsure how to use the power I held over him. Even after my months of training, I had no idea what this was going to be like.

We pulled the prisoner from his isolation. His world, for the last few months, consisted of a tiny windowless cell with four walls and not even bars to look out of. He stood up, but, hunched over in resignation, he never attained his full height. Interrogation was something he'd been through dozens of times before. Prisoners in deep isolation, I would learn, actually look forward to interrogations, even the harsh ones, just for a chance to get out of their oppressive cells and have some human contact.

We sat in the interrogation booth, a sparse room with a few chairs. Davis was severe and direct as he started his questioning, and the Lebanese interpreter, Ahmed, relayed not only the words but the severe tone as well. His Arabic was smooth and efficient. I sat still and tried to keep my eyes fixed on the prisoner, who, for the entire ninety-minute ordeal, never acknowledged my presence. My initial fear and nervousness faded. This was a tightly controlled environment and interaction, and we controlled it.

"What can you tell me about the smugglers who got your family out of Iraq?"[1] Davis started in on a direct approach. We were taught to start with a direct approach in every case, even if we knew it wouldn't work.

"I don't know any smugglers."

"I think you do."

"*Wallah.*"

Wallah, which means "I swear to God," was, I would learn, the most common word uttered during interrogations. Even Americans who had never tried to learn a single word of Arabic knew *wallah*, and it drove them crazy. Davis and Yaqud went through a couple more rounds of questioning and denial before Davis effortlessly shifted tactics.

"How do you think your son is doing?" American intelligence had picked up his twenty-year-old son in the same raid that netted Yaqud. They hadn't seen each other since. The question implied that the son was getting the same treatment as the father. "Do you think he'll ever get out of here?" Yaqud paused before returning to his denials. That pause told Davis he was on the right track. "Do you want your son to go through what you're going through?"

"*La wallah. Sadigini.*" More denials.

We knew Yaqud was lying. We knew when his family was smuggled out of Iraq, by whom, and how. We had the whole thing wrapped up. I knew what Davis was going to do next.

---

[1] In this and other descriptions of interrogations, some of the specifics have been altered in order to protect both the Iraqis involved and information that may be classified.

"Okay, let's go through the timeline again. What were you doing at the time of your capture?" This was classic, and exactly the picture I had of interrogation from the media. Get the prisoner to lie, and then catch him in a lie. The artful part of Davis's technique was the pace. He didn't want to reveal all that we knew at once, but instead would catch Yaqud in so many lies that he gave up on lying. Davis also had another piece of leverage that he pulled out when Yaqud, even after being tripped up a couple times, continued to deny.

"I have this picture of your son." Yaqud's eyes brightened. He trained them on the photograph of a man in prison garb, who looked just as pale and wan as the father. "Do you want it?" Yaqud nodded. "Then answer me."

We got a little cooperation out of that. Yaqud's story started to shift slightly, moving gradually toward the one we knew was true. Then he diverged from the truth again. Davis pulled the picture away and put it in his breast pocket. Yaqud looked crushed. He was ready to break. Now it was only a matter of time. Davis offered him the picture again, and then took it away. Then again. Soon, Yaqud's head was spinning from keeping track of all his lies and contradictions while trying to control his strong emotions. It took about an hour, and then he was ready to admit everything. We spent the next thirty minutes getting the details. Davis never raised his voice or directly threatened him or his son. It was a remarkable performance.

Before he finally collapsed, exhausted, Yaqud said something that surprised all of us. He asked why we didn't believe him, when, after all, he had betrayed his boss (the high-ranking Baathist). We were shocked. That arrest was big news on base. It was one of those arrests that made us think we could actually crack the insurgency. Why didn't we know about this? I asked Davis about it after the interrogation. Why would Yaqud have betrayed his boss, the man he was charged with protecting? Davis explained that the clandestine civilian service known as "Other Government Agencies" (OGA) was behind Yaqud's capture. Before they handed him over to the army, they probably beat him for days. That was their standard practice. Davis knew nothing more than I did, but he guessed that the betrayal must have happened during this time. It wasn't surprising that OGA hadn't told us.

Nor was it surprising to me that they might have beaten Yaqud. I had no strong reaction to the information, and no feelings of sympathy for Yaqud. A beating like that for an asshole like this was expected. As an added bonus, maybe this was a case where the torture worked. He dropped a dime on his former boss, and we got him. For me, at the time, there were no moral complications here.

But when I was in the booth, while Yaqud was lying and when he started to break down, there were times I wanted to believe him. If I hadn't known the facts, I might have. I was worried about this, knowing that I wouldn't always have such a complete picture. I had let my compassion get in the way, and this was a problem. I saw, for that moment, not a Baathist monster but a father weeping for his son. This sympathy crept in despite the fact I had steeled myself against this man. I told Davis about this, and asked him how, in another situation, he would have known Yaqud was lying. Davis, who was a cocky young man, looked at me like I was an idiot. "It was obvious. You couldn't see it? No way was he telling the truth." I wish he'd said more, but clearly I wouldn't understand. I complimented him on a great interrogation. I'd learned a lot.

I still feel it was the best interrogation I ever saw in Iraq, but a few things became clear in hindsight. We didn't actually get any intelligence. Yaqud didn't tell us anything we didn't already know. All we accomplished was an admission. And Yaqud's admission might make us feel like we were making progress, but it would do nothing to help us fight the insurgency.

This was very different from what we'd been trained to do. Army interrogators are not supposed to be like the detectives you see on TV. We weren't trained to investigate crimes, and we weren't expected to even care that much about what an individual had or had not done. Our training was designed for war with the Soviet Union, all based on the idea that we would be questioning uniformed POWs—maybe Russians or East Germans—who would break quickly and gladly provide information on order of battle, tank formations, or plans of attack. We didn't get any useful instruction on how to break insurgents or terrorists, or how to operate in a quasi-investigative function. But in Iraq, I learned from people like Davis, who seemed at the time very competent and professional, and from interrogators returned from Afghanistan, who tried anything that had a chance of working—stress positions, dogs, sexual humiliation, and worse. This is how techniques migrated from Afghanistan to Gitmo

(Guantánamo) to Abu Ghraib and outward. A lot of what I learned, and a lot of what I did, seemed to have been improvised and made policy out of desperation and the desire to prevent another catastrophic attack on the United States.

On September 11, 2001, I was fresh out of basic training and at Fort Huachuca, where we were standing in formation, and I was bitching internally as we waited an unusually long time before the drill sergeant finally strode up to the formation. Something was different about how he walked. He asked if anyone was from New York City. I raised my hand. "Two planes have hit the World Trade Center. We're at war."

It took time for this to sink in. While most of the nation was transfixed on the searing images of the event, we were busy. The base was put on a war footing. We were straight out of basic and not allowed to have TVs or radios and there were no newspapers available. But I was allowed to call my dad, briefly, because he still lived in Manhattan. Wild rumors circulated. Someone told me the White House was on fire. I was still trying to wrap my head around the idea that America had been attacked, what kind of war this would be, and what part I would play.

Anger settled in and a polarizing set of doctrines took root. Here in the army, my left-of-center beliefs and morality were never popular before 9/11, but they were tolerated. Now, any questioning of the prevailing kick-ass mentality was treasonous. It wasn't just me. One of my classmates was, with a group of other soldiers, watching some of the footage in the common room and remarked, morosely, that resentment against America had been building for a long time and now it had finally come to this. He didn't actually blame America for bringing this on itself, and stopped short of the "chickens coming home to roost" argument. What he said was fairly obvious, but it pissed off a lot of people. They chastised the soldier, and then they complained to their superiors, who called in this young man the next day and dressed him down, accused him of being a traitor, and gave him a reprimand.

I got the same treatment when an instructor, baiting any closet liberals in his class, waxed on at length about how glad he was that George W. Bush was president. "Aren't we lucky that it's Bush instead of Jimmy Carter? Who would prefer to have Carter leading us now?" I rose to the bait.

Jimmy Carter made his share of mistakes, I admitted, but he got the hostages home safe without going to war. He served in the military at length and with honor, very unlike our current president.

My instructor was red-faced and furious. He told me that if he were ever forced to share a foxhole with me, he would shoot me in the head.

Things were getting very weird. I became more cautious about sharing my beliefs in public; for example, I never shared my deeper skepticism about where the war on terror would go. I wondered often why it was even being called a war. It seemed more like we were responding to a crime. The military would have to do most of the work in capturing or killing the criminals, and I would be glad to be a part of that. But this was no war, any more than the "war on drugs" was a war. There was no legitimate army—or even a Vietcong-style insurgent army—arrayed against our troops. It wasn't even about territory. Fighting wasn't about "politics by other means." The only appropriate use of force in this "war" was to kill or capture the thugs, not achieve political objectives. Likewise, I realized even then that interrogations would have to be more like investigations, nothing like what we were learning at Fort Huachuca.

Looking around me, and at the training I was receiving, I was very worried about how suited the army was for facing an enemy like al-Qaeda. Our courses in interrogation were based on doctrine established in the late 1940s. We spent class time learning about Soviet weapon systems and memorizing questions relevant to a conventional battlefield. Army interrogators must have learned valuable lessons in Vietnam, but we collectively forgot them. We had only one instructor who had served in that conflict, and he only engaged us in our role-playing games—as a prisoner.

Although most of our instructors had never interrogated an actual prisoner, we had a few veterans from the First Gulf War. Their experiences interrogating POWs led to some very poor lessons. I left interrogation school believing, as I had been told repeatedly, that most prisoners—90 percent of them—break on the direct approach. I have no doubt that happened in the First Gulf War when army interrogators questioned Saddam's demoralized cannon fodder, but an insurgent has very good reasons to keep silent and to lie.

Still, that 90 percent statistic drove the course. We spent all of two days on "approaches." An approach is a tactic to get a prisoner to break. We got a long list of them, all with oddball names like Pride and Ego Up, Love of Family, We Know All, File and Dossier, and, of course, Fear Up Harsh. This was probably the most interesting part of the three-month course. This is where a real interest in this job started to grow within me. The process of matching wits with a prisoner in a mental chess game, developing a customized strategy to attack his ego and psychic makeup, and finally, in a moment of victory, breaking through his defenses and bending him to my will—all of this—was fascinating to me. A little disturbing, but fascinating. I was glad to be training for this job.

Then, when we went to our role-playing, our course fell back to the assumption that 90 percent of our prisoners would cooperate. Very little emphasis was given to the approach during role-playing. I learned in Iraq that in real interrogations, approaches were everything. Very few of my real interrogations actually got past the approach phase. But in school they don't tell you that. The prisoner breaks easily, they said, and he stays broken—that's the assumption that drove the whole course.

Interrogation wasn't my choice when I joined the army. Not even on the short list. As I mentioned, my priority was to get to DLI for Arabic. I'd do whatever it took to get there. Originally, I was slated for a job as an interpreter or linguist, which would have me either working with signals intelligence or poring over captured documents. But it soon became clear that I couldn't get Top Secret security clearance. I had too many student loans outstanding, which I guess made me a target for bribes from Soviet agents. But I only had to have Secret—not Top Secret—clearance to be an interrogator. Fine. Where do I sign?

But once I got to Fort Huachuca I began to think deeply about interrogation and took it seriously. I didn't fully realize it at the time, but the moral and legal questions were also a big draw for someone like me, who'd studied religion and philosophy closely. The official line at the schoolhouse was simple and clear on abuse and torture: don't ever do it. We got ample exposure to the Geneva Convention on prisoners of war and we were expected to follow them in role-playing and if we ever got in the booth with a real prisoner. We got short histories of torture, like what the KGB did, but always with the emphasis on how it was ineffective. Tortured prisoners talk, but they don't give good intel. We heard that, but never really believed it.

These were stern and serious lectures. But they were also punctuated by jokes about hooking people's testicles up to hand-crank generators, pushing a prisoner out of a helicopter while another prisoner watches, or hanging someone by their hands until they dislocate their joints. These came from the instructors as little asides, with enough of a wink that we knew this wasn't the official line. Away from the instructors, students would talk with relish about what the British or Israelis used to do. We all knew where the line was, and we all wanted to push it as much as we could.

I believe now that once I accepted that I was an interrogator, once I decided I wanted to be the most effective interrogator I could be, I started thinking about going down that road. We were talking about how to most fully break a man, which is something extreme and implicitly violent, and then we learned about the restraints and limits. It was only natural for me, and many others, to imagine what was on the other side of those limits. For me, it was yet another boundary to cross, one darker and more chaotic than I had ever known.

CHAPTER 5

Compassion

After a few interrogations, I could see that I was going to have a problem with compassion. Yaqud, who by all rights deserved no compassion, actually got to me. The constant sight of people in cages, all asking for something in the only English they knew—"Mister, mister, mister"—was wearing me down. This normal reaction to someone helpless and in distress, this thing that makes us human, was getting in the way.

I was in my third week at Abu Ghraib. I had by now had close-up contact with dozens of Iraqis, all helpless, all with needs, requests, pains, and a desire for freedom. I was watching myself trying to grow more callous and wondering if I should continue that process. I was sitting in the JIDC (the military intelligence nerve center), writing a report, while a loud conversation about compassion was going on behind me. A senior noncommissioned officer in my company, Sergeant First Class N. Franks, was listening to Eliza P., a civilian contract interrogator, as she described how the Iraqis tried to manipulate her.

Eliza was former military intelligence. She'd left the army and then came back to Iraq with a private firm, making somewhere between a hundred and two hundred thousand dollars per year to do the same thing we were doing. (Actually, these contractors did a lot less; they didn't have guard duty, latrine duty, or any other of the little bullshit jobs that the army uses to put you in your place.) Women have to put up with a lot and have to overcome a lot to serve in the army. So, many of them, like Eliza, apparently make a choice along the way to try to be harder, tougher, and meaner than the men around them, which is hard to do. In Eliza's case the result was a deeply unpleasant person who took every opportunity to advertise the fact that she was proud to be a hard-ass.

Sergeant Franks, on the other hand, had chosen to deal with army life by not only memorizing the rule book and living by it but by *becoming* the rule book. With his clipped and authoritative voice, he even sounded like a rule book. Even his most social interactions came out of his mouth like a series of regulations—announced over a loudspeaker. We got along only because I did my job and followed the rules.

Eliza was complaining about how the Iraqis thought they could play on her feminine compassion. "It never works. There's no way I'd ever feel sorry for any of these guys." Franks, unsurprisingly, agreed. It was a black-and-white world—"Of course not. They're the enemy." Knowing exactly what I was in for, I turned around in my chair and told them both, "I feel sorry for some of them. Sometimes." There was just a moment of pause when they didn't know what to say, and then they both started in on me.

Franks asked me if I'd ever been a prisoner. I had no idea where he was going with this, but no, I hadn't. "Then how can you feel sorry for them? You've never been an Iraqi. You've never been a prisoner. You can't have any sympathy for them." I was stunned at how totally illogical this was, and hoped my expression conveyed to him how little sense he made, but he just looked at me as he leaned back with the air of someone who had just settled an argument with an irrefutable knockout blow. Eliza's response was a lot more revealing.

"Can't you see through these guys? They're just trying to manipulate you. These are their counterinterrogation techniques. They're trained to do that." This wasn't the first time I had heard about these sophisticated counterinterrogation techniques Iraqis allegedly possessed. I never saw any actual evidence of such, but heard lots of assertions that this was so. Not only were Arabs in general born liars, these Iraqis were trained to lie. So don't ever let yourself believe a thing they say.

I tried to reconcile what Eliza told me with what I saw in the holding pens and interrogation booths. I was constantly being peppered with questions: *When can I contact my family? Do they know where I am? How can they survive when I'm here?* Were these all attempts to manipulate me? Was Yaqud's gradual breakdown over his son part of the counterinterrogation training he got? Were they all such excellent actors?

We went around this topic a few more times, and it followed a predictable course. "You have no business feeling that way," Eliza told me. "You're not their psychiatrist. You're not their friend." I wasn't trying to be either—I wasn't *acting* on my compassion, but of course she'd make that leap. I'd been in the army for three years by now, and I had very often been painted as a panty-waist liberal by someone looking for a chance to establish himself or herself as a hard-boiled soldier. The implication that I was soft didn't bother me. I know otherwise. What always amazed me in these conversations was how black-and-white those people thought everything was, when all of us, who had accepted killing and dying as a way of life and who walked a line be-tween interrogation and torture, were completely surrounded by moral co-nundrum and several shades of gray.

Like in this case, Franks and Eliza both tried to tell me, in their own way, that I couldn't feel compassion for an Iraqi. Either my compassion wasn't real or it was based on lies. And we must never forget that they are the enemy. At-titudes like these can help a soldier cope with a complicated mission and with following orders he'd know were wrong if he thought about them more deeply. But these attitudes also probably had a lot to do with why we were so successful at destroying Iraqi and such miserable failures at putting it back together.

Eliza did have a point though, and it was one that I saw coming. I knew that I had to shut out compassion to get my job done. It was a trade-off. I wanted to be effective and I wanted to get great intel. But simply denying that I had any human feelings toward prisoners? I'd be lying to myself. I gradually accepted that I'd never be totally comfortable in a prison, and I finally re-fused to shut out compassion entirely. I would get through this year by shut-ting it out selectively. Of course, this all would have been much easier if the prisoners were all "the enemy" and if they had all been guilty.

Naturally, I was nervous before my first solo interrogation. I wanted to look like I knew what I was doing. I felt I could manage the prisoner and guide the process, but before I could even get into the booth, I had to wade through a stack of previous interrogation reports. They'd matched me up with someone who'd been interrogated for months. I felt like I was jumping into the middle of an ongoing investigation. I worried that the prisoner, Ahmad, would compare me to his previous interrogators, and see an amateur.

I asked my team leader, Staff Sergeant Forbes, what I was going for—what was the objective? Forbes told me to "find gaps" in his story. "He knows more." What? Forbes could not be specific. "He's not telling us something."

So that was how I started the interrogation: "We know you're not telling us something." I glared at Ahmad and leveled my pointed finger at his chest. He blinked, but overall he just looked weary. His cheeks were sunken and his eyes drooped. His answers were slow, giving me the impression of someone not all there. I was still learning the particulars of the Iraqi dialect, but I could tell that Ahmad used much simpler sentences and vocabulary than the Iraqis from Baghdad.

Ahmad was a bachelor who lived north of the capital with his parents. He helped run their farm and did whatever odd jobs he could find. After the fall of Baghdad, he received a visit from his uncle, with whom he had only limited contact. His uncle was a high-ranking member of Saddam's government, a prominent face in the famous deck of cards. Ahmad had not been a part of his uncle's life. His humble means attested to the fact that having a relative close to Saddam did not always mean special treatment. But despite these distant relations, or more likely because of them, Ahmad's uncle showed up at his door not long after the fall of Baghdad. He wanted to be hidden. Ahmad grew up knowing that one does not refuse a Baathist. He did as he was told.

There were a few dozen interrogation reports on Ahmad, but they were all in bits and pieces. My little contribution to this project was to assemble them into a timeline. I planned to use this timeline as a club with which to batter Ahmad's psyche.

"Did you deliver the package to your uncle before or after he received those visitors you talked about?"

"Before."

"Are you sure?"

"Yes."

"You're lying. You told us before that the package came later."

Probably, he just didn't remember. But if I could put him under a certain level of stress and strain, force him to look closely at what he was saying, maybe I could retrieve something new. Basically, I was fishing, but trying to make Ahmad think I knew more than I did.

It was easy to confuse Ahmad. I don't think he had ever had a lot of guile, but it looked like the constant interrogations—not to mention the deep isolation—were taking their toll. Ahmad had been in a windowless cell, under fluorescent lights, for months. In my short time here, I'd seen other prisoners who'd been given the same treatment. Most began to go nuts after a few weeks. All started to change in some way. Mental processes and concentration slowed down, they became emotionally fragile, and found even simple tasks disorienting and confusing. In the case of Ahmad, I wonder if we'd taken this too far. He seemed to be losing touch with reality. Even if he gave me something new, could I trust it?

I stated in my report that I got nothing new, but also that the prisoner had made several mistakes and had a story that was inconsistent in places. I didn't know it then, but this was a red flag. To others, it meant he was lying, and reinforced the perception that he wasn't telling us the whole story. My team leader ordered me back into the booth with Ahmad a day later.

During my second interrogation, we covered more of the same ground, including the information he gave when he was first picked up. Generally, the first interrogations are the best. But I didn't have access to those interrogations, as they were performed by Other Government Agencies. Ahmad didn't want to describe what happened. I thought he was hiding something. Finally he told me.

The beatings, he said, had lasted for days, but he wasn't sure because he was prevented from sleeping and was confined to a small room with no windows. He described being slammed against a wall, thrown to the ground, and kicked. He said that when he wasn't being beaten, he was ordered to kneel for hours at a time. He gave me very little. He said he didn't want to talk about it. I obliged. This was not part of my interrogation plan. We went back to the questions at hand.

Afterward, I went to see Franks; if there was a rule about what to do when a prisoner reports torture, he would know. He didn't hesitate to tell me that I had to file a report. This wasn't an act of compassion; it was a rule. So I went to Forbes, and found him at his usual station—parked in front of a computer solitaire game. I explained that I wanted to file an abuse report. He looked up at me.

"And just what do you expect to happen?" he asked dryly.

It was a good question. If Ahmad had been tortured by OGA, there wasn't much the army's Criminal Investigation Division could do about it. I wasn't sure, but I suspected that was true. Still, I explained, I had to follow regulations, and that meant filing a report. This was the first of several abuse reports I would file. I never heard about this particular case again.

Completing the report meant going back into the booth with Ahmad. He resisted telling me about the torture more than he resisted telling me about his uncle. He didn't understand why I should be concerned. He worried that this would just make more trouble for him. He claimed to have gotten over it. He just wanted to get back to his parents; he was worried about how they were getting by.

We completed the interview, and I placed a sandbag over his head, standard procedure for transporting a prisoner to and from his cell. We didn't want prisoners recognizing him, trying to communicate with him, or vice versa. Besides, the sandbag helped disorient prisoners and usually scared them, even if just a little. Ahmad held his hands in front of him, as he had done so many times before. I cuffed him and put my hand on his shoulder to guide him as we walked across the open ground from the interrogation booth back to the hard site, where he had spent so many months. We were nearly there, when he shifted his weight and paused to ask me something.

"Ooreed an ara al shems." He wanted me to take the sandbag off of his head. Just for a moment, so he could see the sun. For months, he'd seen only fluorescent light. I shouldn't have done this, but by this time he'd convinced me that he had no part in the insurgency and was no threat. Maybe hiding his uncle was a mistake, but I saw him as a very simple man who had no idea of what to do in the moment when his uncle appeared at his door, at a time when the old order had broken down and the new order had yet to establish itself. I felt sorry for the poor bastard.

I removed the sandbag and released my grip on the cuffs. He walked slowly across the muddy ground, looking up at the sky while crying. I walked just behind him and stood by his side when he stopped his puttering. As he held his chin up to let the sun warm his face, I made small talk in Arabic, asking about his life before the invasion, but soon ran out of questions. We both stood there, looking at the prison wall, looking at the sky beyond, and he asked me if I thought he would ever be released. *"Inshallah,"* I told him. Most likely not.

I felt terrible for Ahmad's ordeal, and wondered often about his future, but I don't remember questioning, until much later, whether it was right or wrong to keep him in jail. At that time, it seemed to make sense. He had aided and abetted a well-known fugitive who was now suspected to be leading a vicious insurgency. I might feel sorry for him, but he was on the wrong side. I did, however, question his intelligence value, and the usefulness of keeping him in deep isolation. That seemed to be taking it too far.

Then there was the beating. Why did I report this alleged beating and not follow up on the beating that was allegedly delivered to Yaqud? It just never oc-curred to me that the beating Yaqud received was unjust. That was to be ex-pected, while Ahmad's beating was excessive. I had yet to draw clear lines on what was permissible. I thought I could make exceptions for some. I was not in a hurry to resolve the hazy morality of this war zone and lay down clear lines for myself. I proceeded with my judgments and feelings on a case-by-case basis.

We weren't done with Ahmad, by any means. An army psychiatrist got a chance to read my reports and asked permission to join me in the booth. He was interested in how to best exploit someone in this weakened state. I did my best to show the psychiatrist an authentic interrogation, but my heart wasn't in it. I was definitely uncomfortable with the idea of studying Ahmad to de-velop more enhanced interrogation techniques, and had to wonder what kind of doctor would cooperate with such a project, much less initiate one. The psychiatrist tried his hand at a few approaches, but got no further than I did. A degree in psychiatry doesn't give you an upper hand in the "dark art" of interrogation, apparently.

I reported back to Forbes, for the third time, that Ahmad had given no new information. He ordered me back into the booth, and said he would join me. Apparently, it was time to show the new guy, me, how it was done.

I watched closely and eagerly for a new technique, strategy, or approach, but Forbes just went over the same reports I had already reviewed several times. Every once in a while he'd see a detail that was missing, something I'd forgotten to ask. For example, he paused when he got to the part where Ahmad admitted to delivering groceries, including cans of soda, to his uncle. "What kind of soda does your uncle drink?"

All we had left to ask about were these minute details, but that was enough to keep Ahmad captive and in isolation. My team leader was adhering to the almost mystic philosophy of military intelligence that says it is possible to know all, and no detail should ever be left out. So don't forget to find out if your target drinks Coke or Diet Coke—you never know how that piece of information might fit into the grand puzzle being assembled, even as we speak, by wizardlike analysts in the bowels of the Pentagon.

So clearly, my job was to get something—anything—and lots of it. It was all quantity over quality. (And I understand from news reports that the NSA similarly is willing to vacuum up just about any piece of data from anywhere in the hopes that it might fit into one of their puzzles.) It's a universal philosophy in the intelligence community, and pretty convenient for the collectors, because we don't have to ever wonder about the value of the information. It's all good.

But for someone like Ahmad, this meant that his interrogations could go on forever. And each time he forgot something or left out a detail, and that was reflected on an intelligence report, he could be certain that soon someone like me would be pointing a finger at his chest and shouting, *We know you're not telling us something*. The interrogations for him must seem endless, the interrogators insatiable. With no contact with his family, no lawyer, no inkling of what might be happening outside the prison, interrogators asking him about the soda his uncle drinks, what hope could he have left? Just that occasionally he might get to see the sky between an interrogation and another vast, empty expanse of time in his tiny cell.

CHAPTER 6

Outside

The prospect of spending a year behind the walls of Abu Ghraib was stifling, but others had it worse. The counterintelligence people in my battalion were itching to do the high-contact work they'd been trained for—interacting closely with locals, running agents and informants, setting up surveillance. We could all clearly see the need for this kind of work, but rumor had it that our higher-up officers were determined to return home with zero casualties. They were reluctant to let anyone roam around the country no matter how much they wanted to.

The only way I could get off base was by joining convoys to the airport. Lieutenant Colonel Wright had briefed us, just prior to entering Iraq, that the road to Baghdad International Airport was incredibly safe and secure, wide and well maintained. These kinds of wild misstatements from our officers—intelligence officers, mind you—were surprisingly common.

The road was not safe, but it was my only chance to get outside the walls, so I hopped on as many convoys as I could, sometimes as a driver, sometimes as a gunner. It was a short and fast run, incredibly tense and full of signs of previous attacks: burned-out cars, twisted guardrails, craters, and bridges pockmarked with bullet holes. We were shot at several times on this trip, but I never heard the shots over the roaring engines, and never returned fire. The only sign that we'd been singled out by a sniper were nicks on the steel plates that served as armor.

Being so exposed, so on edge, and backed up by such a large amount of firepower all appealed to my reckless side. This attraction to violence was a little disturbing, but I could tell myself that at least I wasn't one of those soldiers who'd volunteer for the trips so they could take potshots at carloads of Iraqis and brag about it later. There were plenty of those guys around.

I saw more examples of deteriorating humanity, similar to Ahmad, the longer I stayed at Abu Ghraib. Ra'id, a supposed insurgent leader captured in the Sunni Triangle area, reported for interrogation one day supported by two other prisoners. One of them told us he was sick, unable to walk. Ra'id, a stout, bald man, was pale, and a vague gray mist covered his eyes. My more experienced partner didn't buy it. "Bullshit. He can walk." The two prisoners at his side let him go. He took two steps toward us, and fell to the ground. My partner threw up his hands in frustration. He still didn't believe Ra'id was sick, so we went looking for a medic to clear Ra'id for interrogation. Not finding any available, we let it go. Ra'id didn't receive any medical attention. Months later, CID asked me about him. He had allegedly been tortured in the hard site, a process that stopped just before I arrived.

Occasionally I'd interrogate with William, the big friendly guy I'd known since basic training. He let me watch the interrogation of another high-value prisoner—one of two brothers who'd had significant contact with Saddam Hussein when he was in hiding. The brothers were both simple men, shepherds, without strong Baathist affiliations. Saddam had more or less thrust himself into their lives when he was a fugitive. Now, all three were prisoners, the difference being that Saddam had access to lawyers and would get a trial. These two brothers just got our endless questions.

Will had a strange relationship with one of them, Saad, who was maintaining his health and spirits about as well as could be expected. During the interrogation I witnessed, Will playfully poked Saad in the ribs, pushed him into a soft headlock, and gave him noogies with his fist. They seemed to get along famously, and Saad answered everything Will asked him. But days later, as I was walking toward the hard site, I came across Saad walking through deep, cold mud without shoes and Will standing back, arms crossed, watching. Saad had done something to piss off Will and was being punished.

Saad didn't know it, but his brother, Jabbar, was breaking down from the isolation. When I faced Jabbar in the booth, he was skeletal, with lifeless eyes and a dusty gray hue across his skin. He was dirty and foul-smelling. In the booth, he chain-smoked, but the smoking never seemed to relax him. Unable to concentrate on anything I asked him, he just muttered the same thing, over and over. With many prisoners, I felt real compassion; in the booth with Jabbar, I felt only disturbed. He'd become a disgusting, pathetic creature. He had deteriorated so far that it was hard to imagine him as a healthy, normal man. I went to find his mug shot in the file, but couldn't make the connection between the round face, bright eyes, and red hair I saw in the photo and the inhuman presence that we kept in windowless isolation at the hard site.

I wasn't surprised that we were treating people that way, just like I wasn't surprised at hearing about the beatings. I was moved and felt sympathy, sometimes, but I wasn't surprised.

I remembered hearing soldiers talk about how detainees were treated in the war on terror even before I left for Iraq. I had a six-month wait at Fort Gordon, Georgia, between finishing my course at DLI and my deployment to the Middle East. I was assigned to inventory equipment returning from Iraq and clean sand out of tents and computers, and these were probably the most boring six months in my life. The bright spots were the highly informal trainings and briefings from interrogators who'd just returned from Afghanistan and Iraq.

When these veterans talked, we paid close attention. Most of us knew that 90 percent of what we learned in the schoolhouse was bullshit, and the real training would be hands-on, or would come from guys like these. In between the awful mandatory army PowerPoint presentations on tolerance and filmstrips on the dangers of drunk driving, we'd listen to these veterans and learn about how interrogation is really done. This is where I learned about using stress positions, loud music, lights, sleep "adjustment," sexual humiliation, and manipulation of diet and environment, which included using the cold weather to distress the detainee. And it all seemed to make sense. It was also around this time that we read Mark Bowden's article "The Dark Art of Interrogation" in the *Atlantic Monthly*, which introduced us to the term "torture lite," which includes the treatment the veterans described to us. Bowden suggested that these methods of interrogation not only can work, but that they do not constitute torture; they are merely a form of coercion. He also argued that the interrogator should have these techniques, sometimes called "enhancements," at his disposal, albeit with responsibility and limits.

I remember thinking that this is what's going to be required in this war. I remember thinking that these techniques seemed more psychological, just an extension of the mind games we'd briefly studied at Fort Huachuca. The idea was to reduce the detainee to a basic set of needs, like the need for sleep, socialization, and food. Then the interrogator offers fulfillment of those needs in exchange for cooperation. Those things that seemed physical, like the stress positions, only induced discomfort, not pain. So how could any of this amount to torture, or even "cruel, inhuman, or degrading" treatment? Only the sexual humiliation seemed distasteful to me, probably more because of my own prudishness than any real cultural sensitivity. Aside from that, I was ready to try this stuff myself.

Without realizing it, I left for Iraq with a coiled mass of contradictory beliefs and urges inside. I wanted to do whatever it took to get intelligence from prisoners, but was still someone who could feel sympathy for them. I believed that torturing helpless prisoners was morally reprehensible, but believed that the "enhancements" I'd just learned about were fair and legal. I saw lines and boundaries, however vague, and I knew that I should stay within them, but at the same time I desperately wanted to push against them as hard as I could.

I believed that our prisoners would be bad men, hell-bent on the destruction of Iraq, but resisted any suggestion that would lead me to believe that they directly threatened the American way of life. I felt that I was doing a good job of resisting the army's political indoctrination, and so I felt I was also resisting the steady chipping away at my morality. Leaving for Iraq, I still would have preferred to serve under Jimmy Carter than George W. Bush. In Kuwait, Lieutenant Colonel Wright showed us a video that featured the soaring chords of Darryl Worley's "Have You Forgotten?" and images of the Twin Towers falling, flags waving, people crying. When it was done, Wright said, softly and dramatically, that he just wanted to remind us why we were going into Iraq. I wanted to vomit. Iraq had nothing to do with the 9/11 attacks. By the time we shipped over, we knew it had nothing to do with WMD. We were going in to make the best out of a terrible mistake, which I believed was the right thing to do, but showing the towers' collapse just fueled the fire in those who wanted to kill terrorists.

It was easy for me to resist such ham-fisted attempts at indoctrination. But the more subtle influences passed by my defenses unnoticed. So I was unsurprised to learn that Yaqud had been beaten, that we isolated prisoners to the point of mental illness, that stress positions and other enhancements were widespread. It was all part of the culture in which I was immersed. And if I were to be completely honest, when those subtle influences worked their way in, I quietly welcomed them. I knew they would let me see, and even do, certain things that lay beyond the reach of those in civilized society.

During my first month in Abu Ghraib, just as I was getting used to the sound of exploding mortars, a blast bigger than any I'd heard before filled the base. The insurgents had scored a direct hit on a fuel tanker, sending up a serious fireball and raining down shrapnel and pieces of truck. I ran to look, and noticed my buddies on the roof of our living quarters peering down. I climbed up and found the small group in a festive sort of mood, because no one got hurt, and because the sight of the burning tanker, the melted steel, and the secondary explosions were really cool.

I caught myself thanking the insurgents for taking out one of our tankers, because it was now one fewer piece of equipment we would have to drag back to Fort Gordon and spend days washing the sand out of. I hoped they'd hit a few more trucks before giving up. One of my buddies did me one better by wondering, out loud, how we could leak the coordinates of the quarters of our least favorite officer. I knew that our finding this funny was seriously screwed up.

After about four weeks at Abu Ghraib I was transferred to a Mobile Interrogation Team (MIT), which sounded a lot more exciting than my current job. Some of my buddies from DLI, the Arabic speakers, were also assigned to MITs: Tomas was attached to a special forces unit and Fred was assigned to work in the relatively peaceful south. I had no idea where I'd be going, and I didn't especially care as long as it was not here.

The first interrogation I did for this team took me only as far as the front gate of Abu Ghraib. Sergeant Jones, my new team leader, shook me awake in the dark hours one morning and told me an infantry patrol was on its way to the gate with three prisoners. They wanted an interrogator, someone who knew Arabic, to question these Iraqis at the gate before they dropped them into the system. This was unusual and exciting. I rarely got paperwork that adequately explained why someone had been arrested, much less a chance to talk to the arresting infantry. We were going to interrogate them at the gate because bringing Iraqis inside the prison required paperwork, which is exactly what we were trying to avoid. We drove to the gate in a Humvee.

The quiet at the gate, the generator-powered lights casting stark shadows, and the unusual lack of activity gave the scene a desolate, otherworldly atmosphere. As we waited for the patrol to show, I stood there with Specialist Evan N., a lieutenant, and my commanding officer, Captain Richards. They were all counterintelligence, and barely knew me. Sergeant Jones labeled me "the interrogation expert" and said I was going to lead this little assignment. They'd watch and learn.

We heard a car speed up to the wall, just around the corner, which put us on edge. Then came the hiss of a rocket-propelled grenade (RPG). The lieutenant, closest to the concrete bunker, dove first. I followed, landing directly on top of him. My CO, in turn, landed on me. The RPG was aimed at the guard tower above us, but it exploded on the wall. Shrapnel flew toward us, but no one got hit. With my heart racing and my rifle pointed where the car had been, I climbed out of the bunker. This was messed up, but exhilarating. We laughed, embarrassed at having ended up on top of each other, and then we heard another explosion. We dove into the bunker in a pile again. "Outgoing!" said the guard in the tower. We laughed again.

The infantry rolled up shortly after, looking powerful and intimidating with their bristling weapons, night-vision goggles, and laser scopes. I was immersed in the atmosphere, drawn in by the danger, tension, and seriousness of the scene. Two men unloaded three zip-tied prisoners with bags on their heads from the back of the five-ton truck. It was a long way down, and the prisoners fell roughly onto the gravel. The patrol's CO told me about the road-side bomb his men discovered, and what happened next. Two of the prisoners were working in a field slightly removed from the IED but with a good view. They were hundreds of yards away, but they were the closest ones and that was reason enough to pick them up. The patrol then went into town to question people. They got no information, but found one old man who acted evasive and suspicious. They arrested him too.

Now they were my prisoners. The patrol moved on to let us do our job. The prisoners knelt in the gravel. I separated them and got to work. I had no advance plan, so I did what came naturally and what I'd done before—I established a timeline and looked for contradictions. I started with one farmer and asked him to tell me what he did when he got up that morning, when he met the other farmer, and what they did next. Leaving him for a moment, I started in on the second farmer, asking the same questions. Contradictions started to bubble up. I went back to the first prisoner, a few of these contradictions in hand. Since I was new to this team, and supposedly the "interrogation expert," I did my best to put on a show. Lots of yelling, lots of intimidation. The rest of my team ate it up.

One of the prisoners had to piss. He was in great pain and begging for us to untie him. Maybe we would have obliged, but we'd forgotten to bring Zip-Cuffs out with us, so I told him he'd have to wait. It also occurred to me that this could help our interrogation. It was a little extra discomfort, and something to hang over his head. But as my questions went on, his begging got louder and more insistent. Soon, he couldn't think of anything else. I explained this to one of my teammates, who finally said, "Fuck it," and lifted the prisoner up to his full height. He frog-marched him over to the wall, pulled up his dishdasha, pulled down his pants, and stood aside.

A few moments later, the mortars started. We each took a prisoner, threw him roughly into the bunker, and ducked. Outgoing suppressive fire answered the attackers. My teammate, Evan, was fuming. We were all frustrated at being targets and never being able to shoot back. It was usually something we just had to swallow. Just moments before, during the RPG attack, we laughed about it. But now Evan had a prisoner in front of him. "Who the fuck is shooting at us? Where are they?" I translated, and I could see the farmers' eyes fill with fear. I wondered if I would have to push Evan back to keep this interrogation under control. More mortars. We scrambled for cover. The soldier in the guard tower looked down at us and shouted, "Outgoing!" We sheepishly stood back up.

"These guys' stories don't match. They might be involved in something," I explained to Sergeant Jones. My team was impressed and full of praise. All my novice skullduggery and liberal use of Fear Up Harsh looked to them like magic. They were as green as I was and we didn't see that I had performed a bad interrogation. "This guy"—I pointed to the old guy—"isn't involved in anything. We should let him go."

Just like that, my superiors followed my recommendation. We bagged the heads of the two farmers, then grabbed an MRE out of our Humvee and handed it to the old man. I asked him to pardon us for arresting and questioning him. "It is your right," he replied. He was deferential, but he really wanted to know what he was supposed to do when he got arrested again on his way home. It was well past curfew, so this was sure to happen.

"Show them the MRE," Evan offered.

"They'll just say I stole it," he shot back. He was right, but I didn't think to write him a note, so I shrugged and we fell back to the relative safety behind the walls, our prisoners in tow. He shoved the MRE under his dishdasha and walked off.

I don't know what happened next to those two farmers, but I hope they got out quickly. Months later, I thought back to that night, and realized I had made a mistake. I never should have recommended them for detention. There was no evidence linking them to the IED. Their stories were inconsistent only in very minute and mundane details—anyone could have messed up that timeline, especially in the middle of the night, kneeling in gravel, with mortars falling. We just didn't have evidence on them, or any reason to believe they had any intelligence.

Like Evan demonstrated by asking who was shelling us, most soldiers seemed to believe that all Iraqis know who the insurgents are, where the weapons are hidden, and where the next attack will be—they just weren't telling. As if you could pick up anyone off the street at random and, with sufficient interrogation, extract some useful bit of intel from them. That simply wasn't true. The Iraqis suffered at the hands of the insurgents much more than we did, but we still handled the situation as one of us versus them. We were the targets; they were the collaborators.

It didn't occur to me at the time, but the patrol that discovered the IED had no reason to believe these two farmers had anything to do with it. But they were nearby, and so they were worth arresting. Then they were handed to someone like me, who really wanted to believe that the infantry had a good reason to pick them up. I always wanted to give the infantry, who faced the greatest danger and were closest to the situation, the benefit of the doubt. They were, in my mind, truly heroic. Their bravery made them seem honest and professional. And they were on my side.

Back at that moment, when we brought the prisoners into the processing building, and my teammates were telling me I'd done a great job, I was proud and elated. I felt I'd done well, under fire no less. I thought I had done the right thing at the time. It wasn't until much later that I realized I had jumped to conclusions and treated my decision to imprison these farmers far too lightly. But on this night, as I went back to my cot, I was looking forward even more to getting out in the field, where I could do more work like this. Before I lay down, I noticed I was enjoying the sensations of an increasingly familiar mixture of excitement and fear.

PART II

AL-ASAD AND MOSUL
FEBRUARY TO MAY 2004

It is true that a man who refuses to speak does not give himself away,
but on the other hand he may appear more dangerous than he is;
his silence is taken to mean that he must have much to hide . . .
and this makes it seem all the more important to not let him go.
Persistent silence leads to cross-examination and to torture.

—Elias Canetti, *Crowds and Power*

CHAPTER 7

Away from the Flagpole

The helpless must be protected. Even if they are dangerous, murderous, vile, or insurgent, their captors must protect them. This axiom is the basis of international law, especially pertaining to prisoners. It does not differentiate between the helpless who are innocent and the helpless who are heinous.

As a moral principle, the axiom is transcendent. It goes far beyond practical morality and gut instinct. It lies in a moral plane so far above us that we often resent it. Why should we protect evil and monstrosity, even as it is being punished by imprisonment? Why do jailed murderers deserve to be free from pain and fear? Why do the condemned deserve a painless and tightly regulated death?

Then there is the moral hypothetical, the "What would you do if" that includes a ticking bomb and countless civilian deaths. The hypothetical pulls the axiom from its lofty plane and drags it through the mud of our own recent history.

The idea of protecting the helpless is central to the Geneva and Hague conventions. These two projects were born from emotional reactions—visceral worldwide horror over modern combat—but were accepted by nations for practical reasons—namely, reciprocity. If we don't use chemical weapons on their civilian populations, for instance, ours won't suffer the same fate. If we don't kill their civilians, they won't kill ours. If we don't torture their soldiers, when our soldiers are captured, they will come home safe and unharmed. In this way, the argument goes, we can rationalize and humanize warfare. Those who carry arms are fair game, but those who are helpless will be protected.

By wrapping a transcendent idea in a package of practical morality, we doomed the project to failure. We so watered down the idea that a White House lawyer (later attorney general), Alberto Gonzales, dismissively called the protections "quaint." We opened the door to exceptions. Instead of one law for all, we developed a set of laws for "enemy combatants," another for "persons under control," and another, very ad hoc, set of rules for Iraqis.

The big moral hypothetical used to almost always involve a dictator, a Hitler or a Stalin. In the age of terror, the moral hypothetical is the "ticking bomb." Do you torture someone if they have knowledge of where the bomb is located? Or do you just let it explode and sacrifice hundreds or thousands of innocents? Do you avoid inflicting pain on one person, and in the process allow many more to suffer or die? Who is more moral, the person who tortures this prisoner or the person who appeals to a transcendent idea that refuses to discriminate between innocence and evil?

In Iraq I came to believe, as did many others, that the ticking bomb was not a hypothetical. We were hearing and seeing the results of actual bombs every day. When the infantry brought us a prisoner, and said that he was an insurgent, oftentimes all we could hear was the ticking of a bomb.

"Away from the flagpole" is that blissful state of being when a soldier leaves the bases where his commanders gather together and try to dream up new ways to make his life suck. Even if you leave your base and go to another, the units at the other base tend not to bother about you. You are fairly well left alone. Petty regulations and detail-oriented oversight tighten in direct proportion to your proximity to the flagpole, and relax the farther away you get. Because it was crawling with brass and VIPs, Abu Ghraib had as big a flagpole as any base in the United States, but few of the perks, and plenty of incoming mortars and rocket-propelled grenades. So, as strange as it seems, a lot of us preferred the idea of being in the field, maybe closer to the enemy but farther away from the brass.

This helped temper the fear of traveling in a lightly armed and lightly armored convoy up to the northern reaches of Iraq. This was our mobile interrogation team's first mission. Our convoy from Kuwait was massive. By comparison, this convoy, just three vehicles, was puny. Our civilian contract interpreter, Daoud, was scared out of his wits, especially after he found out that he was sitting on all our extra ammo. He hadn't signed up for this. He thought he'd be on a safe base for a year, not driving through the night with his life in the hands of very green military intelligence guys who were desperate to get off base.

After a short stay in Al Ramadi, we reached al-Asad Airfield. Where Abu Ghraib was confined, al-Asad was expansive. Where Abu Ghraib was muddy and foul, al-Asad was beautiful desert under bright blue skies. The perimeter was wide, and the desert beyond largely unpopulated, so we were safe from mortars and snipers. We didn't have to wear helmets and body armor everywhere we went—again, very different from Abu Ghraib. The relaxed atmosphere was immediately evident in the way the Third Armored Cavalry Regiment strutted around base in their traditional wide-brimmed cowboy hats instead of the helmets we wore everywhere back at Abu Ghraib. *Too strange*, I thought, as I wondered how they deployed with these huge hats. Did they have special army-issued hatboxes?

Saddam built this base as a warning to Syria and called it al-Asad, "the lion," though he probably also wanted to thumb his nose at Syrian president Hafez al-Assad with this christening. Huge earth-reinforced aircraft hangars, each several stories high, broke up the flat desert. Before long, we climbed these hangars to watch the American helicopters come and go, and the C-130s drop paratroopers on training runs. Exploring this huge base by Humvee, we found all kinds of Iraqi bunkers and antiaircraft positions, some destroyed, some intact. These were sometimes stocked with ammo and food. The Iraqis who once manned them had obviously been hunkered down for a while. It seemed like a number of them had just walked away, leaving their supplies barely touched.

We had time to explore like this because we really had no reason to be here. On arrival, we reported to the lead interrogator for this base, who had no idea we were coming and had no need for extra hands. We never found out who requested extra interrogators. A young Sergeant, T. Gordon, whom I knew from Monterey, and a specialist, N. Packer, were running HUMINT (intelligence from human sources) for the base all on their own, and didn't think they needed help. But if we were willing to pitch in, lightening their load even further, that was fine. "Just look through the files. If you feel like you want to talk to a prisoner, go ahead," Gordon said and shrugged, setting the tone for what would be a very lenient three weeks.

The prison area, tucked into a corner of one of the enormous hangars, was anything but relaxed. Walking into the hangar was like stepping into a Gothic cathedral. Light and sound were altered and the space seemed large enough to support its own climate. As I walked across the long empty space to the prison, my footfalls echoed slowly, calling attention to my presence. A guard faced the concertina wire that enclosed his prisoners. They were lined up in rows, sitting, facing forward. They weren't allowed to speak to guards or to each other and could change positions only insofar as they stayed in formation. It was very different from the bedlam of Abu Ghraib— no one reaching out through the wires, no one shouting, "Mister!" But the silence and imposed order had an eeriness all its own. A prisoner could spend weeks like this, sitting in rows, prohibited to speak, staring straight ahead.

I pulled a prisoner who had been identified as former Mukhabarat (Iraqi intelligence). He had an interrogation report in his file that read, in emphatic bold capitals, "He should never be let out of prison. He says he's a farmer, but he's Iraqi intelligence." In the booth, the prisoner, Amer, seemed confused, not just by his situation or by my accusations, but by everything. He spoke slowly and stumbled over his own words. He was ill fed, bony, and his callused hands and feet spoke of a lifetime of manual labor and shoeless field-work. He said he was a farmer. I insisted that we *knew* he was a former intelligence officer.

It didn't take long before I slipped into Fear Up Harsh—yelling at him in Arabic, slamming my fist, pointing my finger, and in general doing my best to scare the living shit out of him without directly threatening him. Fear Up Harsh was all I had. The previous interrogator insisted he was a bad guy, but when I looked in the file again, there was nothing. No evidence, no hearsay, nothing. Just the story of what happened when they picked him up. I had no leverage, nothing with which to trap him, no way to subtly lead him to the information I wanted. I kept yelling.

Soon he was crying. It was hard to tell if he was crying because my act was so good or because he came to the conclusion, sitting there, that he was never going to see his family again. I stormed out and filed a report. *Prisoner refuses to cooperate. Recommend transfer to Abu Ghraib for further interrogation.* This interrogation set the pattern. I did almost nothing but this for three weeks.

I should mention that once a prisoner was sent to Abu Ghraib, he might languish there for six months before anybody reviewed his case at all. Many stayed there for much longer. There was a huge backlog, and the guys in the field were under pressure to keep a steady flow of prisoners. It looked like progress.

For someone who was supposed to be the interrogation expert on this small team, I was very inexperienced, and admitted as much. Interrogation, however, has this aura of mystery around it. The uninitiated often believe the process is about discovering the best path through a labyrinth of deception built up around a prisoner's mind or finding a key to unlock the secrets hidden inside.

At the time, I still believed some of this myself. So when I fell into a pattern that looked nothing like the expectation, I started becoming frustrated. Over and over, I'd try a psychological approach based on whatever scanty information I had from the arrest report, listen to denials, run into a dead end, jump up to yell and badger, storm out, and recommend that the prisoner be sent to Abu Ghraib. If there is a high art to the dark art of interrogation, I was missing it.

My team leader, however, knew less about interrogation than I did. Sergeant T. Jones had been trained in counterintelligence and, I believe, would have done a great job developing contacts and running agents, if he had been allowed outside the base, as he was during his first tour in Iraq in 2003. Jones is a businessman now, but had been in the army for six years. He was born and bred in the South in an African-American middle-class family that valued military service. Smart, disciplined, and personable, Jones was promoted fast and did his job well. But what made him really stand out is the fact that it was clear he had nothing to prove. He was the most straight-ahead, no-nonsense guy I met in the army. I served under Jones for most of my year in Iraq.

We had two other team members, Bill Bates and Lisa M. Bill was a great guy to work with, psyched about the mission and deeply dedicated to helping the Iraqis. He was staunchly Republican and very religious; we got along well except when the topic of the 2004 elections came up, and that was always my fault. The closer we got to November, the more pissed off I became. Also, I don't think he ever got used to me asking him questions about his religion. I was honestly curious, but I think he took a lot of ribbing about his strict beliefs and assumed I was setting him up. Bill was smart, methodical, and a natural at interrogation. He also had good instincts about the prisoners. His hunches were often more valuable than my training.

The first occasion I spent any length of time with Lisa, I tried to get her to yell at me. She was very uncomfortable interrogating, so I played the role of a prisoner. We sat in the middle of one of the hangars as I put on my very best "belligerent Arab" act. She could hardly make eye contact. Over the next few months she got better, but she never really gained the confidence of the team. One reason: she prohibited us from watching her interrogations. So we never really knew what was going on in the booth.

"Something bad" had happened at al-Asad as well, but unlike at Abu Ghraib, we didn't get this from official channels, and no one told us not to talk about it. I found out from Sergeant Jones that someone had killed a prisoner. That's all he knew. This time, I didn't even bother trying to learn more. I still hadn't heard anything about what happened at Abu Ghraib. I'd accepted that I would probably never know.

There were signs all around me that something was wrong: the rumors of homicide, the fear and hopelessness of the prisoners, the arrest reports that asserted someone was a terrorist but gave no evidence other than some anti-American graffiti, and the corruption of the Iraqi police, which was widespread throughout Iraq, but which I learned about during my second week at al-Asad.

The prisoners were a father and his two adult sons. Their crime was serious—they were accused of killing some twenty Iraqis. I went into the booth with the father, Jallal, ready to tear apart whatever lies he put forth. "Do you know why you're here?" Of course, he said he didn't. Or to be more specific, he said he didn't know why I thought he was there, but knew how he had ended up there. I listened to his story.

The Iraqi policeman who fingered Jallal and his sons had bought a truck from the family and still owed them quite a bit of money. He'd warned Jallal to forget about it, or face jail time. Instead, Jallal complained to the authorities. Okay, I thought, this is probably bullshit. But lies like these can be useful when you have two other prisoners. Let him lie, and let the others contradict. Wrap him up in his own lies and the others' contradictions, and let them all hang themselves.

I gathered minute details about the truck and the purchase and took them to the sons, one at a time. I was surprised to find that every detail matched. I tried another round, focusing on details that the two sons offered that the father had not. It all checked out. The level of detail—for example, specific threats made by the policeman—was not something that the three would have been likely to fabricate beforehand.

I checked on the crime. Indeed, a number of murders had occurred in the area recently. But not twenty. This was a tough call. The charges were serious and came from someone closer to the people than even our infantry patrols. But the policeman's story was full of holes, and the family's story was airtight. I wrote this up in a report, noting that the prisoners did not show any signs of deception. Two weeks later, they were released. This was one of the first cases where I felt I had done the right thing and continue to feel that way today.

In Abu Ghraib, I saw how the U.S. forces arrested, detained, and interrogated family and associates of high-value targets if they had contact or if they aided and abetted the one we really wanted. It bothered me that these prisoners had no chance at freedom, or even a fair trial, but I understood why we were doing it. I had a harder time understanding the justification for the detention of Iraqis like Alim, a small, skinny fourteen-year-old from the city of Qaim.

Intelligence had targeted Alim's second cousin, but since they couldn't find him, they picked up Alim instead. Another interrogator, Sergeant Michaels, took the lead, and I went into the booth as an observer. Neither of us was prepared for Alim's response to our questions:

"Yes. I don't know if he is an insurgent, but he has rifles and rockets and bombs. I'll show you where he keeps them."

Sergeant Michaels and I looked at each other, and I ran to get a map. Alim did a surprisingly good job reading the map. We only had to show him a few landmarks before he could navigate it on his own. Few rural Iraqis could do this. "The weapons are buried here, buried in the land."

"Who does he associate with?" Sergeant Michaels continued. Alim started giving us names and locations of the people he suspected of being insurgents. The kid was amazingly precise and forthcoming. I was excited because we were finally getting intelligence from a prisoner, and I admired Alim for taking what he knew must be serious risks.

"Where is your cousin?" Sergeant Michaels brought the interrogation back to our original objective. And this is where it all started to go horribly wrong.

"*Wallah, ma'arif,*" Alim replied. I could see Sergeant Michaels's face register disgust. We all had heard "I swear to God I don't know" so many times. We were all tired of it.

"You're lying," Sergeant Michaels shot back. I could see where this would lead, but could do nothing to interfere. Within moments, Sergeant Michaels was in full Fear Up Harsh mode, and Alim was in tears. Sergeant Michaels asked him if he knew what would happen if he didn't cooperate. Of course he knew. All Iraqis knew. Abu Ghraib was the destination before we invaded, and was the destination still. He nodded as he sobbed.

That was Sergeant Michaels's last card, and he declared the interview over. He went to file his report as I escorted Alim to his new home behind the wire. He cried the whole way.

The next day I heard that Alim had collapsed in the prison compound. I double-timed over to the medic's office and found him writhing on a table as MPs tried to hold him down. He was screaming and his eyes darted around without seeing. He looked like he was possessed. Alim had not been allowed to take his medication with him when he was arrested. Without it, he told me later, he would suffer regular seizures.

Although this was an unusually busy time for us, I looked up Alim's file. My heart sank as I read a recommendation written by Sergeant Michaels for transfer to Abu Ghraib. I stared at the report in disbelief. I had wanted to believe Michaels was bluffing about sending Alim to Abu Ghraib. Things were becoming clearer. In this war, we refused to distinguish between witnesses and criminals. If someone had information, no matter how it was they came about it, they were as good as guilty. Alim had cooperated extensively; we learned things from him we didn't even know to ask. No one ever suspected him of being involved in the insurgency. And yet, his information seemed to be so good that we couldn't let him go. If he knew a little, he must know more. That made him worth keeping.

I put in a request to interrogate Alim myself. My plan was to file a separate report commending him for his cooperation and recommending release. The next day, I sat down with Alim in the booth. He was already crying, begging not to go to Abu Ghraib. And how would his family know where he was? And how would he get back? It took me several minutes to assure him. I then took some time to ask him questions about himself, as a way to calm him down.

Alim lived with his parents and older brother. He had a moped that he used to run errands and messages for other people in his city. It was all he had as far as a job, and he wanted to be able to be more help to his family. I asked him what he wanted to do when he became an adult. He hoped that maybe someday he would find a wife and earn enough to support a family. He had never seen an American movie, and had few ideas about America. I asked him if he would ever want to visit there. "Do you think they would let me?"

We clarified a few of the intelligence items he'd given us already. He was much calmer. I told him I'd try to get him released. With Alim back behind the wire, I started typing a report as quickly as possible, wondering all the while what the hell we were doing to this kid and his family and for what possible reason. I hid my disgust from my superiors and filed the report just as I had any other.

I was too late. The decision had already been made. Alim was soon on his way to Abu Ghraib. In talking to my superiors about this, I saw the same assumptions at play—all Iraqis know where the insurgents are, all Iraqis are liars. These were good men, but they had clearly made an awful mistake. In any case, the deed was done and there was nothing I could do. The bureaucracy of the army was a leviathan, slow and unstoppable. I'd never felt so helpless.

When I got back to Abu Ghraib a few weeks later I searched the database for Alim, and got no hits. Probably someone had screwed up the transliteration of his name—entered Aleem instead of the more standard Alim—and his prisoner number would have changed when he was processed at Abu Ghraib. Alim, at fourteen years old, had disappeared into Abu Ghraib's throng.

At al-Asad I was seeing more children than at Abu Ghraib, and this bothered me. I remembered one family—a father and two sons, ages eight and eleven—who earned a living fishing and making deliveries on the Euphrates. They shut off their running lights as an American patrol passed, and that was enough to arouse suspicions and get them arrested. I'll never be able to forget how the eight-year-old reacted to the medical exam. He assumed the worst—probably something he'd heard about before. There's nothing like the unchecked fear that pours out of a child when they fear what's going to happen next and they *know* how bad things can get. It took a very soothing female Arabic speaker to calm him enough to get the exam done.

I talked to the father and sons and could see no reason why they should be detained. Still, it took three weeks before they were released. That, unfortunately, was normal. Slow-moving paperwork, of course, was the culprit.

Things didn't work quite right at Al-Asad, but I was only dimly aware at the time of what was wrong. I tended to blame the problems I saw on a lack of communication between the arresting infantry and the interrogators or a lack of oversight or classic snafu. When confronted with something extremely disturbing, I closed my eyes.

Specialist Dan, one of the interrogators who had been there a year, was a boisterous, friendly guy. So I was shocked when, one day as we sat in the office, feet up on the desks, he told me about various "pressure points" he'd discovered that aided his interrogations. He laughed as he told me about kneeling on a prisoner while probing these pressure points. He thought it was funny because of the way the prisoner howled with pain under his touch. Even torture lite, which I now believe to be brutal, recognizes a sharp line between inflicting pain without touching the detainee, as with stress positions, and an interrogator actually causing pain with his own hands, like Dan was doing. I knew that using "pressure points" was not allowed even under a liberal reading of the rules, but in one of my more cowardly moments, I didn't say anything. I just nodded.

I knew that Dan's methods were over the line, but still, one day about a week later, I asked Dan for advice. I'd been given a prisoner who was almost certainly, I believed, a dangerous insurgent—a warrant officer who had interrogated the detainee in the field had said so. One of the first things the prisoner, Habib, did was lift his shirt to show me how he had been tortured by Saddam's henchmen. Either a fast whip or a sharp knife had left scars across his chest and back. Showing his scars was his way of explaining that he hated Saddam as much as we did, that he loved America for setting Iraq free, and that he would never lift a finger against us. I was not convinced, but the scars were cause for concern. There was nothing I could do that could match the torture he'd already been through. Habib would be tough to break.

After about thirty minutes of yelling and invective, I left the booth and asked Dan what he had in his toolbox for prisoners who wouldn't talk. "Well, first I take them into one of those aircraft hangars. Leave him in the dark for a while. That freaks them right out."

I cuffed Habib and walked him to an empty hangar. As I opened the door, light poured into the cavernous space but did not fill it. Our footfalls echoed through the emptiness. The air was deathly still. It felt like a tomb. Habib stiffened. In his mind, I thought, he must be reminded of previous torture. Why else would I take him to this place except to really work him over? We walked into a small enclosed room with no windows.

I chained Habib to a bed frame that had been fastened to the wall, I believe, just to have something to chain prisoners to. I felt something like the presence of ghosts, but it was just the feeling that many other prisoners had been here before Habib. Without a word, I walked away from Habib and closed the door, leaving him alone with his thoughts in utter darkness.

I returned after a half hour. Habib had a different look in his eyes, but had the same responses to my questions. This was clearly not working. Was I doing something wrong? I found Dan. "Shut the door and stand in there with him. Talk to him. He won't know where you are or what you are doing. That scares the hell out of them."

After another half hour in the darkness, with me standing there talking to him in intimidating tones, I started to feel foolish. Habib was not going to break. This haunted house treatment was going nowhere. I could only imagine what he was thinking as he compared his torture at the hands of Saddam's agents to my pale imitation. I thought briefly about taking this to the next level, but I didn't know what that might be. I returned Habib to the prison. Let the guys at Abu Ghraib take their best shot. (Looking at his file later, with a more critical eye, I actually could find no evidence that he was an insurgent. He may well have been totally innocent.)

That dim awareness was back. I had crossed a line somewhere, I knew, but it wasn't until much later that I saw clearly what that line was. At the time it was easy to justify. It clearly wasn't torture, in my thinking at the time. We even had fancy names for what I'd done—Environmental Manipulation or Change of Scenery Down—and they were approved techniques. No one ever talked about putting someone in the dark, but my actions seemed to fall neatly into this category. So what line had I crossed?

My intention was to induce a panic attack. While I'd yelled at prisoners before, and implied dire consequences if they didn't cooperate, I'd never deliberately tried to fill someone with so much fear that his reason and resistance collapsed entirely. This was something new for me, and for reasons I couldn't explain at the time, it didn't sit right. I knew, I must have known, that something was wrong when I sent an e-mail to a close friend describing what I'd done. "Where is this going?" I asked, more to myself than to her, and then answered my own question. "I don't know."

CHAPTER 8

Shadows

The marines came to al-Asad to replace the army, and once they arrived, the marines had no use for us. *Too bad*, I thought, because I'd grown used to this place and I would have gladly served with the jarheads. The ones I'd known back at DLI were outstanding, serious servicemen who had an aversion to the bureaucratic inertia that was as strong as the army's attraction to it. The marines' advance men looked around the interrogation center and the prison and immediately started making changes for the better. By the time I left, it was starting to look like a very tightly run ship.

I reported back to Abu Ghraib, which I hated even more than when I'd left. Nothing appeared to have changed, but there were a few more prisoners who were accused of insurgency instead of merely being remnants of the old order. Intrigued, I joined my DLI buddy Fareed (né Fred) in an interrogation of a very hardened insurgent—Majid al-Din, a veteran of Afghanistan and Chechnya—who had come to Iraq to meet with al-Zarqawi. I wanted to see and hear an actual insurgent fighter to see what I was up against.

Fareed was more knowledgeable than most of us about Arab affairs and Muslim sects, because he was really deeply interested. He'd cultivated an interrogation style that tried to pull the prisoner into a wide-ranging conversation about politics, religion, and society, gain trust, and develop a relationship that he could later exploit. Nothing could have been more inappropriate for Mr. Majid al-Din. He could easily see how inexperienced we were and how little Fred actually knew about his world. He played us like fiddles. He told us plainly that he came to Iraq to fight Americans and confirmed what we knew about him. We left the booth thinking we had a cooperative prisoner and a selection of good intelligence. The intel turned out to be half-truths, and al-Din managed to slickly escape from Abu Ghraib not long after. Escapes were pretty common. There were so many Iraqi contractors walking around base without IDs displayed that all a prisoner needed was to get out of his cage and out of his jumpsuit, and he could blend right in. But in the case of a prisoner like al-Din, an escape was absolutely unforgivable.

Fred got a transfer to work in southern Iraq, where his knowledge and approach actually had a chance of working. He was much better suited to work with willing subjects, winning friends and contacts, hearts and minds. He later sent me pictures of himself sitting cross-legged on rugs surrounded by Iraqis and traditional food. He looked like he was having a great time. Myself, I was going back north.

This period of time, spring 2004, was a critical few months for Iraq. The Iraqi Governing Council had signed an interim constitution, which provoked more frequent and more intense attacks. We saw violence continually ramp up considerably through April. We also saw the pictures of the four contractors killed in Fallujah, their charred bodies strung from a bridge. From that point on, there was steady talk about the impending attack on Fallujah. I listened closely because I got word that I was certain to be assigned there, and I felt both concern and fascination.

It turned out that one of our other mobile teams was sent to Fallujah, while our team was whisked away to Mosul in a C-130. In the hull of this massive transport plane, Lisa fidgeted, I read a book, and Jones, always thinking about his team, ran checklists and organization plans through his mind. Specialist Evan N. replaced Bill Bates, who had gone to Fallujah. I would work closely with Evan in Mosul. He was also a counterintelligence guy, not trained in the interrogation schoolhouse, but he picked things up quickly. Evan was a classic Long Island dude, complete with the L.I. accent, a deep love of Led Zeppelin, and pictures of himself with his baby (his Mustang). He always moved with an awareness of his newly acquired muscles from weight lifting. Everyone liked him, and he absolutely loved the army.

As a Mobile Interrogation Team, we traveled with our own laptops, communications equipment, and supplies, ready to rush off a plane or helicopter and into action within moments. We landed at Mosul International Airport, which was now an army base, ready to do business. As with al-Asad, we were there to supplement an existing interrogation operation, ready to jump in midstream.

But meeting the chief warrant officer, S. Pitt, we figured out that we weren't going to be a supplement. We were it. Chief Pitt was presiding over a nearly nonexistent operation. Of course he was glad to see us. Pitt was a stocky guy with a gray mustache and a strong handshake. All smiles, and with a real eagerness to see us get started, Pitt showed us the prison facility.

This camp was not very built up. The prison perimeter was a mass of concertina wire strung in a wide oval. The guard shack stood in the center. To one side there were four holding pens sectioned off by wire. One was empty, and was generally used as a temporary isolation pen. The other three had plywood shacks and were full of our subjects. Walk to the other side of the circle, and there one would find three interrogation booths, also made of plywood.

The perimeter of the prison area brushed against the perimeter of the base. While Abu Ghraib was claustrophobic, and al-Asad was wide open but isolated, this perimeter was just another set of wires. On the other side was Mosul. Close enough to reach out and touch, it seemed. We could see groups of Iraqis walking, driving, talking, or playing soccer, and they could see us, or shoot at us, if they were so inclined. Even worse, there was a five-story abandoned factory just meters from the perimeter that cast a shadow over the prison and interrogation booths. It looked like an ideal place to set up business as a sniper.

We walked over to our quarters. Not only was our new home a complete mess, full of army junk and trash, but it was merely a tent that offered no protection from mortars and was alarmingly close to the base perimeter. What insurgent could ask for more?

We awoke that night to extremely close and loud gunfire outside the fence. We could hear footfalls and shouting. Our side responded with brief, directed bursts. More gunfire from outside. We looked at each other. No one was sure how to respond. Poking our heads out in the middle of cross fire seemed kind of dumb. So we sat it out. It passed, and we went to sleep.

My first and very positive impression of Chief Pitt started to fade within days. I suppose that rank has its privileges, but I still felt there was something wrong with our pulling twelve-hour shifts while he holed up in the office watching a DVD of *Joe Dirt* for the fifth time. Probably just jealousy, but it grated, especially because he was keeping the pressure on us. He desperately wanted intelligence from these prisoners and couldn't figure out why we weren't getting anything from day one. Here was another guy who believed that there was some magic to interrogation, that we interrogators "have ways to make you talk."

But what really bothered me about Pitt was how he'd talk about the prisoners. It was never "the prisoner" or "the detainee" or "the suspect." It was always "numbnuts" or "the dirtbag" or "Hey—what did you get out of fuck-face?" We had Iraqis behind the wire for all sorts of reasons. Some we really believed were insurgents, some were suspected of having information but were not thought to be actual enemies. Most, I believe now, were totally innocent. But to him, they were all "dickweed."

We held meetings every day to debrief and work out plans and assignments. Pitt never left these meetings satisfied. Within the first week, his initial excitement about our team was gone. He couldn't understand why we weren't sending up intelligence reports.

The reason was totally obvious to me. We weren't getting good prisoners. Most of the hapless Iraqis we interrogated were arrested for minor "infractions" like possession of an AK-47 or mild anti-American propaganda. We had a lot of prisoners who were fingered by informants, or turned in by neighbors. Usually, this was their way of settling a grudge. Then there was a substantial class of prisoners who were there for God knows what reason. Mus'ad, for example, came to me with the thinnest arrest report I'd ever seen. It had nothing except "Suspect is a farmer in Tel Afar." So I asked him, "Are you a farmer?" Yes. "In Tel Afar?" Yes. "Gotcha."

Still another class of prisoners was there because the person who arrested them was ignorant. Our S-2, Captain Perry, sent word to our office one day with an urgent assignment. They said they had the brother of a well-known insurgent, Majid Ali Raad al-Jaboori. "We need you guys to get on him right away." They weren't even close. This guy wasn't a brother to any insurgent.

He had been mistakenly picked up at a checkpoint because he was from the same region as the guy we wanted.

Iraqi names work like this: your first name is your given name. Your second name is your father's first name. Your third name is your grandfather's first name, and your fourth name is your tribal name, usually similar to the name of the area where you were born. There were probably 100,000 people around Mosul with the tribal name al-Jaboori. They were not necessarily related by blood at all. If the detainee was the target's brother, it wouldn't have been uncommon or unreasonable to bring him in for questioning, but that wasn't the case at all.

So what happened here was this guy, Thamir Abood Hamid al-Jaboori, pulls up to a checkpoint and has to show ID. A buck private compares his ID to a blacklist. Aha! They have the same last name! By the time I heard about it, of course, the fact of their having the same tribal name had been exaggerated to the point where they were brothers. So Thamir gets arrested and has to explain this whole story to me because everyone else, from the private to the S-2, doesn't know this simple fact about Iraqi life. *And*, to add insult to injury, my report, which emphatically states that he is the wrong guy, takes weeks to be processed. Two to three weeks later, Thamir is a free man. At least until the next checkpoint.

There was this other prisoner whose son's name was Jaish—the same as the Arabic word for "army." So the prisoner was also known as Abu Jaish. Imagine how happy one of our more ignorant officers was to learn that the "father of the army" was in his prison! It took a lot of explaining to convince him otherwise. Same thing happened with anyone unlucky enough to have as their name the Arabic word meaning "struggle, strive, or utmost effort." "So, the prisoner's name is *Jihad*. Make sure he talks."

Each week seemed to bring fresh absurdity. Once, I interrogated three men who had been arrested at the gate. Two of them had been shot. One was crippled from birth and dragged his foot around behind him. They approached the gate and claimed compensation for their injuries and their car. They were driving through Mosul when they were caught in a cross fire. I guess they were lucky to be alive, but they were so poor that the car, lost wages, and medical care amounted to a small fortune.

The U.S. forces gave out money pretty liberally if they accidentally shot someone up or totaled their car or killed a family member. I don't know how the process of obtaining compensation worked, but it wasn't common to have people come up to the gate with fresh bullet wounds. So what did the guards do? Arrest them. They're wounded, so they must be involved in something. These three were comparatively lucky in that they didn't get sent to Abu Ghraib. They were not so lucky in that we detained them for several weeks. They didn't get the compensation they asked for, needless to say, and left our custody having lost almost a month of work, so they were even further behind.

It was probably three weeks into my stay at Mosul that I started to feel burnout and seething aggravation. I had a warrant officer who expected war-winning intelligence from every prisoner, a stream of shoddy arrest reports that gave me either no reason for detention or reasons that were absurd, and two to three prisoners a day who were often as baffled as I was about why they were in the system.

To these prisoners, I was their only hope. For most of them, I was the only person they would actually talk to, their only chance to make their case. The pleas, begging, and tears were constant. I heard about how their babies were starving, their mothers were sick, their wives were unable to fend for themselves. They told me about how Mosul was lawless and how they were at the mercy of gangs and thugs, about the lack of jobs, electricity, clean water, and the utter lack of any American assistance.

The sympathy I first felt for prisoners—even for prisoners who didn't deserve it—was fading away. My compassion was overexercised and fatigued, and I was shedding it not only because it was overburdened but also because it was pointless. No matter how I explained in my reports that there was no evident reason to hold these men captive, the odds were against them. My paperwork would stand in a queue at headquarters, be reviewed by officers trained not to judge guilt or innocence but only to assess intelligence value. If there was even a remote chance the prisoner had even an iota of intel (like maybe what kind of soda an insurgent preferred), they were worth keeping. If they were actually helpful, they could expect not a reward but a longer stay and more frequent interrogations.

I was craving alcohol for the first time since I'd arrived in Iraq. I wanted to be drunk and numb. Only once did I get any while we were in Mosul. Jones and I once convinced a female soldier who was a little desperate for our approval to wander the base and flirt with one soldier or other to score some strictly contraband booze. It was a real testament to her loyalty that she brought it back to us. So we sat in the trailer that I called home and drank, comparing horror stories. I secretly wished I was alone, and with a lot more liquor.

Most of the soldiers spent their free time watching movies. If Sergeant Jones and I had a chance, we'd play cribbage. If not that, I'd try to read. If I couldn't read, I'd end up back at the prison compound, talking to prisoners through the wire. Sometimes I'd pull one of them out, hand over a pack of cigarettes, sit down, and talk. The prisoners usually liked it because they could smoke and saw it as a chance to ingratiate themselves to someone who might help them. I liked it because this was my informal, self-directed class in Iraqi people and customs, and it taught me how far apart we are.

Iraqis knew America not through our cultural exports, like movies, TV, and fast food, but through our weapons. Our displays of power during the First Gulf War and during Shock and Awe had left an impression. Iraqis took note of the precision and lethality of our bombs. When our soldiers rolled through town in their Strykers, loaded down with expensive equipment, seemingly impervious to bullets and well protected from bombs, Iraqis felt helpless. Our power was evident; our show of strength was awesome.

To speak generally, Iraqis reacted to this in two different ways. They either feared us or hated us. To the proud and formerly powerful, or to those who lost a loved one at our hands, our presence was a slap in the face, a direct challenge. To the humble and simple, we were just the new Saddam. There were just too few examples of our power being used in benevolent ways. But whether they hated or feared us, no Iraqi could figure out, with American power, money, and know-how on constant display, why we couldn't keep their lights on.

*   *   *

When we entered the prison compound, we left our weapons in the bunker we used as an office. A loose weapon in the hands of a prisoner . . . well, that's something to avoid. So there I was, in the middle of the compound, in the middle of the night, watching five men in black ski masks walking purposefully toward the guard shack, and I was thinking about my rifle back in the bunker, the words "Fuck, fuck, fuck" ringing through my head. I ventured a question, "What are you doing?," and waited for them to pull pistols from their waistbands. Instead, one of them said, "We have business here." And with that they were inside the guard shack.

Special forces. Who else would run around a base in the dead of night in a war zone dressed in ninja outfits and without a speck of insignia? These guys slipped on and off base like shadows and answered to no one. A guard told me they were SEALs, but I honestly never saw an insignia or patch that could identify them as such. They had their own small compound near ours that was off-limits, and a little plywood shack where they took their captives before turning them over to the regular prison, after they were finished. On this night, they decided they wanted another crack at a prisoner they had already turned over, so they came in and took him.

We never saw their interrogation reports, if there were any, and sworn statements from the arrests were sparse. They never shared their intelligence or deigned to tell us what they were up to. Their prisoners were mysteries to us, but the assumption was that if the special forces guys brought them in, they must be high-value. Chief Pitt, especially, directed us to focus on these prisoners. *They must know something.*

One of the first of these was a skinny, impressively articulate young man named Fadel. The SEALs dumped him in the prison one morning, so another interrogator and I went to his pen and called out his number in Arabic. Two prisoners supported him as he walked with us to the interrogation booth. His feet were swollen and black and he had burns on his legs.

Once we were in the booth, Fadel's fear left his eyes when Evan asked him what happened to his feet. I think he assumed he was about to get beaten or worse. Fadel spoke at length and answered every question we had. I had no reason to believe he was lying.

After the fall of Baghdad, Mosul fell into chaos as the Americans, spread thinly across northern Iraq, approached the city with a minimal force. The Baathist government, police, and army melted away. Thugs, looters, and killers ruled the streets. Fadel was a small man, an academic with a Ph.D. in engineering. He feared for his safety and for his family. He feared the Peshmerga, a Kurdish militia, who swept into town and threatened to take over the homes of Arabs. He asked a casual acquaintance where he could buy a gun.

This brought him into the orbit of Ghazi, one of those industrious Iraqis who quickly perceived the opportunities in the chaos. We knew Ghazi as an arms dealer. We all wanted him dead or in jail. But back then, he had to borrow Fadel's car and take Fadel's money in advance to score a rifle from suppliers unknown. When he returned, he handed Fadel an AK-47, some ammo, and Fadel's car keys. Fadel drove home and Ghazi walked away. Fadel never saw him again.

Fast-forward to March 2004, almost a year after the fall of Baghdad. In the middle of the night, men in ski masks snatch Fadel from his home. He is blindfolded and has no idea where he is going, but hears men muttering in English. After a long drive, he's forcefully walked to a seat. A man with a Lebanese accent asks him questions about Ghazi. He tells what he knows, explains what he did and why. His captors don't believe him. The voice tells him that his story is false and he must know where Ghazi is. *We know you haven't told us everything.*

Fadel, still blindfolded, is stripped naked and placed prone on the plywood floor. He feels cold water and ice poured over him. As he starts to shiver, he feels a small, thin tube inserted in his ass. It's left there. He hears laughter.

Next Fadel is bombarded with sound. Grating noises, distorted and only slightly resembling music. His blindfold is removed, but he can't see anything because a flashing light is right in front of his eyes. His head spins, and he's still very cold.

Fadel loses track of the questions. He still can't say anything but that he doesn't know where Ghazi is. He's moved to a chair, where, he says, someone beat his feet with a blunt object and burned his legs.

The other interrogator and I let him talk. We were silent. Fadel cried the entire time.

✳   ✳   ✳

I failed to file a report on what Fadel told us. I'm not sure why; maybe I was too busy, or wanted someone else to take that responsibility Later, though, the memory of Fadel got to me and I asked a buddy, back at Abu Ghraib, about him. Fadel had been transferred to Abu, and someone actually had filed an abuse report. That was the last I heard of him.

It was not the last I heard about these techniques. At least half a dozen prisoners told me about ice water, beatings, or the strobe and music treatment. These prisoners were separated by space and time, so I believe these were not coordinated stories. I also heard them from a guard, someone trusted to join these special ops guys in their plywood shack. He told me about the lights and the music and how a prisoner had ice water poured over him, and how one of them applied a rectal thermometer as a way of making sure his body temperature didn't drop too low. Then they stood around the prisoner, who was cold, wet, and shivering, with a thermometer in his ass. They laughed as they puffed on cigars.

Over the course of the next few weeks, we found ourselves getting rougher and rougher in the interrogation booth. Little by little we adopted what we heard about the SEALs' techniques until there wasn't much difference between us.

CHAPTER 9

Departure

Mosul is incredibly, surprisingly green. It first struck me as we flew in on a C-130, and continued to surprise me for the first few weeks of my stay. The green was fed by the Tigris, which had sustained people here for eight thousand years. The land here was stable enough for a bridge, and so this area had been, for centuries, an indispensable trade passage between east and west before the Suez Canal was built. The Arab conquerors of the eighth century thus called it Mosul, "the place of connection." Before that, Mosul was known as Nineveh.

On our airport compound, we were surrounded by 1.7 million Iraqis, a volatile mix of Arabs, Kurds, Turkomen, and Assyrians. (Mosul also had the highest proportion of Christians in Iraq.) The University of Mosul, one of the largest universities in the Middle East, at one time drew a diverse mix of peoples with its advanced research facilities. Fadel was just one of many highly educated Iraqis who called Mosul home.

Days after the fall of Baghdad, the Iraqi Fifth Army, stationed in Mosul, vanished. It just melted away. Since Turkey had prohibited the United States to invade from its territory, there were few coalition troops here in the north, and the city fell into chaos as serious as that seen in Baghdad. The Kurdish Peshmerga occupied towns to the north, and their drive to Mosul was a serious concern for Arabs, Turkey, and the U.S. forces. A tiny component of coalition special forces stopped them and entered Mosul, but their small numbers could hardly be counted on to provide security. A contingent of marines trickled into the city, but, according to the account given by Michael R.

Gordon and General Bernard E. Trainor in their book about the invasion, *Cobra II*, the flow of marines was suddenly cut off from above. Higher-ups at the Pentagon believed in a small footprint. The fewer boots on the ground, the better. I think you'd find few soldiers in Iraq who'd agree with that doctrine.

A component of this minuscule force found themselves, on April 14, 2003, trying to control a massive crowd downtown. Then they made the mistake of allowing a widely despised racketeer with Baathist ties a chance to address the crowd. They just didn't know better, and how could they? When the mob surged, the marines fired, killing between seven and ten Iraqis. Suddenly, the Americans were hated, and the city was in turmoil.

By the time the 101st Airborne (which had never planned on going near Mosul) arrived, they found a mere 750 marines holed up around the airport. According to Trainor and Gordon, the 101st Airborne's Major General David Petraeus calmed things down by acting as a go-between for diverse ethnic and tribal groups. He sat, listened, and negotiated. He made a point of walking through the city without a helmet or body armor. Eventually, he was able to cobble together a caucus that could provide the kernel of a local government. In a number of places in Iraq, there were signs of hope like this, for a brief moment. In the beginning, the U.S. military didn't believe the Iraqi people were the enemy, and didn't treat them as such. That started to change, with a change in leadership at the top.

Unfortunately, the Coalition Provisional Authority's Paul Bremer undid Petraeus's work in Mosul by halting the formation of local governments and then dissolving the Iraqi army. The protesters in Mosul rose up again, wounding sixteen U.S. soldiers. The reserves of goodwill washed away, and now our troops had to face an entire corps of disgruntled former soldiers who had never surrendered their weapons. Then, the 101st rotated out and was replaced by units that had to start more or less from scratch. So things were bad when I got there, though not as bad as they would get.

I kept trying to devise unique approaches to attack individual psychological defenses. We still didn't get much in the arrest reports, so I was frequently off the mark. One prisoner, I remember, I assumed would be a real tough guy. He was huge—around six feet three and 280 pounds—and looked like an

Iraqi Samoan. Another interrogator and I thought that this guy probably wasn't used to people disrespecting him, so we went for Pride and Ego Down, a series of pointed insults delivered with the objective of getting someone to admit to something to salvage their pride. Essentially, it's the line that goes, "No, he's too stupid to do something like that." It's a hard approach to pull off, and would only work with a certain type of prisoner, if it could work at all. I'm not sure why interrogators think insults and humiliation produce results. I think now that it is based on the mistaken belief that it's a way of establishing absolute power over the detainee.

So we started in on this bruiser. An informant had accused him of spray-painting something to the effect of "Yankee go home" on a wall, and that "tip" was enough to get him arrested. Maybe he had some insurgent connections he could tell us about. We told him we didn't believe the report because clearly he was illiterate and stupid, besides being fat and lazy, and so on. I guess we touched a nerve. The big bruiser broke down crying almost immediately. He was anything but a tough guy.

I bring this guy up because he was one of the first prisoners I apologized to. As my tactics became ever more harsh, I found myself more frequently out by the cages, talking to the prisoners I'd just tormented, trying to connect on a more human level and seeking some kind of forgiveness. I only did this when I was convinced that I'd just gone harsh on an innocent man, and only after I was sure that our interrogations were done. But it was strange. Prisoners thought it was strange also, though some of them, like this big guy, welcomed it.

In the booth, however, I was still acting badly. In some cases I thought that increasing the detainee's fear and helplessness was the key to breaking him. And even though that inconvenient compassion was still at play, as evidenced by my apologies, I wanted to take interrogation further. Actually, I wanted to take it as far as I could. If we had the freedom, we could certainly break the prisoners, I thought. Soon we would be granted that freedom.

Chief Pitt, when he wasn't watching movies, was demanding results. As we came back from the interrogation booth empty-handed, he wanted to know what else we could do to ramp up the intensity. The methods used by the men in ski masks seemed promising. They were, he felt, getting great intelligence. They never actually shared any of that great intelligence with us, and we had no reason to believe that they were getting results, but I think people in regular forces are a little in awe of elite forces. If they were using more intense tactics, it must be because they work.

This was all talk for a while, and I managed to resist the demands for prolonged stress positions and other enhancements because I knew that it wasn't worth it. We weren't getting prisoners that had any information to extract.

About three weeks after we arrived in Mosul, two cousins showed up in our prison. Special forces had dropped them off there, and, as usual, we had no idea where they came from or why they were in custody. Then, one guy who worked with them, who knew Sergeant Jones from training in Huachuca, delivered a transcript. If it was all true, it was a gold mine.

The transcript appeared to be a conversation between the two cousins and a third party. They talked about whom they were going to recruit, what their group had already done, where they were going to get money, where their weapons were stashed away, and what they were going to blow up. Great stuff. Far above and beyond anything I'd seen before. If this was all legit, who knew how far this could go?

Pitt was almost salivating as he described what he wanted to do. Coincidentally, interrogators from his unit had just joined us, but instead of letting them relieve us, Pitt decided to keep his shop open twenty-four hours. Our focus was on these two cousins, and our assignment was to put the pressure on and never let up.

The three new interrogators were a tight-knit group and I never got a very good read on them. Their leader, Staff Sergeant J. Edwin, who had worked in Guantánamo, probably had more hands-on interrogation practice than anyone I'd served with. He loved to talk, but rarely gave specifics. He preferred to try and impress rather than inform. I did benefit from him, however, in that he advised us to be very cautious about accepting orders and to get questionable orders in writing. Edwin had been doing interrogation for a while: he'd seen political fallout from enhancements and experienced the frustration of working in an intelligence operation that could not produce intelligence. He knew it wasn't worth getting in trouble for playing the fool in the interrogation booth. He also knew that when the trouble comes, it rolls downhill and the leaders hide behind their subordinates, who take the fall.

We sat around a table with Chief Pitt, and he told us what he wanted us to do. First, we soften them up. Don't bother doing a serious interrogation at first. Throw some questions at them, but mainly focus on breaking down their will to resist. Start by keeping them up all night—in stress positions.

This brought us to the Interrogation Rules of Engagement (IROE). At the time I was in Iraq, there were different IROE depending on where you were, with whom you were serving, and when. The IROE at Abu Ghraib (which have been leaked and published), for example, kept changing and shifting. Various army investigators pointed out that it was difficult, if not impossible, for interrogators to keep up—we had different IROE at Mosul than we had at al-Asad. Elite forces worked from yet another IROE. But while the particulars varied, there was one central purpose to all of them—to permit us to push the limits of what we learned in school, what was in the army interrogation manual, and what was in the Geneva Conventions. They were broad, self-contradictory, and malleable. A reporter who reviewed a leaked IROE from Abu Ghraib was very accurate in saying that it was "almost Talmudic in its intricacy."[1]

We had to let our prisoners have at least four hours of sleep a night. But, Chief Pitt pointed out, it didn't say that those four hours had to be continuous. So he suggested we break those four hours into five pieces. I suspected that wasn't what the IROE intended, but I offered only the weakest arguments against his plan. I felt a little queasy about where this was going, but just like everyone else in the room, I was eager to have a go at these guys. They seemed to deserve it, and we certainly deserved the latitude we needed to finally get some results.

More than any other prisoners I'd encountered, these two actually looked sinister, especially the one named Mustafa, who had a pointed chin and ac-

---

[1] Mark Danner, *Torture and Truth: America, Abu Ghraib, and the War on Terror* (New York: New York Review Books, 2004).

tive eyes that darted around behind his squinting expression. His cousin, Bashr, looked slightly more vulnerable, but nevertheless gave off an aura of wickedness. I was glad they were in jail.

We separated Mustafa and Bashr and put our plan into action. We roused each from sleep—from the deepest sleep either of them would get for the next four weeks. Each faced an interrogator in a separate booth, who yelled questions that we knew they wouldn't answer, hardly waiting for a response. Then the interrogator stormed out in disgust. A guard flexicuffed the prisoner, bagged his head, led him out behind the booth, and ordered him to his knees. The prisoner didn't know it at the time, but he was in for a long wait, as the cold crept into his body.

Forty-five minutes later, the interrogator returned. Back in the booth, more yelling, posturing, and fear. Quickly, it was over, and Mustafa or Bashr was outside, wondering what exactly was going on. Eventually, when they were exhausted, it was nap time. We escorted each to a separate pen and told them to lie down in the dirt, still cuffed. Maybe they slept, probably not. Either way, we roughly jolted them from their repose forty-five minutes later and put them through the same routine. This went on all night, and all through the next day. Since there were six of us, we never had to let up.

What is the longest you have ever spent on your knees? Do you remember the stiffness when you stood up? Could you do it, with your hands tied behind your back, for an hour?

What's the coldest you've ever been? The desert's thin, dry air drops below forty degrees at night. If you've ever been in that kind of cold wearing a single thin cotton layer, how long was it before you got to a place you could warm up?

What's the longest you've gone without sleep? What do you remember about the craving for sleep? What do you remember about the disorientation? Was it similar to this description?

> In the head of the interrogated prisoner, a haze begins to form.
> His spirit is wearied to death, his legs are unsteady, and he has
> one sole desire: to sleep, to sleep just a little, not to get up, to lie,

to rest, to forget. . . . Anyone who has experienced this desire knows that not even hunger or thirst are comparable with it.[2]

The words are those of Menachem Begin, former prime minister of Israel, who was tortured by the Soviets. Sleep deprivation was one of their most widely used techniques.

Maybe stress positions, sleep deprivation, and cold don't seem like such horrible things to subject a prisoner to because we've all experienced them to some small degree. But hardly any of us have experienced all of these in combination, and hopefully never for a prolonged period of time.

Mustafa and Bashr got it for four weeks, and I watched them deteriorate. I remembered the first few prisoners I'd interrogated at Abu Ghraib. I remembered how their faces looked mummified, how lifeless their eyes were. I remembered their slow reactions and how devoid they seemed of character, personality, or humanity, like someone had hollowed out their insides with an ice cream scoop. The same thing was happening to Mustafa and Bashr, and I found that I really didn't care. Within days, I was sick of the sight of them kneeling outside the interrogation booths. All I really wanted was for them to break.

The first week went by. We gradually increased the intensity and questioning during the interrogations themselves, hoping they would talk now that they were appropriately softened up. I spent some time on Bashr, the one with the softer face and the one who seemed to be taking the sleepless nights a little harder. With so much material in the transcript, I was sure to catch him in a lie. And with Bashr so disoriented, it didn't really matter if he lied or not. I could just tell him that he'd contradicted himself, and, in his befuddled state, he'd probably believe me.

At first Bashr denied that the conversation recorded in the transcript had ever taken place. Then he said that it had taken place, but he and his cousin were just humoring the third man. He effortlessly slid from one story to an alternative contradictory story without a pause, as if he had convinced

---

[2] Menachem Begin, quoted in John Conroy, *Unspeakable Acts, Ordinary People: The Dynamics of Torture*, 1st ed. (New York: Knopf, 2000), p. 34.

himself that his first lie had never been uttered. All the while, even as he was visibly deteriorating, he was polite and kind. I could wrap him up in his web of lies all day, and he didn't care. He was comfortable there.

About this time, we started slacking off. Our first wave of torture lite had failed, and I, for one, was losing confidence in these enhancements. Chief Pitt was growing impatient. We all were. None of us liked this round-the-clock routine. Other prisoners kept trickling in and I had to keep up. Pitt talked more about ramping up the intensity. Nothing specific. The cousins got a little break—two or three days—and then we went at them full-bore once again.

A few days after their reprieve, I walked through the prison yard and saw Mustafa doing deep knee bends in the yard while Glick, Morris, and a guard yelled at him like a band of drill sergeants. After a full set of these aerobics, they had Mustafa lift water bottles like free weights, all the while insulting his strength and manliness. The worst part came when they had him roll through the limestone gravel. This was something we did in basic training, and it's not as easy as it looks. I imagine it would be harder if your knees and elbows were aching from stress positions. (Pitt put a stop to this pretty quick. The gravel might leave marks.) I shook my head and walked away from the bizarre scene. This whole program of torture lite wasn't working. And now a physical training routine was going to break them? We were just grasping at straws.

Soon after that, Glick and Morris lost interest. Not only were they losing the battle of wills, they had inherited the night shift. I came around one night to find Mustafa in the same stress position outside, in the cold, right where they had left him hours before. When I tracked down the dynamic duo, they were in the bunker we used as an office, watching *Austin Powers in Goldmember* and half asleep. We'd set a limit on stress positions of forty-five minutes, but they'd let that slide, more from laziness and forgetfulness, I believe, than from sadism. They shrugged when I complained. Mustafa moved like a ninety-year-old man when I lifted him to his feet and returned him to his cage. His joints were shot. I don't know how long he'd been kneeling, but clearly it was too long.

I started making a point of checking in on Mustafa and Bashr. They were spending too much time outside, too much time in stress positions. I worried sometimes that they'd suffer permanent damage—or worse. Finding them in their usual spot, I'd pull them into the interrogation booth for a break. There was a heater, and they could warm up a bit. Inevitably, I'd get bored and try to practice Arabic (the Mosul dialect was yet another challenge for me). They hated me for this. All they wanted was to go to bed, and here I was trying to make conversation.

One night I noted a contusion on Mustafa's head. He said one of the guards had bashed his sandbagged head into a post. I figured this was probably an accident. Just carelessness, but I had to report it. The guard, a good guy and not one I'd ever suspect of deliberately beating a prisoner, was whisked away from the prison in a swift disciplinary action. Never saw him again.

Here was another puzzle for me. The damage we were doing to these guys, both physical and psychological, was much more serious and lasting than a bump on the head. But it wasn't the injuries that caused the guard to be on one side of the line and for us to be safely on the other. It was the degree of separation.

I put the prisoner in a stress position, but it was his own weight that caused the pain. I left him out all night, but it was the cold that caused him discomfort. I kept him from sleeping, but it was his own weariness that scrambled his psyche. I was separated from his pain by at least one causal link. It's the same sort of flawed reasoning reflected in Chris Rock's facetious statement, "Guns don't kill people—bullets kill people." The guard, on the other hand, directly caused a prisoner pain, so he crossed the line. Such is torture's tortured logic. The bottom line is that we all followed this twisted mental path because we wanted to.

Edwin took the lead on the case in their third week of torment. He devised a good cop–bad cop plan, which wasn't too sophisticated but was far more thought out than what we'd been doing. He was the good cop—everyone else was bad. Clearly, it was time to give these guys a way out. Their health was visibly slipping, they'd both lost a frightening amount of weight, and their eyes were getting that gray, glazed-over look I'd seen at Abu Ghraib. "Look," Edwin said, "we obviously know a lot about you guys. The only way I can help you is if you start cooperating. This will go on forever if you don't give me a chance to help you."

I suddenly had a lot less to do with these two prisoners. My only assigned task was to keep them awake, which I did sometimes by continuing the pointless conversations we'd already started. It was during one of these that Bashr claimed a guard had pissed on him while Glick watched. For the first time, I saw him really upset about his treatment. In his mind, somehow, all the sleep deprivation and stress positions were to be expected, but this humiliation on top of it all was too much.

Glick denied it, the guard denied it, and the translator who was with them told me the guard had poured warm water on him while he was hooded. I believed the translator. That didn't make the slightest difference to Bashr, who still to this day probably believes the Americans used him for a urinal.

As the third week became the fourth week, I wondered how our good cop–bad cop routine was working. During a regular meeting it became clear that not only were these interrogations going nowhere, they had stopped altogether. We had all become distracted, bored, busy, or lazy, and had just given up. But the torture lite treatment continued. We started by keeping these guys awake so they'd be good and soft for our questions. Now we were doing it for nothing.

At the end of my wits, I went into the booth with Mustafa and ran a very unofficial approach—I'll call it Desperate Interrogator. I was almost begging this very evil man for any scrap of information. It was clear now who was really in control. "Come on, you have to be tired of this. Just give me something and I'll see what I can do." I took him back to the transcript. I reminded him of his lies and tipped my hand, revealing that we had a transcript of his conversations. "*Eh Naam,*" he finally sighed. *Yes. It was me.*

This confession was deeply unsatisfying. It had taken four weeks of torture to get to this place, and it was nothing we didn't already know. On a much deeper level, one I wasn't aware of at the time, the confession was unsatisfying because I got it by ceding control. I had let go of the absolute power I had over this prisoner by showing a weakness. Here he was, this asshole, this murderer (maybe), broken down physically and mentally, hardly able to stand and hardly able to think straight. I had so much power over him, but he wouldn't give up his lies until I exposed my own weakness. I hated him for that.

It had taken time, but from the moment I arrived at Abu Ghraib I had started getting used to having this kind of power. Then I started demanding it.

CHAPTER 10

Proliferation

The techniques we used on the cousins inevitably spread. As the stress positions, sleep deprivation, and isolation spread to other prisoners, I hardly noticed. The bleed-over was unremarkable. It was as natural as water running downhill or an ink stain spreading slowly across fabric. In a tight-knit and interdependent community like prison, this is simply inevitable. Nothing happens in isolation. The deeds of a few bad apples can't be contained. What the special forces were allegedly doing in their shack spread slowly to the interrogations we did on Mustafa and Bashr, and from there to the other prisoners.

A new interrogator, Stephan, showed up about this time. I'm sure that he was, like me back at Abu Ghraib, uncertain about his new environment and unsure of how to act toward prisoners. He learned by watching us. Within days he was using stress positions. But what we'd started as special treatment for Mustafa and Bashr he used on *every single prisoner* he was assigned. Stephan was a nice kid, eager to please, willing to help, but he had absolutely no interest in the prisoners, interrogation, or any work beyond what was absolutely necessary. So he'd check a prisoner out, do the required paperwork, and have the guards put him on his knees in the holding pen, bag over his head, wrists firmly cuffed. A couple hours later, Stephan would amble back to the holding pen and retrieve the prisoner for interrogation.

In his mind, he was softening up the prisoners for interrogation. I thought he was being lazy. Even worse, I was aware by this time that there were a lot of innocents mixed into our prison population. In his unreflective, careless way, Stephan was using harsh, physical tactics on everyone, guilty or not. What we'd started as a set of special treatments had become routine.

I was doing it too. If a prisoner displeased me, he went into a stress position. We had a pretty limited number of these positions and none of them was too sophisticated. We used kneeling the most. Standing still is also a stress position. Donald Rumsfeld may do it eight hours a day at his little podium desk (as he bragged in a note on proposed torture techniques), but he didn't have a guard standing next to him to make sure he didn't move in the slightest—even to shift his weight. The worst was the position that had the prisoner's back to the wall, feet flat, and knees bent ninety degrees. We did this in basic training as an exercise to build thigh strength. But we never had to do it for more than two minutes, which was very difficult and ultimately painful. The longest I could do it without severe discomfort was four minutes. We forced prisoners to do it for up to twenty minutes.

"Prisoner was defiant and answered me sarcastically. At this point I should have put the prisoner in a stress position," I wrote on one of my interrogation reports. The prisoner had mocked my authority, and deserved to be punished. As I was writing my report, I realized that I'd failed to use one of the tools my superiors had granted me and I casually made note of it. The prisoner was low-value, the interrogation of no consequence. I sent the report up thinking it would be filed away and forgotten, just like nine-tenths of the others.

The next day, officers from battalion were in our office talking to Chief Pitt. "Who the fuck is this fucking Lagouranis idiot who put up this fucking report!!"

"That's me, sir."

There had been some trouble with my reports in the past. At Abu Ghraib, I had been trained to always list approaches and techniques in a section on the form called "Interrogation Notes." This was not information for the analysts or the officers, but was very useful information for the next interrogator. If Pride and Ego Down had been an effective technique, for example, the next interrogator would appreciate knowing that. We'd get better interrogations and not waste so much time in trial and error.

Chief Pitt hated seeing this. "What is this bullshit?" he asked me after reading my very first report in Mosul. When I explained, he snorted. As my time in Mosul wore on, I never stopped putting down these notes and he never stopped bitching about it. When we started using stress positions and sleep deprivation, I started putting that down too. Seems that these techniques always got redacted before they went up to battalion, but that was not my decision. There was nothing I could do.

But this time, after interrogating an unimportant prisoner, the report went straight through with all my comments. The officer demanded to know what I thought I was doing.

"I don't understand, sir."

"You lost control of the interrogation. You let the prisoner sass you."

"Yes, sir. I noted that in my report," I replied evenly, but I was worried. Something about this reaction was totally out of proportion.

"You also wrote down that you should have used a stress position."

"Yes, sir."

"Don't ever let me see that shit again. Understood?"

No. It was not understood. "Sir, do you not want me to use stress positions?" By now he had calmed down slightly, but not because he was less angry. He was getting out onto shaky moral ground. He wanted to choose his words carefully.

"Just don't write it down."

I said, "Roger, sir," and went back to my computer. I was pissed. It was 100 percent clear that they were happy to have enlisted men doing torture lite, but they didn't want anything controversial to pass before their eyes. Basically, the command didn't want their hands dirty. Basically, they were trying to screw me. Just don't write it down? No way. After this little episode, I put it *all* in writing. If they were going to have me do this stuff, they were going to read about it.

I had lost control of the interrogation that the battalion officers reacted to. This is one of the worst things that can happen during an interrogation. Control over the prisoner and the situation is the foundation. All scripts, plans, techniques, and questions are possible only if the interrogator retains control.

It's so essential that it's easy to forget that the kind of control interrogators seek is really just an illusion.

Entering an interrogation booth, an interrogator wants the prisoner to believe he has any number of tools at his disposal. That he determines the prisoner's fate. As the interrogator spins out a series of promises and implied threats, the process will only move forward if the prisoner really believes that good things will come if he talks, and that bad things will happen if he doesn't.

But we didn't really have that much power or very many tools at our disposal. There were little things we could promise and actually deliver on, like cigarettes, although they were only allowed in the booth and not in the prison. Likewise, the implied threats we could actually deliver on were few. Stress positions, a night out in the cold, or a night without sleep—these were things we could do, and things prisoners hated, but once a prisoner who's resolved to stay silent makes it through the night, and gets over his initial fear of the thing we threatened, he just deals with it. Serious torture requires steady escalation. As bad as things are, the prisoner has to believe that what's coming next will be worse. Torture victims don't break on the pain they're experiencing, they break on the fear of more and worse pain to come.

So even though we were pushing the boundaries, we really didn't have enough harsh techniques to make any kind of difference. There were still limits. If a prisoner called me on my implied threat that things were going further, and if I actually didn't go further, the game was pretty much over. I could still yell and bluster, but my power was deflated. If they figured out where the limit was, and if they could endure anything up to that limit, they'd won. I hated it when this happened. I felt naked and unarmed standing before these prisoners, and I knew I would catch hell from Pitt for losing control of the interrogation. It made me want to escalate. It made me want to go further.

It's hard to reconcile this with how I feel now, but in Mosul I was still pretty psyched about interrogation. I was working closely with Evan, and we felt we were doing a good job—or the best job we could with the prisoners we had. I suppose I would have questioned my effectiveness if I'd counted how many intelligence reports we sent up. (As opposed to interrogation reports, we only sent up intelligence reports if we actually had something.) But in the blur of these busy, twelve-hour days, I sort of lost track of the real goal. I was interrogating a lot, I was getting people to break down and cry and beg. So in my mind I was doing a good job.

Habib was one of those rare prisoners who looked like he might really have something, and even more rare, we knew exactly what we needed from him: just one name. There was this house, and in the house was an arsenal. It was absolutely ridiculous how many weapons were in this house—RPGs, antitank mines, mortars, artillery shells, shoulder-fired missiles, and of course AK-47s and plenty of bullets. It was a reminder of how the Iraqi army here had not actually been defeated; they just slipped away.

Special forces hit the house, and finding no one there, they went looking for the owner. They somehow extracted from neighbors that the owner of the house didn't live there, and hadn't lived there for some time, but he rented it out to someone who came and went and who no one could identify. They searched further for the owner, and learned he was in Doha, Qatar. So then they went looking for family members of the owner and came up with Habib, the owner's brother.

Once he was in custody, little hints and clues expanded into a full-blown conspiracy. The unknown renter of the house was tied to a man who had foreign contacts. And Habib, we learned, was a professor of chemistry at the University of Mosul. Just the kind of knowledge that could be put to use building IEDs and blowing up Americans. It all made perfect sense. And now we had him.

Special forces got a first crack at Habib, and, he told me, they used their standard set of techniques—strobe lights, music, and ice water—to get him to drop a dime on the renter. Gaining nothing for their efforts, they sent Habib to our prison. Chief Pitt got word of all this, and directed us to go hard on this "dirtbag." When I read the file on Habib, I thought this idea of a conspiracy was specious. There was only circumstantial evidence linking Habib to anything going on in the house, and he was twice removed. And so what if he taught chemistry? Dismissing the conspiracy theory, I decided to do a very focused interrogation. I wanted the name, just the name, of the guy renting the house. He was our real target.

Another interrogator, John, and I set up a performance of "Mutt and Jeff," a.k.a. good cop–bad cop. I was the good cop. My job was to set the stage and appear nonthreatening (but not overly friendly) to gain Habib's confidence and let him feel comfortable. Then John would enter stage right, playing the role of an infantryman who had just lost a friend to a roadside bomb. His job was to convince Habib that he was overwhelmed with anger and out of control—ready to seriously hurt Habib, if not kill him, in a fit of rage. I would then push John offstage and return to Habib. He would now face a choice: cooperate with me and maybe get out of prison, or be interrogated by John with no one to protect him from John's wrath. So that was the plan. Worth a try, anyway.

The moment I saw Habib as I picked him up from the holding pen, I knew we'd made the wrong choice. I expected to see a graying professor, but I also expected someone physically fit enough to take an active part in a guerrilla war. Habib was old and feeble. Visibly weakened from the treatment he got from special forces, he trembled slightly. I wondered if he would survive the fear we were about to induce. But when I looked him in the eye, I could see reserves of strength and composure. Even in his dirty clothes, flexicuffs, and sleep-deprived state, he projected dignity. The compassion I'd managed to stifle hit me again, but it was too late to go back now.

I cut his flexicuffs and sat before him in the interrogation booth, eye to eye. In that moment, before my questions began, we were simply two men sitting down for a conversation. He reminded me of professors I'd had in the past, people I admired and learned from. In different contexts, I would have deferred to this man and shown him respect due to his age and position. This, however, was my booth and a performance was under way.

I began asking him basic questions about his job, his relationship with his brother, and the rental property. All I saw in his eyes was weariness and apprehension. The same thing I'd seen from other prisoners who'd been given the treatment by special forces. It was a gaze that tried to divine what would happen next. The look of shock and fear on his face when John burst in told me that he'd failed.

John's face was red and his hand trembled as he picked up a chair and hurled it out the door. "Is this the motherfucker? Is this the guy that had a house full of weapons?" The table flew out the door next, tumbling and crashing loudly. "He didn't deserve to die. You and your friends killed my goddamn friend." Habib stood up quickly and cowered in the corner, hands slightly raised at the waist level. John was delivering a totally convincing performance. Even I was moved. He was really good.

It was part of the plan that I push John out the door, but because I was worried about Habib's heart faltering, I ejected him a little sooner. "He needs to get these guys who killed his friend," I said calmly. "I don't know what he's capable of doing." Habib, only a little calmer, said, "I'm sorry." I got to the point.

"We know you don't have anything to do with these weapons. We know you don't own the house. We also know your brother is in Doha, or he'd be here instead of you. All we need is the name of the guy who rents the house. And you can go."

Habib returned to his seat. I'd told John to leave at least one chair in place so the interrogation could continue. He collected himself and fixed me with a no-nonsense gaze.

"I know, but I'm not going to tell you."

And the only thing that went through my head was "Fuck."

No one had ever said that to me before. Prisoner after prisoner had pled ignorance with *"Wallah ma'arif"—I swear to God I don't know.* Most of the time, they probably didn't know. In a few cases I was sure they were lying. This was something new, this complete acknowledgment and total defiance. It was insane, and insanely brave.

I dropped all pretense. The power had shifted to the prisoner. I had nothing left. But that didn't mean we were just going to let him go. He had to be punished for his defiance. His punishment would be justified as our seeking intelligence, but that was a charade. He wasn't going to tell us anything.

"You know what's going to happen to you?"

"Yes." He certainly knew—he'd just recently been a guest of the men in ski masks.

"Then why not give me the name?"

Habib explained himself patiently, like he was talking to a student who'd asked him a question. "I know who he is, but I don't know if he's involved with the weapons you found. But if I give you his name, your soldiers will arrest him in his home and bring him here, and they will do to him what they did to me."

That was it. Habib and I were done. I cuffed him and took him outside with a bag over his head and put him on his knees in the dirt. I left him with a guard and reported back to Pitt. The plan John and I worked out had failed, and the prisoner was defiant. I knew what was coming next: a program of sleep deprivation, stress positions, and cold nights in the open air. I left with an awful knot in my gut and Habib's words ringing in my ears.

Before I put the bag over his head, he looked at me one more time and said, "Tell the soldier who came in here that I'm sorry for his loss." The air temperature dropped into the low forties that night, and then the rains came, soaking Professor Habib as he knelt in the mud.

As much as I wanted to hate Habib for protecting a man likely behind the deaths of our soldiers, I could see his point. As we swept through Mosul (or Baghdad, or Fallujah), we treated Iraqis we wanted to question as criminals. Habib had tenuous connections to the actual suspects. In any American city, the police would have questioned him. But in no American city would they have swept him up in a commando-style raid, bagged his head, cuffed him, and held him incommunicado (not to mention the torture). If we had set up a system where rights were honored and protected, and Iraqis had a shot at actually proving their innocence, Habib would have had no problem giving us a name. But he knew that once we had that name, that guy would be treated as a convicted criminal. Case closed.

Now that he'd admitted he knew what we wanted to know, Habib had almost no chance of getting out of jail. He'd be sent to Abu Ghraib and we'd never let him go. I tried to explain this to him as I went to check up on him. But he already knew this. I soon gave up. The guilt I felt over this whole situation—both the parts I was responsible for and the parts that were out of my control—was crushing. I offered my apology, and he was gracious in accepting. But I could still see resentment in his eyes, and it pained me. At the same time, he asked about John. He was more concerned about the "bad cop" and his loss than the "good cop" and his guilt.

Fortunately we got the name we were looking for from another detainee. I brought Habib back into the interrogation booth at around three a.m. and told him the name. Habib nodded, almost involuntarily, and that was all I needed to write a report that stated that Habib was fully cooperative and should be released.

It was now in the hands of the bureaucracy, which was slow to act on my recommendation. As the days passed, Habib's students organized and thousands of them peacefully demonstrated for his release. He was well known and loved by Sunni, Shia, and Kurds, and they united in his cause. It turned out that the man we'd arrested for someone else's name preached tolerance and nonviolence. While opposed to continued American occupation, he spoke openly against the insurgency and violent solutions. This presented us with a serious problem. It wasn't like we needed more Iraqis to hate us. He was released after a few days.

I wonder if Habib shared his experiences with his students—if he told them about the stress positions and the cold and not being allowed to sleep. I tend to think he did not. He was much more active in trying to dissuade people from violence than he was in trying to get people to hate Americans. But if he was the vindictive type, we really screwed up by giving him such stories to tell. He wasn't just another farmer. He had a large audience and powerful connections. He looked so old and feeble that he could have really painted us as monsters by sharing his stories with insurgent-age students. *This is how they treat a respectable professor?* I hope we didn't push him off of his moderate stance, but I'm sure we taught him some unfortunate truths about the occupation—namely, that it didn't necessarily matter how far removed one is from the cache of weapons. A few degrees of separation are still enough to warrant detention and torture.

As the professor left us, I marveled at how he'd held up, this weak man with a strong mind, against our battering, both psychological and physical. The Iraqis often cried during interrogation and torture, and often begged for water, news, or just attention. A lot of guards thought they were

pussies. A lot of my superiors thought they should be easy to crack. After
spending these months with hundreds of Iraqis, however, I'd seen them
stumble but never fall. There was always an impenetrable center that I
couldn't break.

Mohammed Ghani, a Baghdad sculptor, spoke to an American reporter
before the invasion, looking forward to the fall of Saddam but already dis-
trustful of the Americans: "We'll bend but we are not broken. They can bend
us but they cannot break us. We are like palm trees. The wind will bend
them but it never breaks them. We live. This is the Iraqi character. We cannot be broken."[1] That was certainly true of the professor, the cousins Mustafa
and Bashr, and countless others. Increasingly, this project of interrogation,
even the whole project of remaking Iraq in our own image, was looking like
an unstoppable force against an immovable object.

---

[1] Mohammed Ghani, quoted in Anthony Shadid, *Night Draws Near: Iraq's People in the
Shadow of America's War,* 1st ed. (New York: Henry Holt, 2005), p. 43.

CHAPTER 11

Firing Blind

O ne day in April, the Iraqis who worked on base didn't show up. This was alarming, because we had been hearing rumors of a planned attack by the insurgents, something much bigger than the regular mortars and potshots. We took it as a sign that in the evening we would be overrun, the enemy bursting through our flimsy perimeter and killing as many Americans as possible before being killed themselves.

Nothing of the sort happened, but in April things definitely changed. The tempo of attacks increased and we started hearing more about foreign fighters taking on U.S. troops in suicidal attacks. April 2004 became the deadliest month for U.S. forces to that point. One hundred thirty-five dead. We definitely noticed that things were getting worse.

We in military intelligence should have had a better idea of who the insurgents were. Even I, a lowly specialist, should have had some picture of who the enemy was, but I found that our internal information was much more muddled than even open sources like CNN or Al Jazeera. I was really no better informed than a dedicated viewer back in the States. When I talked to analysts or military intelligence officers, I heard a variety of opinions about these insurgents, and never any synthesis. They were Baathists. They were pissed-off Iraqis. They were thugs and nascent warlords. A lot of soldiers had just given up on trying to figure it out: "These are just violent people."

So even when we did get someone we strongly suspected was doing harm to Americans and Iraqis, we had almost no idea why they'd turned against us, or which group they might belong to. A savvy prisoner in this situation can figure out pretty quickly that his interrogator has no idea what's going on. I often had no idea what was going on, and I was trying harder than most. Some didn't seem to try at all. One interrogator, who was especially fond of using stress positions, once asked me, after he came back from an interrogation, "What's the Baath Party?"

There were plenty of uncurious, intellectually lazy people in military intelligence, and then there were others who were just lazy, period. Two other interrogators on base discovered that they could avoid doing interrogations entirely if they put up a Request for Information (RFI) pertaining to the prisoner. If anyone asked why they hadn't interrogated the prisoner, they could say they were waiting for the RFI. Now, any response to these requests was bound to take three weeks, and we could only hold a prisoner for two weeks unless we had a compelling reason. If, at that point, there was no reason to hold the prisoner, and the interrogator didn't make a strong case for releasing the prisoner, he got transferred to Abu Ghraib. So laziness was partly responsible for the growing ranks of innocent detainees crowding Iraq's largest prison. That created a backlog, and it was generally months before interrogators there would take a shot at them. By that time, if they had any intelligence (which most did not), it was stale.

I was disturbed by people like this, people who avoided work just so they could watch yet another *Matrix* DVD. Besides not helping the innocent detainees, by not actively seeking to gather intelligence, they were allowing the insurgency to grow. I couldn't allow myself to get too angry, though, since increasingly I recognized that my own incompetence as an interrogator allowed me to call the innocent guilty and to allow intelligence to slip by me. Human Intelligence Collection should have been the best tool the coalition forces had in the war, yet we were failing miserably. We watched as the attacks on U.S. troops increased, security for Iraqis deteriorated, and snipers' bullets sailed past us. My interrogations weren't helping anything. Nothing was helping anything. Why not just watch *Finding Nemo* again and microwave another bag of popcorn? The interrogators who chose that route, and there were quite a few of them, probably accomplished as much as I did, and maybe didn't do as much harm.

*　*　*

Speaking of snipers' bullets, I'd been convinced we'd take some from that factory, the one just outside the perimeter, ever since I arrived in Mosul. Finally, one day in April, snipers used it for cover as I was transporting a prisoner. I was outside the wire of the prison. The prisoner was cuffed and his head sandbagged. I didn't have my weapon because I was guarding a prisoner. Their shots came wildly; if they had known how to shoot, they would have been deadly.

All I could do was take cover. I was so sick of being shot at and so ready to kill. . . . And here I was without my rifle. We took fire for half an hour.

The only time I thought I had even a remote chance of killing a sniper was back at Abu Ghraib. I had to take a turn in the guard towers, which were vulnerable and open. We took small-arms fire from the field directly in front of us. I opened up on the field with my machine gun. I didn't hit anything, but maybe it got the sniper to put his head down and clear out.

The infantry on base at Mosul, mostly Stryker teams, were solid professionals, but when it came to peacekeeping operations, they delivered mixed results. A lot of this had to do with training, a lot had to do with the fact that we weren't giving them good intelligence, and in some cases it was because they didn't care. Sergeant Patterson, a very intense man who seemed to always run off a mixture of caffeine and adrenaline, was smart enough to not need the training, produced his own intelligence, and really did care. He was downtown all the time, despite the fact that they'd often greet him and his men with firefights. He was also one of the remarkably few infantry guys who'd personally brief us on the prisoners he brought in.

"Be careful. He's a bad, bad man. A real thug. A total badass. Definitely has information." He fixed me with an intense, serious stare and told me about how the prisoner, Abu Hatem, had been blackmailing Iraqi cops, beating them up, stealing, fencing stolen goods, and associating with insurgents. Patterson talked fast, delivered his information, turned and was off, two privates double-timing to keep up with him. I admired this sergeant, but just listening to him was exhausting.

The guards brought in Abu Hatem wearing the standard sandbag and cuffs. He wasn't tall, but he had a solid chest and burly arms; he seemed to take up more space than he actually occupied. Evan and I were frankly a little scared. Having been told by Patterson that Abu Hatem was the biggest badass in Mosul, and now seeing his intimidating build, we went straight to harsh. Without taking the sandbag off, we had him lean against the wall and we started yelling. We'd barely gotten our dander up when he started spewing a stream of information, singing like no other prisoner we'd ever heard before.

"I know these two brothers . . . they're dealing weapons . . . they have rockets, grenade launchers, antiaircraft guns, Stinger missiles . . . can I have a cigarette? . . . they hate each other but live across the street and shoot at each other all the time . . . and there's this other guy who has cars he looted from the Baath Party and he's selling them and wanted me to sell them . . . please can I have a cigarette? . . . and I know this other guy, he came to me because I'm the guy you go to in Mosul and he's selling mustard gas . . . come on, I'm helping you, give me a cigarette . . . he's got a ton of mustard gas and . . ."

Evan and I were frantically trying to write this stuff down, but when Abu Hatem got to the mustard gas, we froze. WMD! We found the WMD! Abu clearly had all kinds of information, and some of it seemed completely nuts, but here was something we could focus on. We cut his cuffs, sat him down at the table, slapped a pack of cigarettes on the table, and pulled off the sandbag.

Abu lit up and started puffing, calming down instantly. It was like he became a different person. He fixed us with a powerful, winning smile and the charisma absolutely oozed out of him. The smile, one I'm sure he used all the time to similar effect, conveyed specific information and presented a choice. First, it said, clearly and profoundly, "I'm not afraid of you. At all." Then, once that was established, the smile said, "And anyway, wouldn't you rather be my friend?" He was clearly a dangerous man, but also irresistible. Evan and I loved Abu Hatem from this point on.

We turned to the matter at hand—the mustard gas. As Abu Hatem chain-smoked, we pored over maps and wrote down his description of the seller and his résumé. Pitt was jazzed, Evan was beaming, and I was thrilled that we finally got to send up an intelligence report, pinpointing actionable intelligence that could save lives. Finally.

Abu Hatem spent almost six weeks with us, and it wasn't until the end of his time that I fully realized that 90 percent of the information he fed us was total bullshit. He was an amazing liar. Not only did he make everything he said sound convincing, he kept all his lies straight in his head. He never contradicted himself. He never seemed uncomfortable if one of his leads didn't pan out, and somehow made us feel it was our fault if the stuff he told us was wrong. Early on, he established himself as being on "our side" and never showed the slightest animosity or lack of cooperation. He never acted like a prisoner should, and that's one of the reasons we loved him.

Abu Hatem went on to win over every guard in the prison and wrangled all sorts of special treatment. We kept him separate from the general population, in his own cage and his own shack off to the side. He could see the other prisoners in the adjacent pen and hold a loud conversation with them, but he was essentially alone. This was for his own safety. We pulled him out for interrogation so often that it was obvious he was talking to us.

Being alone drove him nuts, so he'd always try to get a guard or interpreter over to his cage for a conversation—or a cigarette. Abu Hatem was an absolute fiend for tobacco, the worst case I'd ever seen. He wasn't allowed to smoke in his pen, so I showed him how to use chewing tobacco and left him a few tins. He hated it, but went through my gift in two days. The guards, the guys who'd turn into monsters over any other prisoner's most minor infraction, soon started supplying him with cigarettes and let him smoke in his cage. After his first week with us, I never saw him without one of those awful, stinking Iraqi cigarettes in his hand, no matter where he was. Often, he was holding court with a small group of guards, telling them through an interpreter about one of his amazing sexual exploits.

Sex was his other big obsession. Abu Hatem was fascinated by our female interrogators—actually by the whole idea of women in the army. Like most Iraqis, he first assumed that they were merely prostitutes who traveled with us. He was astounded when I told him that no, I hadn't slept with any of them and didn't plan on it. Every time I pulled him out of his cage, he asked, "Hey, did you fuck those girls yet?"

"No. I'm not going to fuck those girls."

He'd click his tongue to let me know how disappointed he was.

He had seen American and European TV and was fascinated by the behavior of Western women. Evan offered him some soft porn in exchange for information. He cooperated, as always, and later on Evan dropped off a couple issues of *Maxim*. Abu Hatem absolutely loved it.

Abu Hatem had created a little piece of paradise in his cage. While other prisoners were coping with mind-numbing boredom and pissed-off guards, Abu Hatem had guards entertaining him if not sucking up to him, an endless supply of cigarettes, and a pile of soft porn magazines. No one ever messed with him. No one could even give him orders. I saw a new guard try once, yelling at him for smoking. Abu turned and gave him that look, laughing a little and asking, "Come on, what the hell? Are you serious?" The guard backed down. They became friends.

I think we all failed to understand how completely sociopathic, manipulative, and dangerous this man really was. He watched carefully what we responded to, and used it to his advantage. In one episode, he pulled me aside quietly. "Pssst! You see that guy over there?" He pointed to a prisoner in the adjacent cage. Someone I'd never interrogated before. "He used to be in the Mukhabarat. I saw him walking around with Uday, pistol in his belt, whole thing."

So I pulled the other prisoner, Salman, into the booth and started in. "We know who you are."

Abu Hatem had made it all up. Somehow, Salman had pissed him off, and Abu was using me to get even. "No, really," Salman insisted, "I've given you so much information. I've cooperated." We went around a few times, and, getting nowhere, I put Salman outside in the cold, kneeling, hands behind his back. It didn't occur to me at the time, but where I left Salman was right in full view of Abu Hatem. I went to look at Salman's file (which reported that he *had* been very cooperative), and when I got back, Abu was sitting there, smoking, laughing at Salman with gleeful satisfaction.

Bashr and Mustafa were still with us, and still getting the treatment, but by now, none of us expected them to break. We'd made one last grand effort after I got the confession from Mustafa, and they started hinting that they would talk. Trying to break through their last lines of defense, we put them into a room together for the first time in four weeks. They were obviously close and cared for each other; maybe the sight of the other, so pitiful and obviously tormented, would crack their last resistance.

Well, we were completely wrong. They both shut down completely. Maybe each of them resented us for torturing a beloved family member, maybe each drew strength from seeing his comrade, or maybe it helped them remember a pact they'd made before capture. In any event, they stopped hinting that they would talk. They rejected the good cop and his overtures. We had no room to maneuver, and no new tactics to surprise them with.

Pitt was ready to take this to the next level. In our next morning meeting, the officer in command of interrogation, Captain Lamb, joined us. Pitt explained what he wanted us to do. He'd already set it up. It was time to exploit the supposed, and highly suspect, "Arab fear of dogs."

The suggestion to use dogs—"Using detainees' individual phobias (such as fear of dogs) to induce stress"[1]—was approved by Donald Rumsfeld for Guantánamo prisoners back in November 2002. The approval was later rescinded, but the technique migrated to Abu Ghraib. Many have reported and testified that Major General Geoffrey Miller, who had been in charge of the detention facility at Gitmo and visited Abu Ghraib, recommended dogs for Iraqi prisoners. Miller denied this, but in any event he believed, as he testified himself, that there is "a cultural fear of dogs in Arab culture,"[2] and an IROE at Abu Ghraib permitted the "Presence of [a] Military Working Dog" because it "Exploits Arab fear of dogs while maintaining security during interrogations."[3]

By the time I got to Abu Ghraib, no one was using dogs, and we got specific instructions not to. But out here in Mosul, Chief Pitt could point directly to a document that permitted this technique, and he could talk about

---

[1] The famous "I stand for 8–10 hours a day" memo: William J. Haynes II, General Counsel, to Secretary of Defense, "Counter-Resistance Techniques," November 27, 2002; www.humanrightsfirst.org/us_law/etn/pdf/dod-memos-120202.pdf (accessed on June 29, 2006).

[2] U.S. Senate Committee on Armed Services, Testimony on Allegations of Mistreatment of Iraqi Prisoners, May 19, 2004.

[3] Ricardo S. Sanchez, Lieutenant General, U.S. Army, to Commander, U.S. Central Command, "CJTF-7 Interrogation and Counter-Resistance Policy," September 14, 2003; www.aclu.org/FilesPDFs/september%20sanchez%20memo.pdf (accessed May 6, 2006).

it openly with his commander, Captain Lamb, in the room. There was clearly no legal issue here, he said. If he wanted us to do this, he'd obviously been granted that authority.

No legal issue, I thought, *but what a completely crazy idea.* Who ever came up with the notion that Arabs are inordinately afraid of dogs? I saw mangy curs everywhere in Iraq. They didn't seem to be afraid of Iraqis, and Iraqis certainly weren't afraid of them. This was just more of the same racist bullshit that we saw in the Arab mind lecture. Some genius, somewhere, saw an Arab running from a dog and made it into a theory. Then the army took it up as doctrine. Again, it looked to me like we were so uncomfortable with this culture, and it looked to us so alien and remote, that we were ready to believe any bold assertion. Arabs are afraid of dogs. Sure. That makes sense. Anyway, if we're talking about a large, growling German shepherd, who wouldn't be afraid?

So Chief Pitt wanted to use dogs on the two cousins. Fine. We would follow the rules. The dog had to be muzzled at all times, and under the control of a trained dog handler. At no time would it touch the prisoner. The muzzle, we knew, would lessen the prisoners' fear, so we agreed to keep the prisoners' heads bagged. They could hear the dog, but not see it. At most, they could see a blurry, lunging form through the gauze of the sandbag. Pitt had already secured two eager dog handlers and we were ready to go. I thought this was all a very stupid idea, but there was another part of me that was drawn to it. It was another level, another line we were crossing. Some twisted part of my psyche, one totally divorced from the rational side that knew that this would never work, wanted to take things further. It wanted to see where this path would go.

After the meeting, Staff Sergeant Edwin, the leader of the other interrogation team, pulled me aside. He hadn't been selected for this little mission, and he made it clear that was fine with him. "Whenever you do this stuff, I don't want to have anything to do with it." I was surprised. I'd heard about some of the things they were doing at Gitmo, where Edwin had interrogated, and all that sounded a lot worse than what we were going to try here. What was he worried about? What had he seen or done? He didn't say, but he had some advice for me: "If he's ordering you to do this, you get every little detail in writing." I pointed out that what we were doing was legal, according to the written rules. "Look," he finished, "you just don't want this to come bite you in the ass ten years from now."

I went about the interrogation very halfheartedly. In the booth with Mustafa, I started in with my questions, the same questions he had heard many times before. When he gave his stock reply, "*La wallah*," I gave a signal to the dog handler. Just a little wave. The dog handler gave an even more subtle signal to his muscular German shepherd, and the dog lunged forward, straining at the leash. The prisoner stepped back and reflexively lifted his right leg to shield his genitals. There was fear, and it seemed the dog could smell it. He strained harder at his leash.

Part of me knew that Mustafa was not about to break just because a dog was barking at him, and that this was just pointless violence. A darker, less rational part of me liked seeing the man who had defied us for so long try to cover his balls in fear. We went through the routine again, focusing on a name in the transcript: "*Niha'iyan, wain Malik!*" For the last time, where is Malik! "What's his involvement?! You better start cooperating!"

"*Ma'arifih.*" More emphatic denials. Another signal to the handler, and the dog lunged again. This time, I didn't notice an increase in fear. After only a few minutes of this, had Mustafa's fear plateaued? Were we so transparent that he'd already figured out we weren't going to let the dog actually attack him?

The first rush I got from seeing Mustafa cower completely emptied out of me. There was no reason to keep going, but I put on a show just to be able to tell Pitt I'd done it. It was all over in about fifteen minutes. We did the same thing with Mustafa's cousin, and my apathy turned to depression as he sobbed behind his sandbag. He also didn't break. No new information, no actionable intelligence. But we'd started down this road, and these two prisoners would not be the last who would face our dogs.

After this, we were done with Mustafa and Bashr. We were sick of them, so we just left them in isolation until their paperwork completed its painfully slow cycle and they were transferred to Abu Ghraib. One of the last times I saw Mustafa was when he motioned me over as I walked by the prison. He was hunched over, as he always was after so many weeks of our treatments, but he tried to straighten himself to look me in the eye. "You know," he said, peering out through the wan and rubbery mask that had once been a healthy-looking face, "I wasn't afraid of those dogs."

CHAPTER 12

Regression

I was having trouble sleeping. Even after twelve-hour days that involved the interrogation of four or five prisoners, I couldn't get my mind to shut down. I should have recognized my problem as a nagging conscience, the feeble voice of my deeply suppressed morality crying to be heard. But what place does morality have in war? This is no place to ponder or turn over and examine the right or wrong of what you are ordered to do. The army doesn't want you to do that. It replaces morality with a system of regulations. It's either by the book or not. Your orders are either legal or not. Don't question whether they are moral. That can get you killed.

So when Jones, Evan, and I sat together over a cribbage board and discussed our different cases and experiences, we talked the regulations up and down, examined them from every angle, and wondered if we were doing the legal thing, but we never talked about doing the right thing. One problem, however, was crystallizing: the vast majority of our prisoners were probably innocent. We saw too many cases involving mistaken identity, distant relatives of suspected insurgents, people who were close to a bomb when it went off, and Iraqis who were picked up for God knows what reason. This was a problem. It tugged at my conscience, but, even worse, it fell outside our regulations.

We weren't set up to function as a criminal justice system. We weren't trained to run investigations. We weren't even authorized to run investigations. Our job was to extract intelligence from human sources. At some point, our job turned into extracting confessions. This happened slowly and naturally. In the absence of any real criminal investigation, the only suitable evidence is a confession. When a confession is not forthcoming, the interrogation becomes increasingly harsh.

When I was convinced that I had a prisoner who was not guilty of any crime, and this happened often, I could not write that in my report. There was no place on the form for my assessment of guilt or innocence, only whether I got intelligence or not. Since the system was set up to deal with uniformed POWs, the system did not question the value of holding the prisoner versus releasing him. Of course, we hold prisoners until the war's over. The only question is whether to continue interrogating or not.

So the very best I could do for a prisoner, to give them a shot at being released, was to write "No Further Intelligence Value" on the interrogation report. If an intelligence officer above me disagreed—say they compared my report to the report of an arresting infantry private who insisted that this guy was a dangerous insurgent—then they would rule that the prisoner was guilty and therefore did have intelligence value. So it was Abu Ghraib for them.

Iraq's own criminal justice system was gone, or barely functioning, so we got the petty criminals and mixed them in with the suspected insurgents. If the criminal had possession of a weapon, he was automatically treated as an insurgent. I had no problem keeping some of these guys in jail, if it really seemed like they were looting, stealing, or killing, but I had a real problem with seeing them interrogated and tortured when they should have been put through a trial.

Wafeeq, I felt, deserved to be in jail and deserved a trial. The infantry brought him in because he was shooting up the street, and his wife came out to thank the Americans for taking him in. She'd been beaten repeatedly by Wafeeq, and said she was now going to take the children away and just disappear. So we'd taken a dangerous and unstable man off the streets of Mosul. We'd done good.

But once he was in our system, we reflexively went after him for intelligence. I don't think Pitt put a high value on this particular guy, as evidenced by the fact that he gave the responsibility for interrogation to a known slacker. Still, Wafeeq got the treatment.

I kept coming across him in my nocturnal wanderings, and he was always outside, in a stress position, under guard, and shivering from cold while his interrogator slept or watched a stupid movie. I had no sympathy for him, but I'd pull him into the interrogation booth, in front of the heater, just like I'd done for the cousins Mustafa and Bashr. He was fat and pampered, soft and weak, and always sobbing. Maybe he deserved what we were doing to him, but it was dangerous for people like us—untrained, often lazy, and sometimes incompetent—to mete out his just deserts.

He wanted to go to bed and so I made a deal. Sing me a song, and you can sleep. He knew several songs by his favorite pop singer, Kathem El-Saher, and he had a sonorous voice. Night after night, he'd sing, and then I'd take him back to his cage to sleep.

I always did this after Pitt had gone to sleep and I always tried to cover my tracks. I didn't want to be accused of being weak or sympathetic. But it was harder to hide what I was doing from the guards.

The guards here were great guys who took their jobs seriously. I always made sure they knew I respected and valued them—in part because they had it harder than we did and were under tighter scrutiny, and in part because my life depended on them every day. I knew that they would have my back even if they hated my guts, because they were just that kind of soldier, but obviously it was better to let them know that the loyalty ran both ways.

Seeing me bring this prisoner out of the cold repeatedly, one of the guards would talk shop with me. He was an actual prison guard in his civilian life, and thought the Iraqi prisoners had it good. "It's much colder in Pennsylvania," he said once, telling me how they'd leave prisoners outside in the cold with no shirt on. "We're way too soft." The guards and I talked, often, about their cynical view of the war. *The problems here go back thousands of years. We'll never solve them. The Arabs understand only force. We're too nice to work in this part of the world.* Standard stuff.

But even though the guards had these views, they rarely acted on them. They were, to a man, remarkably restrained and treated the prisoners with dignity. Only when specific orders were given did the prisoners suffer at their hands.

It was a new commander (in their chain of command, not ours) who came in one day and decided that each prisoner needed a shave and a haircut. The guards did as they were told, shaving heads, the beards that were for many a religious requirement, and the mustaches that for many others were evidence of their manhood. The guards almost sparked a riot. The prisoners were literally howling as they were strapped down into this little barbershop of horrors. The guards got through only about half of the prisoners before their commander's superior found out and put an immediate stop to it. The guy who gave the order was gone ASAP. This sparked another round of bitching from the guards, more assertions that Iraqis understand only force, complaints that now we looked weak because they didn't get to finish the job. For me, once again, it was strange that an officer got removed for ordering that the prisoners get haircuts, while we were totally sanctioned to use dogs to scare the living shit out of them. It added to the notion, already swirling through our ranks, that military intelligence was being given a very wide berth and we were expected to use it.

Putting a barking dog in a prisoner's face wasn't working, so where to now? Across the camp, in their off-limits compound, the elite forces among us were supposedly getting great intelligence. At least they went on a lot of raids and scooped up plenty of prisoners. Few of us ever saw what went on there, but descriptions of their techniques kept coming back, from both guards and prisoners. These reports served as inspiration for our next escalation.

Pitt pointed to a shipping container right outside the wire of the prison and described what he wanted us to do. He obtained a strobe light from aviation and a boom box from a private. He asked the guards for CDs of the most awful death metal music they had. He gave us these new tools and told Evan and me to clear the container out and get it ready for use as an interrogation chamber, saying, with finality, "I want to do this."

Once again, the IROE seemed to support Pitt—though it occurred to me now that this document was giving us way too much latitude. As with the dogs, I was skeptical, but I was also just as frustrated as everyone else. I shrugged and decided to see where this would lead, but I also remembered the advice I'd received from Edwin when we first used the dogs. Once the shipping container was set up, I wrote a plan for our first subject, naming all the techniques Pitt had asked for. Then I had him sign off. Pitt signed

without complaint, which tells me he believed in the legality of these techniques as much as I did.

Umar, the first Iraqi to join us in the shipping container, was a big, dumb
guy with a soft face and sad eyes. After bagging his head while checking him
out of the prison late at night, we threw him roughly in the back of a pickup
truck. Evan drove while I sat with him. He was already scared. "Where are
we going? What's going on?" he kept asking, his soft voice trembling a little
more after each repetition. I tried to sound just slightly intimidating when I
replied, "*La taqluq, tsadiki.*" Don't worry about it, buddy.

We drove him around base for about twenty minutes, even though our
destination was right outside the prison wire. We dragged him out of the
truck and forced him to stand in the middle of the container. His breathing
was heavy after hearing the metal doors slam and the bolt fall into place. It
was completely dark. We'd staged it perfectly. In his mind, we were getting
ready to seriously mess him up.

As Umar knelt, we put the flashing light directly in front of his sandbagged
face and the boom box, at full volume, just off to the side. The music, such as
it was, consisted of industrial-style guitars, beating drums, and lyrics delivered in a moan/shout style, the singer obviously trying to sound like the
Prince of Darkness himself. It blasted out of the speakers and ricocheted
around the container. Even though his head was bagged, we knew Umar
could see the light flashing, even if his eyes were closed. I knew because I
tried it myself. It was disorienting to look at, even through the plastic mesh of
the sandbag.

And as Umar knelt, we took turns yelling our questions into his ears. His
head twisted around as he tried to figure out where we were. After about a
half hour, he started moaning. I imagined he was crying behind his sandbag.
We pushed forward, getting harsher with our words. My throat was sore, my
ears were ringing, and the lights were disorienting. I realized I wasn't going to
be able to stand this much longer. The music and the lights were making me
increasingly more aggressive. The prisoner, still not cooperating, was making
me increasingly angry.

As we moved into our second hour of this treatment, Umar still on his
knees, Evan and I were jolted by a huge *boom* and a series of screams outside

the container. It took a second to register that this was someone—no, a bunch of people—banging on the container walls and yelling at the top of their lungs. Someone was hitting the outside with a rifle butt or a piece of lumber, someone else was whooping, "Yeee haa," and someone else figured out how to climb up to the roof, where he jumped up and down, slamming his boots on the container with extra force when he landed.

Some soldiers had obviously heard the music, figured out what was going on, and decided to join the party. I couldn't say, in front of the prisoner, what I thought, but I tried to give Evan a look that conveyed how screwed up I thought this was. He seemed to agree. Umar let his head hang low and limp, like he was offering it to the executioner's axe, and let loose with a series of resigned sobs. He could hear the wrath and chaos in their screams. He must have thought we were going to kill him.

There was some theory behind all of these enhancements, of which I was only vaguely aware at the time. All I knew is that we were trying to prolong the "shock of capture," the moment of maximum disorientation when a prisoner feels most vulnerable. Imagine this: hooded soldiers snatch you in a raid. The guy next to you, your friend, is killed. You're beaten, kicked, a bag is thrown over your head, and you're transported in a swiftly moving car. Suddenly the car stops, you're carried indoors, thrown to the floor, stripped naked, and you get a strobe light in your face, music blasting through your head, and the same guys who killed your buddy are screaming questions at you. I don't think there would be any question in your mind that your captors are capable of doing anything to you. So you start talking. That's the theory anyway.

I think that's where we got the idea that the strobe light and the music would be effective. And if it worked for special forces, I could see why. They didn't just look like super-badass ninja killers in their black hoods; they could actually play the part. But we weren't special forces. We had prisoners come in and slowly be in-processed. I'd ask them a set list of standard questions in my bad Arabic—Where do you live? What's your father's name?—while filling out a form. Then they'd get a jumpsuit and maybe a meal and a chance to relax. Then, when it was time to interrogate, I'd check them out of the prison. This always involved stripping them naked, which could have been an effective way to humiliate them, but I never used it as such. Instead, I would explain to them that we were looking for wounds and bruises to make sure they hadn't been mistreated, and they'd be checked again when I brought them back. Only after all this did we try to "prolong the shock of capture" with strobe lights and music.

Needless to say, this hardly worked. Even though we scared the shit out of Umar, he never gave us intelligence. Most prisoners were terribly confused and very annoyed by what we did, but hardly pressed to the breaking point. We'd tried to fit a set of tactics meant to be brutal into a set of regulations established to force us to be humane. The result was that we were just inept. It was so typical of the army that it was laughable.

I didn't find out until much later that these techniques had their genesis in CIA research done in the 1950s. The techniques developed were in the arena of "psychological torture." (Americans seem to generally avoid direct physical torture, or at least the bureaucrats who write the regulations do.) Isolation, stress positions, sensory deprivation, and manipulation of lights and sounds were all studied and sometimes tested on unwitting subjects. The goal was "regression." That is, according to the CIA's 1963 interrogation handbook, the goal was "inducing regression of the personality to whatever earlier and weaker level is required for the dissolution of resistance and the inculcation of dependence."[1] These techniques lie at the crossroads of torture and brainwashing. When I was doing this stuff, however, I had no idea.

Of course, we never succeed in actually brainwashing anyone. But here's what's interesting. These techniques were propagated throughout the Cold War, picked up again after 9/11, used by CIA, filtered down to army interrogators at Guantánamo, filtered again through Abu Ghraib, and used, apparently, around the country by special forces. Probably someone in this chain was a real professional, and if torture works—which is debatable—maybe they had the training to make sure it worked. But at our end of the chain, we

---

[1] Quoted in Alfred W. McCoy, *A Question of Torture: CIA Interrogation, from the Cold War to the War on Terror* (New York: Metropolitan Books/Henry Holt and Co., 2006), p. 53.

had no idea what we were doing. We were just a bunch of frustrated enlisted men picking approved techniques off a menu. We weren't grounded in the history or theory; we were just trying shit out to see if it worked, venting our frustration, and acting like badasses when, in the dark art of torture, we were really just a bunch of rank amateurs.

We watched the prisoners who were transferred over to us by the special forces very carefully, looking for signs that they were passing notes or any other bad behavior. While watching one guy, Jafar Ali Abdul Naser, one of the interrogators thought she heard another prisoner call him by another name, which she didn't catch. Now, that could have been a nickname or his patrimonial name (Abu something-or-other, meaning father of . . .) or a formal address or an insult. The report came from someone who didn't speak Arabic and didn't know how complicated these names are. But Pitt took the bait. That night, Evan and I took him to our little discotheque.

"What's your real name?!"

"Jafar Ali Abdul Naser!"

"No, asshole, your *real* name!"

We were giving Jafar Ali Abdul Naser (which was his real name, I later came to believe), the full treatment. We had the strobes going and the music blaring.

"My name is Jafar Ali Abdul Naser!" he shouted over the grinding guitars. "I have ID at home. I can prove this to you!"

"Bullshit! We know you're using a fake name! What's your real name?"

"Jafar Ali Abdul Naser!"

After about an hour, we opened the door and let in the dog and his handler. This had been prearranged. Jafar was going to get everything we could throw at him. I asked again, "Time to start cooperating. What's your real name?"

"Jafar Ali Abdul Naser!"

I signaled the dog handler, and the hairs on the animal's back bristled as he lunged forward, barking. Jafar knelt on the ground and I held the collar of his jumpsuit. We kept yelling. His responses were now inaudible, but I didn't care. He kept shaking his head. We signaled the dog handler to come forward. As the barking started again, Jafar whimpered and a wet stain spread out from the crotch of his jumpsuit. A second later, there was a puddle on the floor. Evan and I looked at each other, stunned. We were astounded that this charade had actually succeeded in scaring someone. We pushed forward.

"Why'd you piss on our floor, asshole?"

"What's your fucking problem?"

"Who do you think is going to clean this up?"

"What are you so afraid of, big man?"

He seemed to barely notice us; he was so fixated on the dog (which of course he couldn't see through his sandbag). We kept him on his knees. We kept pushing at him, trying to keep the pressure escalating, but all he would say is "Jafar Ali Abdul Naser." By morning we were exhausted and knew we had no place left to go. I marched him back to his cage. He was a muscular guy, not very flexible to begin with, and much stiffer now from the stress positions. I checked him in with a guard. Every prisoner filled out a form in Mosul after each interrogation that asked him to detail his treatment. All he said was "It was a very long night. My arms hurt from being handcuffed." I wrote it for him in Arabic and English because he refused to write it himself.

Jafar didn't get much sleep. The special forces team came for him not long after in their ski masks and pulled him back to their compound. I knew Pitt would want me to take another crack at him when he returned, so I made sure to rest up for another long night.

When I pulled him from his cage for a second night in our little house of horrors, he looked exhausted and resigned. I had no idea how long the special forces guys had kept him up or what they'd done to him. I put him in the shipping container again with the music and strobe lights and stress positions. I decided not to even talk to him until he spent some time in there. He begged to talk to me for three hours before I started asking him questions. "Yes, I'm involved in an insurgent group. But my name really is Jafar Ali Abdul Naser. Why are you doing this? I told the men last night everything I know." And then he told us who the insurgent leaders were, who the other members were, where to find them, what they'd done, and what they were planning to do. "This is the same thing I told the men last night. That's all I know. Now can I go to bed?" I took as much information from him as I could until I let him go to bed.

Whatever the men in black ski masks had done, it had worked. He broke for them when he wouldn't break for us—no matter how terrified he was over the dog. As much as I wished I could have taken credit for this intelligence, I noted in my report that he claimed he'd given this all to the special forces interrogators. I went to bed and made plans to interrogate him again the next night.

When I asked Pitt the following afternoon to sign off on my interrogation plan, he said, "Oh, that guy? He's been slated for release." *What the fuck are you talking about? This is the only guy here who's admitted to being an insurgent, and we're letting him go?* It made absolutely no sense. We were shipping dozens of people who were probably innocent off to Abu Ghraib. Here, we have someone who is providing real, actionable intelligence, and he walks out the gate?

Pitt said it sounded crazy, but it was probably an administrative screwup. He shrugged, as if to say, "Oh, well, what are you going to do?" Jafar Ali Abdul Naser was a free man later that day. Amazing, because I could never get our innocents released that quickly. No one told special forces. They came around to interrogate him yet again, and when they learned he was walking freely through the streets of Mosul, they went ballistic, yelled at Pitt, and stormed off to see if they could find Jafar.

As incredible as it sounds, they probably did find him. At least someone did. Months later, the army's Criminal Investigation Division wanted to ask me about a prisoner's complaint—it was just sort of a sideline to a much more serious investigation, but the special agent wanted to check it out. He had no idea at that point that I'd had contact with the prisoner who made the complaint. He read me a sworn statement, in which the prisoner claimed that men in black ski masks had dowsed him with ice water. Then two men with dogs put him in a large metal box and played music. . . . I interrupted, "Is this Jafar Ali Abdul Naser?" He'd repeated his name so many times it was burned into my memory. The special agent looked at me with surprise. "How did you know?"

CHAPTER 13

Dark Corners

The second half of April was a low.

I'd developed an abscess on my right butt cheek that swelled to an obnoxious size and made sitting painful. When I showed it to the nurse at the infirmary, she flipped. "Oh my *God*! Wait right here. I'll get the doctor." He came in to find me where she'd left me, prone on a gurney, pants around my knees. "Oh my *God*!" the doctor shouted, and now I started to worry.

They put me under for the operation, and removed a third of a liter of fluids out of the cavity. In the weeks following, I had to make a trip to the infirmary twice a day to get the hole repacked with gauze. Every day, it seemed like there was someone new behind the desk, so I got to repeat the embarrassing story for a new audience. Once I'd explained to them what they had to do, and assumed the position, I'd inevitably hear, "Oh my *God*! What the fuck!" Then they'd have to go get the doctor, who was also usually new to my plight. Meanwhile, as I waited for the doctor, I'd spend up to twenty minutes on the gurney, ass in the air, with people walking by and blurting out, "Oh my *God*! Dude! Is that from shrapnel?" In those moments, I almost wished it was something so glamorous. It was really just a garden-variety infection that had gotten out of hand.

The only good thing about this whole situation was the way the doctors threw painkillers at me. The days had been grinding on and I'd been having trouble sleeping. The painkillers took some of the edge off, though I was careful not to use them in advance of my shift. A Percocet-addled interrogator would have been even less effective than I was.

They were building a new detention and interrogation facility on base, one of those permanent structures that Iraqis could point to and say, "See, the Americans aren't leaving. Never intended to." During some of the morning meetings, we'd be asked for input on the design. Our officer in charge, Captain Lamb, who didn't interrogate and wasn't trained in interrogation, jumped in one morning with a flash of brilliance. He wanted a few booths designed so prisoners could hear what was going on in the next booth. That way, we could pretend to torture someone—probably a translator or someone would scream for his mother in Arabic—and the real prisoner would hear all this and be moved to talk. He also had some amazing ideas about performing mock executions and how facilities for this could be incorporated into the building design.

I was glad that most of the other interrogators backed me up when I protested. We'd had direct lectures back at Huachuca on why mock torture and executions were totally illegal—against army policy, against Geneva, and a sure ticket to Fort Leavenworth. So we dodged that suggestion. I was careful, of course, to couch my objections in the language of regulation, rather than morality or, God forbid, because we should have some sympathy for these prisoners. I could always win an argument by pulling out the regulations, but I'd never win on moral or humanistic grounds.

It was raining and the camp was a sea of mud, which reflected my despondence. We continued with our stress positions and general Fear Up tactics, despite our lack of outcomes. I had more or less given up on everything. An e-mail home to a close friend captured my mood: "The weather sucks. It is rainy and cold right now. That is good for interrogators because it is no fun to leave the prisoners standing with a bag over their heads in the yard if the air is balmy." He'd offered to send me a care package. Did I need anything? Yes. "A big fucking bottle of vodka."

The FBI showed up one day, with about a dozen prisoners in tow. The agents asked us to help interrogate. The poor fools they brought in (none of whom breathed a word of intelligence) were kept in our holding pen, where they slept in the dirt when they were lucky and in the mud when they were not. The special agents were pleased, I guess, with our help. They gave us patches commemorating their mission. I said thanks and looked at this piece of fabric in my hand. A skull and crossbones adorned this rather somber patch that honored the FBI's "Search for WMD—Iraq 2004."

Right. The WMD. At this point I'd forgotten all about that. Remember? The "reason" we were all sent to war. How long had it been since we seriously thought we were going after WMD? And what about the mirage of "spreading freedom" that followed the disappearance of the WMD story? How long had it been since I felt we were really bringing democracy to the Middle East? And what was the plan now? What exactly were we doing here again? What meaning did this war have? The steady tempo of killings, by U.S. troops and by the hydra-headed insurgency, what were they for? And for what did those people die?

We weren't, any of us, fully aware of how this moment in history had taken a horrible turn into a dark and dangerously active nihilism.

American troops near the border with Syria had been fired on. They got one of the suspects and transferred him here. Pitt wanted him in the shipping container posthaste, and wanted me to get what he knew. We were desperate for intel about cross-border smuggling routes, safe houses, who transports, and who buys. Foreign fighters and smugglers were a priority, even though they constituted a small part of our problem.

I handled him roughly as we disappeared into the shipping container around sundown. I was alone. I closed the door and prepared myself for a long night.

Khalid was about twenty-four or twenty-five, skinny, a little on the tall side. He had a strikingly handsome angular face that contrasted with very soft eyes. Even as I pulled him from the prison, I never saw a hint of resentment or fear in those eyes. They were passive, somewhat lost in a world of their own making. Now they were covered with goggles that I'd blacked out with duct tape. He stood in the middle of the container, hands cuffed. I started:

"Why did you fire on the Americans?" I wanted him to know that he was in serious trouble.

"I didn't. I was just watching my sheep when—"

"Liar. You were picked up with a rifle right after Americans came under fire. You were smuggling benzene."

"I swear to God, no."

The arrest report on Khalid was a lot more detailed than most. A patrol spotted a small group of figures walking over the rough terrain, away from the Syrian border. They were carrying gas cans. The Americans drove toward them in their Humvees, and suddenly came under fire. They traded fire from a distance, and no one was hit. The group dispersed, dropping their cans. By the time the patrol cautiously moved forward and recovered the cans, the smugglers had disappeared. The patrol followed one likely escape route, and that's how they found Khalid.

The Americans accused him of aiding the benzene smugglers, or smuggling himself. It wasn't clear which. His captors and his guards had kept him awake, so he'd probably been twenty-four hours without sleep. And now he was in my shipping container.

I didn't get his side of the story because I'd never let him finish a sentence. The heavy metal was bellowing in his ears and the strobe light was flashing, visible even through the goggles. I changed his stress position. Now his arms and back were flat against the wall, his knees bent at a right angle, and his feet flat on the ground. He was losing his composure because this was a very hard stress position to maintain. Every time he relaxed a little, I'd yell at him to sit up straight. I kept peppering him with questions.

"Who buys the benzene?"

"Who are you working with?"

None of this was serious questioning. Just enough to keep him guessing, just enough to show him who was in control. After about three hours, I pulled him out of the container. It was time to see if he would talk.

We sat in a small shack off to the side. There were bunk beds in there, but no one used them except the translators, who'd sometimes come in here for a quick nap. The small, cramped space stunk of Iraqi cigarettes. I pulled off Khalid's goggles and looked him in the eye.

"Are you ready to tell me what happened?"

Khalid's side of the story: he was sitting on a blanket with his AK-47 in his lap. He heard gunfire in the distance. He heard gunfire often. He knew that his land—his parents' land, where they raised sheep—was a smuggling route. The smugglers stole from them and killed their sheep, so he was watching his flock as the sun went down. The Americans rolled up. The Americans came by often. He was glad they were there, because when they were known to be close, the smugglers wouldn't come. When the Americans would come, he would give them water and food. But he'd never seen the men in this patrol before, and they'd never seen him.

At this point in an interrogation, most prisoners would either beg for sleep or try to suck up to me or increase the emphasis of their denials. They really wanted me to believe them. Khalid didn't do any of this. He presented his story in an even tone, looking me straight in the eye, but without trying to read my reaction. He presented his story as if it was something I could take or leave and it was all the same to him, either way. That pissed me off. We went back into the disco for another round.

I was sick of the death metal and put in something that was possibly more torturous—an audio version of Ben Stiller and Janeane Garofalo's *Feel This Book*. Their long discussion of relationships was lost on my prisoners, but their high voices and inane antics, when echoed and amplified through the interior of the shipping container, became distorted and painful, at least to me. If the goal was disorientation, this would do just as well as anything—and probably would do the job better than the James Taylor albums that I forced some prisoners to listen to.

Khalid had been on his knees for about an hour when we heard a banging on the door. Either the dog handler was early or I'd lost track of time. Khalid still hadn't cracked, or even shown an opening. He was clearly disoriented, uncomfortable, and sometimes winced when I shouted at him, but it wasn't the kind of fear I could sustain and exploit. It was close to eleven at night. I hoped the dog would help me wrap this up soon.

"Who did you meet in Syria?"

"I don't go there."

The dog's reaction came almost immediately after my signal, and Khalid leaned back as the deep, menacing barking echoed through the chamber, competing effectively with Ben and Janeane. I wondered if I was going to see yet another prisoner wet himself. I let the barking go on a little longer than usual, then signaled it to stop. The dog stopped immediately, as if it was now taking commands from me, not just its handler. *I have so much power over this man*, I thought. I felt he was ready to break, and I yelled my question again. Nothing.

Khalid's fear peaked and quickly subsided. You could see him, even without being able to see his expression, return to the peaceful center he occupied before the dog started barking. He had all the right reactions. He was clearly afraid of me and the dog and for his future, but he simply accepted his fear and absorbed it. There was plenty of fear, but not the kind I could use. So I let the dog go at him again. And again. My head was spinning. I had never been so angry. *Break, you asshole. Just fucking break.*

It was close to one in the morning. I let the dog handler go. I'd made no progress and had exhausted my tools. I left him in the container, in a stress position, and went outside. The base was quiet, except for the voices of Ben and Janeane bouncing off the walls of the shipping container. It was cold and I was completely alone, except for this prisoner inside, who not only wouldn't talk but wouldn't acknowledge the absolute power I held over him. It was just me and him. No one else was out here, no one was watching.

Khalid was right where I left him, calm and serene. When I looked at him, the anger surged, amplified by the flashing lights and the booming noise. A thought flashed through my head: *Chop his fucking fingers off.*

And why not? I'd been pushed for weeks to ramp up the pressure, to hit these shitbags harder and harder. Why had I been putting on the brakes? The only thing that held me back was this inconvenient compassion I'd been lugging around since I got to Abu Ghraib. By now, there were only shreds of it left. I didn't care anymore when prisoners cried in front of me, when they wept for their families left behind, or from the pain of stress positions. Wasn't it time to lighten the load? Break whatever remaining threads of sympathy still hung between me and these Iraqis? And who would care? This whole miserable country was insane, and getting worse. If I wanted to cut off Khalid's fingers, why the hell not?

※　　※　　※

The thing about Khalid that drove me crazy was his clear sense of self-control and poise, which let me know I had no mastery over him and that my power was mere illusion. Khalid was Yazidi, an ancient religion that was here long before the Arab conquest. Yazidi trace their roots back to 2000 BC, and for millennia they've been persecuted by every ethnic group they've come in contact with, and every empire that's ever governed this land. There is something about their beliefs that other religions cannot seem to abide.

There's a lot of mystery surrounding the Yazidi, and a lot of contradictory information. But I was drawn to this aspect of their beliefs: Yazidi don't have a Satan. Malak Ta'us, an archangel, God's favorite, was not thrown out of heaven the way Satan was. Instead, he descended, saw the suffering and pain of the world, and cried. His tears, thousands of years' worth, fell on the fires of hell, extinguishing them. If there is evil in the world, it does not come from a fallen angel or from the fires of hell. The evil in this world is man-made. Nevertheless, humans can, like Malak Ta'us, live in this world but still be good.

Humans fear pain, but we fear evil more. Why do torture victims suffer such long-lasting psychological damage while victims of accidents suffer little more than post-traumatic stress disorder? It's the presence of evil. The torture victim is aware of another consciousness, someone like them, deliberately inflicting pain and summoning hate. The sane, domesticated mind rebels against the idea that there are people out there who can torture (and even worse, can enjoy it). Evil is something we don't understand. We can't know what it's capable of, or what it will do next. We fear most not what evil will do to our bodies, but what it will do to our orderly, civilized worldview, our fragile psychology that's so dependent on predictability and a belief in the goodness of human souls.

In a way, Khalid saw my evil as pre-forgiven. It didn't figure into how he interpreted what I was doing to him. I was just another in a long line of invaders, more akin to a natural disaster or a historical inevitability. True, I was another consciousness, just like him, but I wasn't irredeemably evil. So my acts were just something he would have to endure, and I, too, would pass. His fear was just the reflexive fear of pain; I saw it ebb and flow as I tried my techniques, but it never became the deep, uncontrollable fear of evil and what evil people can do. It never became the fear that can make torture effective.

Khalid kept his fingers. The thought of mutilating him enjoyed a brief flash of life. For that moment, it made perfect sense to cut his fingers off, but then the impulse dimly flickered and died away. For a moment after, I was sorry to see it go, because now I was back in a place where very little made sense, and I still had to figure out what to do with Khalid.

One of my biggest problems with Fear Up Harsh was the way it boxed me in. Once I started down this road, any deviation could be perceived as weakness. I had to keep hammering on Khalid's defenses with lights and sound and yelling, even though I knew by now that nothing would come of it. By now, it was torment done for its own sake, and so I could put down on my report that I did this all night.

At about two in the morning, I was ready to give up. The lights and noise had affected me as well. The cruelty and the role I was forced to play were mentally draining. I took off Khalid's goggles and looked at him. I'd become convinced during the night that Khalid was just as he said he was—a simple man who had done nothing wrong and knew nothing of wrongdoing. But someone was banging on the door.

Four infantry sergeants were standing outside. "What's going on in there?" one asked me as they invited themselves in. I thought for a moment that I was in trouble, but they'd come for Khalid. Before I could protest, they surrounded him.

Khalid's eyes showed fear again. Four large men with guns were yelling at him. One was banging the wall. He couldn't understand a thing they were saying, but it was clear to both of us why they were here. Months of patrols in Mosul, the stress of never knowing when or where the next IED would go off, the injury or deaths of close friends, all that anger. And here was one of "them," a real insurgent, helpless and at hand.

I didn't recognize any of these men, and all of them outranked me, but this was my interrogation and I was supposed to maintain control. That control was now slipping away. One of them was poking Khalid in the chest with his finger while yelling in his face, drill-sergeant style, with ample spittle flying. Another had his fist cocked back, locked and loaded. I pushed my way in between them, saying, "I've got this, guys."

"Sure," one of them replied. "Why don't you take a nap? We'll take care of him for you. . . ." The sergeant who seemed to be the leader of this pack winked at me and the words "take care of him" went through me with a chill. I refused, but what more could I do? I wanted to leave and find someone who outranked these guys, but that meant leaving Khalid alone with them. I realized how alone and isolated I was, and now I was not in control. Stupid, stupid situation, one that now might end in Khalid getting seriously fucked up.

"No, really, it's okay. He's cooperating. We're fine." My voice felt meek, without authority. There were too many of them. I could get in between Khalid and one of them, but another would come from the side. We started to tussle slightly, getting a little more physical as they tried to close in on the prisoner.

And then they just stopped. Their unofficial leader gave in just before this became a real test of wills. "Okay, let's go," he said, and they started to file out. "Let us know if you need any help." I locked the door behind them, and turned back to Khalid, bathed in the flashing white light.

Khalid slept in the shipping container while I stood guard outside, waiting for the sun to come up. I couldn't take him back to the prison. Some of Mosul's city council members were due here in the morning, on a regularly scheduled visit, and Pitt wanted to keep anyone who'd gotten rough treatment hidden away. I'd have to stand guard here for hours, but that was fine. I wanted to make sure the four visitors didn't return.

Something very wrong had happened here. The idea of cutting his fingers off was something I quickly dismissed, but the fact that it even crossed my mind . . .

Here was a signal that it was time to pull myself out of this abyss. I'd been skeptical of all the things we were doing—the whole torture lite package—and I'd been following orders, and I tried to make sure we didn't go too far. Maybe I liked the pain and distress I caused. It gave me power, but there was something else. I saw my cruelty reflected in the cruelty of the four men I had just restrained from beating Khalid.

Like that nineteen-year-old soldier in Kuwait who said he couldn't wait to shoot a terrorist, I'd come here looking for an extreme experience. Something that normal people just never get a chance to even glimpse. Back in the schoolhouse, I'd become fascinated with interrogation, and here in the field, I wanted the whole thing. As the regulations and our reading of the regulations got more and more permissive, I saw a chance to really put myself in a situation where I was not in control, and where much darker impulses took over.

As I swam through this abyss, I think, on that night, I brushed up against something not just unpleasant or cruel or sadistic, but something thoroughly evil. Now, if I *really* wanted to give up control, all I had to do was grab on to it.

I found that I wasn't capable of that level of cruelty. I found that there were boundaries on what I was willing to do. This made me feel somewhat better, but the things I was willing to do up to those boundaries were still very bad. I was still willing to do those things to people even without compelling evidence that they were guilty of anything. I did these things, basically, for my own amusement. Just to see how far I would go, just to seek out an extreme of experience. Here I was in a god-awful war zone, the most dangerous and vile place on earth, and I was acting like a tourist.

I woke up in the late afternoon and found that Khalid had spent the entire day in the shipping container, which usually got as hot as ninety-five degrees with no air movement. Not only that, the dozen or so guys the FBI brought in were stashed away in there as well. They were still being hidden away from the Mosul city officials who were touring the facility with an American colonel.

Over the next few days, I talked frequently to Khalid. He missed his family. He worried about his parents, who needed his help. I asked him a little about his religion. I'd asked friends at home to send me whatever they could find on the Internet about the Yazidi, because Khalid gave me very short answers. Yazidi are very reclusive, and don't seek converts. He was more expansive about his family, and his hopes that he could one day save enough money to get married. He never tried to provoke my compassion or draw attention to his plight. He never complained. He always looked me in the eye, but always without penetrating; it was a very friendly gaze that I tried to interpret as forgiveness. I got the strong impression that Khalid was a very good man. Much better than myself.

After a couple weeks, Khalid's file went before the battalion decision makers. Unknown eyes compared my interrogation report (which included the key phrase "No Further Intelligence Value") to the sworn statements produced by the arresting soldiers, which implied he fired on U.S. troops. There was nothing else in his file. No further interrogations or inquiries were made. The decision makers felt they had enough. A small group of guards came for Khalid and several other prisoners one morning. With head bagged and arms tied, Khalid boarded a helicopter for the long trip to Abu Ghraib.

CHAPTER 14

Bad Apples

One of the goals of the torture lite techniques, according to a CIA manual that defined and promoted them, is to inflict pain and disorientation in such a way that the victim does not blame the interrogator. The victim would not resent the interrogator for the pain from stress positions, for example, but would ultimately blame himself. If the plan also includes disorientation techniques, cutting the subject off from the known and familiar, and successfully induces "regression," the subject is supposed to blame himself for his suffering, and even experience guilt.

This twisted theory must count as one of the wackier ideas promulgated by our central intelligence service. Prisoners aren't going to blame themselves. Unless they're already prone to self-loathing, they will always blame their captors. This self-blame idea, and its brethren, was born in a paranoid era when we really believed that people could successfully be subjects of brainwashing and mind control. The same era produced CIA-sponsored LSD and deep-isolation experiments on unwitting subjects. Some of them went insane, but none of their minds was controlled, none of their brains was washed. But the CIA did manage to develop a set of techniques that looked clinical rather than brutal, clean and scientific instead of messy and sadistic. Those who practiced the techniques could try to heighten guilt in their prisoners while avoiding feeling guilty themselves.

It was a nice try; in my case it didn't work at all. I failed to get any of my prisoners to feel guilty, and I failed to avoid feeling guilt myself. After my torment of Khalid, after I reflected on the steady escalation I'd been a part of, the guilt came on slowly and steadily. Within days, it was crushing.

I talked to Jones about the shipping container and how I wasn't going back out there. I pointed out the problems with doing interrogations outside the wire. I explained that I was isolated and not really in control. I told him about the guys who showed up the night before, looking for an Iraqi captive to put the hurt on, and how I was almost helpless to stop them. (At the time, I thought Chief Pitt put them up to this—I was wrong.) Jones listened and showed the concern a leader should. He could see the problem. His heart had never been in this process anyway. He told Pitt that we were shutting the disco down. And that was that.

Not long after, the NCO in charge of the dog handlers, whom I'd never seen or even heard about, found out what we were asking her men to do. She pulled the rug out with finality. No more dogs during interrogations.

The steady escalation was over, and Pitt seemed to accept it. It was so easy it made me wonder why I didn't kill this project long ago. This led me down another path of self-recrimination that I still struggle with daily. How did I become a moral failure?

I could have stopped this anytime. I could see now that the strides we took into extreme techniques were hesitant and fragile. If I had stood up at any point in this process and said, "This is wrong," it would have lurched to a halt. Why didn't I do this?

The hackneyed excuses of a torturer were all available to me, and none of them worked. None of them convinced me that I was ever in the right.

The pressure to do these things was clearly present, from Pitt's references to prisoners as "shitbags" to the demand for actionable intelligence, but it was pressure I could have resisted.

Other U.S. troops were doing much worse things. But my restraint wasn't a moral stand. It was just circumstantial.

The insurgents were bombing us almost every day. I'd been the target of one of their snipers, true, but I couldn't use this as a justification when my victims had probably nothing to do with it, or, if they did, our techniques weren't working anyway.

The insurgents were doing much worse things to our troops and to

Iraqis—not just torturing, but killing. Why couldn't this fact help me accept my own cruelty, which paled in comparison? It seemed to work for other people. Unfortunately, I learned, I believed in the highest moral principles embodied in the international ban on torture. I believed them, but I didn't live up to them.

In the end, I did what I did because I wanted to. That has been very hard to accept.

I'd almost forgotten about how "something bad" had happened at Abu Ghraib. At this point, I'd written it off. Either it wasn't really bad or the army had done a superb job covering it up. Since I wasn't watching TV, I heard about it slowly. Some MPs had done some stupid stuff, and even more stupid, they had taken pictures. The backlash was coming here, I heard the guards complain. "Now we're going to have to give them [the prisoners] chocolate bars," one guard quipped.

It was a busy time, so it was days before I got away to the Internet tent. I knew that this story, no matter how small, would at least be on Al Jazeera, so I went to their Web site first. The first picture I saw was one of the naked pyramids. My stomach turned. It felt like I was watching a bomb going off.

I knew this would be explosive, incredibly damaging to our reputation in the Arab world, and would lead to courts-martial and new rules for MPs and guards (though not involving candy bars, probably). In the end, though, wasn't it just a bunch of stupid kids acting up? That's what I thought at the time, and just about everyone on base in Mosul would have agreed with me. We were so isolated from the anger that erupted back in the civilian world. In our world of constant violence and a steady stream of prisoners, this episode was comparatively minor. But this was the most amazing part: I didn't connect it to interrogation or what we were doing, at all. At least not at first.

When I heard there were going to be Senate hearings, I saw that this was bigger than I first thought. When I caught some of the hearings on CNN, it started to dawn on me that I wasn't so different from the MPs run amok at Abu Ghraib. As the scandal's deeper roots revealed themselves, connections between the photos and our interrogations became clear. And as everyone—

from the pundits to the senators to the secretary of defense to the president— roundly condemned the guards' actions in the harshest terms, I started to wonder what they'd think of our little forays into the darker side of interrogation.

Finally, I was able to look at what we'd done from the outside. In our military cocoon, it all made sense. Of course we should keep someone up all night, freeze him in stress positions until his joints failed, and by all means, pull out the dogs. Use all tools at our disposal to defeat the enemy. But from stateside, if someone had seen broadcast pictures of what we were doing, the only difference they would have noticed between our prison and Abu Ghraib was that our prisoners had their clothes on. The senators were shocked, *shocked*, to learn that stress positions and dogs were part of interrogation practice and appeared on IROE. One of these IROE was on display in the Senate hearing room as a chart. When pressed on the harsher practices listed, Colonel Marc Warren, a judge advocate general (JAG), agreed that they didn't look too good: "[To use a] term I've learned in the past week in Washington, the optics are bad on that chart."[1] No kidding.

I also learned a few things about the army's civilian leadership. For one thing, they often didn't know what they were talking about. Stephen Cambone, the undersecretary of defense for intelligence, testified that hooding, sleep deprivation, and stress positions were "techniques in army doctrine," which is bullshit. Nowhere in the army interrogation manual are these techniques endorsed.

Rumsfeld repeatedly claimed, "The Geneva Conventions apply to all of the individuals there in one way or another." The uniformed soldiers, of which there were very few, were protected as POWs, and the rest were protected under the Fourth Geneva Convention, pertaining to civilians. There was no such protection. Under Geneva, a competent tribunal is supposed to determine if imprisoned civilians are an "imperative" security threat. They have the right to appeal their imprisonment and their case must be reviewed twice a year. None of this was going on, anywhere. Our prisoners were with-

---

[1] U.S. Senate Committee on Armed Services, Testimony on Allegations of Mistreatment of Iraqi Prisoners, May 19, 2004.

out status. The JAG who testified before the Senate once referred to them as "unlawful combatants," making them sound like they'd received the same dreaded status reserved for the "worst of the worst" at Gitmo—no lawyer, no appeal, no communication, no writ of habeas corpus. Just endless questioning and indefinite imprisonment.

Rumsfeld knew this breach of Geneva was taking place. Human Rights Watch told him about it in February 2004, just after I got to Abu Ghraib.

The policy-makers who'd done their best to undermine the Geneva Conventions now evoked them. The techniques that Rumsfeld signed off on for Gitmo, and which migrated to Iraq, were now, according to his undersecretary, "army doctrine." It was clear what was happening here. We, who had faithfully executed the policies after being told they were perfectly legal, who had our asses on the line every day, who made Bush's insane war possible, were being hung out to dry. Thanks for your service, boys. Now, as Dick Cheney might say, go fuck yourselves.

As I dug deeper, I found that the Abu Ghraib photos were the least of the abuse. Of course, they got the most attention because they were immediate, sensational, and gripping. After the Taguba Report was leaked, however, there was no question that this was much more than a series of crazy pranks. Our soldiers had committed rape, sodomy with chemical lights and nightsticks, severe beatings that required medical attention, and homicide. One dozen dead Iraqis, labeled by the U.S. Army as either homicide or unexplained.

The most famous, and still most mysterious, was the death of Manadel al-Jamadi, a prisoner captured by SEALs and interrogated by OGA at Abu Ghraib. He had been beaten severely during arrest. He was shackled with his arms high above him in a shower room during the interrogation. The army ruled that the homicide was caused by a combination of blunt force injuries to his torso and compromised respiration. Manadel al-Jamadi's dead body appears in the Abu Ghraib photos, with two of the MPs hovering over him, giving the thumbs-up sign.

This happened on November 4, a little over two months before I arrived at Abu Ghraib. Weeks before I arrived at al-Asad, a prisoner died in custody there. Abdul Jaleel was shackled to a doorframe, in a manner similar to my shackling of Habib to a bed frame months later. Soldiers kicked and punched him while he was gagged and shackled. Someone jammed a baton under his throat and lifted him up. He died of "blunt force injuries and asphyxia," according to his autopsy report. Were the soldiers prosecuted? Army investigators recommended it, but commanders overruled it because Abdul's death was the logical "result of a series of lawful applications of force in response to repeated aggression and misconduct by the detainee."[2] Really? The guy was shackled and gagged. What kind of aggression and misconduct could he commit in that moment?

Another prisoner was killed at Mosul, this one during my stay there. I barely heard hushed rumors about this. It happened in the SEALs' compound. The victim was allegedly hooded, cuffed, and got the same ice water treatment I'd heard so much about, in addition to being sleep-deprived. The cause of death, the autopsy reported, was "undetermined." Maybe, the report went on, the hypothermia had something to do with it.

Three assignments, three dead prisoners, all either just before I got there or not long after, and it's not surprising at all. This is where torture leads. Only one thing gave me pause. If I'd gone ahead and cut Khalid's fingers off, where would that have led? What else would I have been capable of?

I was full of guilt and trying to come to grips with my moral failures, but I kept this to myself. Not a good time or place to get a reputation as a pussy. Instead of vocalizing the self-loathing growing inside me, I took my frustrations out on Donald Rumsfeld, with rants and missives—"Goddamn liar, arrogant prick"—that should have had me sent up for insubordination. My team noticed, and so did Pitt. But we'd learned that a new assignment was on the way. Soon we'd leave Mosul, and all we'd accomplished here, behind.

The word was that we were shipping out to Fallujah after reporting back to Abu Ghraib. The thought of returning to the flagpole now, with the scandal still fresh, was beyond depressing. One of my buddies had gone down and

---

[2] USA Amnesty International's Supplementary Briefing to the UN Committee Against Torture, May 3, 2006, p. 2.

back on a mail run, and reported that the insurgents had ramped up the attacks even more. Iraqi contractors had been killed at the gate; now they wouldn't come to work. The insurgents successfully cut off supply lines of food, fuel, and water. Shit was cresting over the tops of the portable toilets. As awful as the place had become, it was now world-famous, and so a much more attractive target.

We flew back to Baghdad and convoyed to Abu Ghraib. Donald Rumsfeld was coming into Abu Ghraib just as we arrived. Black Hawks and armored vehicles were everywhere. Sergeant Jones ordered me, in mock seriousness, to turn over my ammo. He didn't want me to draw a court-martial. I laughed and turned my eyes back to the road. "No, really. Hand it over," he demanded. Why? Like I was seriously going to take a shot at the SecDef? Maybe, reflecting on my anti-Rumsfeld rants, I should tone it down.

PART III

ABU GHRAIB AND LEAVE
MAY TO SEPTEMBER 2004

Unless a group is prepared to totally dedicate itself to the twisted logic of atrocity, it will not gain even the shortsighted advantages of that logic, but will instead be immediately weakened and confused by its own inconsistency and hypocrisy. There are no half measures when one sells one's soul.

—Lt. Col. Dave Grossman, *On Killing*

CHAPTER 15

In Hiding

The roof of the hard site where we lived at Abu Ghraib was extensive, multileveled, dark, with places to hide, and easy to climb to. Soldiers knew it well as the perfect place to escape. One night, shortly after I got back from Mosul, Tomas and I climbed up to discuss how we were going to get out of the army.

The building wasn't so tall, just two stories high, so we couldn't see the town over the wall, but it gave us a great view of the sky above. Just like any other night, the air was full of gunfire and the tracers slashed knifelike across the sky. I could watch the tracers for hours and never get over how fast these red flashes were. They were faster than shooting stars, faster than the lasers of science-fiction movies. Because their momentum was almost supernatural, and because I knew that each tracer had three bullets behind it, flying at the same speed, they were horrifying. But from a distance, they were also beautiful.

Explosions punctuated the tracers with their thunder, flashes of light, and the occasional fireball. Our gunships would sometimes fly in low and open up on a neighborhood, providing more fireworks. But whatever form the destruction took, it happened every night. Baghdad was a violent and lawless place; you could see that even from out here.

Tomas and I slowly sipped vodka from tin canteen cups and quietly mourned the demise of Baghdad and the evident failure of our mission. Tomas had been my favorite right-winger back at language school—the young guy I argued with extensively and respected deeply. He'd come to Iraq at about the same time, but served as an interrogator in a unit involved in highly sensitive, kinetic, and violent operations. He was much closer to the action and served with a smaller unit, but we still had very similar experiences when it came to detainees.

Tomas told me about hypothermia techniques used on prisoners. I'd seen the lips of prisoners turn blue when they were left outside in the rain, but Tomas described a man's entire body shaking like an epileptic. He recalled how one time he left his tent and saw half a dozen naked prisoners chained to poles in different stress positions, sort of hanging there like overripe tomatoes on vines supported by stakes. There were other things he didn't tell me about until much later, when he felt it was safe. These were the beatings—the blows to the crotch, face, and gut—all delivered by American interrogators for the purpose of gathering information.

He did his job, and had commendations to prove it. But he was sickened by what he saw and how his commanders sanctioned it. When he came back to Abu Ghraib (he arrived a little before I returned from Mosul), he stopped seeing abuse, but continued to see that the overwhelming majority of prisoners he interrogated were held on slim to zero evidence. Like me, he had almost no chance of getting them released, no matter how much he tried.

He hated the PowerPoint slides, repeatedly foisted on us by officers who wanted to show how, through massive detentions, we were "winning" the war. He hated hearing from them and from his peers how our prisoners were all guilty. He was sick of the repeated references to 9/11 and the global war on terror, because he knew that this occupation had nothing to do with either.

I saw Tomas change his moral and political stance drastically over the years I knew him. His experience learning Arabic and following the news and constantly talking to and challenging other people changed him. He had traded Ann Coulter for Noam Chomsky and intelligent design for evolution. And now, sitting on that rooftop, he told me that he was so sick of seeing what this war was doing to people that he was ready to apply for conscientious objector status.

I'd like to say that Tomas changed because of the irrefutable points I scored during our arguments back at DLI, but I believe I really had little to do with it. As I thought about the last time I'd seen Tomas and about the issues he was grappling with, I realized that one of the early influences on his transformation was Al Jazeera. We watched this station constantly at DLI, and I remember Tomas starting to see that Middle Eastern issues were actually very complex. That the Palestinians had legitimate grievances, that the Saudis weren't always the best allies, that everyone did not see America as a paragon of virtue.

This was the first chink in his right-wing armor. Once he started questioning whether America was always right in its conduct abroad, doubt started worming its way into his moral fabric. Instead of rejecting the intruder, he listened.

The army was not a hospitable place for this kind of exploration. Tomas was surrounded by peers and commanders who expected and reinforced fealty to each and every Republican policy—social, economic, and foreign— and rejected any semblance of leftist thought as immoral weakness. It was remarkable that Tomas had changed so much, but the fact that he did so by swimming against the tide of thousands of angry men and women at war was nothing short of stunning.

Though it's entirely possible that they accidentally helped him along. So many of our peers spat out such vicious bile on such a regular basis that Tomas clearly saw the ugly side of the American right wing, and recognized it as totally incompatible with the Christianity that these people also professed. When soldiers talked loudly about turning Baghdad into a parking lot, or about the pleasure they got from seeing the guts of an Iraqi blown from his torso, they identified themselves as part of a tribe that Tomas wanted no part of. Then he went out into the field and saw for himself what actions spring from these beliefs. He learned, as he watched a soldier beat a defenseless prisoner, the end result of American exceptionalism. *This* is what we do when we believe God favors America. *This* is what happens when we believe we are powerful only because we are good. *This* is what we mean when we say "My country, right or wrong."

Tomas didn't announce to me that night that he was a new person. I simply learned it by listening to him. His jaw clenched as he told me about his NCO, who talked about how he couldn't wait to get back to Arizona, sit on his porch, and shoot illegal aliens. He got in a shouting match with a group of sergeants who ordered him to turn off *Fahrenheit 9/11*. He was also engaged in a constant debate over politics with the lieutenant in his company. They always exchanged a jab or two when they saw each other. His curses at the top brass testifying before Congress on the Abu Ghraib scandal took him to the edge of insubordination. I deeply respected Tomas that night and I still do.

Both Tomas and I had questioned our officers and NCOs about Geneva, because what we were doing or seeing was clearly outside the bounds. We both heard from our officers, in almost the exact same terms, that the United States did not consider these Iraqi prisoners to be protected by Geneva. This went against army doctrine and everything we'd learned in training, but we accepted it and did our jobs. We trusted our commanders to give us legal orders and accurate information. As we watched the Abu Ghraib hearings, we saw that this was a mistake. Rumsfeld and his generals repeatedly said that these prisoners *were* covered by Geneva, without exception. Later, in an interview with Matt Lauer, Rumsfeld claimed that "the decision was made that the Geneva Convention did not apply precisely," but there was general agreement that prisoners would be "treated as though the Geneva Convention did apply."[1]

It was clear to Tomas and me what these convoluted statements meant. Bush, Rumsfeld, and Cheney had been deliberately undermining Geneva ever since the war in Afghanistan, but once it made them look bad, they ran for cover. The generals and other top brass followed suit. Everyone's ass was covered, except for those asses attached to the lowly specialists who'd carried out the policies that the policy-makers now disavowed. Okay, so if this played out for Mosul like it did for Abu Ghraib, I was screwed. I'd be Lynndie England. I'd be Charles Graner.

At this point in our service, we both saw the army as corrupt, hypocritical, abusive, totally unsuited to the reconstruction of Iraq, and disloyal to its own troops. These were not just failures of the system, but a wide-ranging collapse of values.

The mechanical sounds of Kalashnikovs exchanging fire, muted by a mile of humid air, echoed off the hard site. Tomas sipped his vodka. I stared

[1] Secretary Rumsfeld Interview with Matt Lauer, NBC *Today*, Department of Defense News Transcript, May 5, 2004; www.defenselink.mil/transcripts/2004/tr20040505-secdef1425.html (accessed August 1, 2006).

straight ahead. My hands were shaking. Tomas had reminded me of how immoral I'd become in Mosul, and of all the anger I'd harbored over how deeply we'd fucked the Iraqis over with our arrogance and incompetence.

"I'm going to apply for CO status," Tomas finally announced. I agreed to join him. We'd finish our year in Iraq and then exit the army as conscientious objectors.

Six months later, I learned what this meant. I would have to swear before a review panel that I was morally opposed to war. I realized at that point that I couldn't go through with the pact I'd made with my friend. I hated war, but I still felt that a just and competently fought war was possible (unlikely under the current administration, but still possible nonetheless). I wanted out of the army, more than I'd wanted anything in my life thus far, but I wasn't going to lie to make it happen.

Tomas felt differently. He'd built a new belief system, and he honestly believed that war, all war, was immoral, period. I'm still not convinced on that point. I deeply respect Tomas's conviction, though, and I'm certain he came to it honestly and after looking deeply into the implications of it.

I was at Abu Ghraib waiting for either my next field assignment or my standard two weeks' leave, whichever came first. I soon discovered that there was some confusion about whether I was working for Alpha Company or Bravo Company, which I exploited terribly. By letting each company believe I was working for the other, I could disappear. My new quarters was a cell in a hard site, and my roommate soon left for a field assignment. No one came up there, and no one paid attention to where I was.

When I checked in at the mailroom, it was like Christmas in June. Family and friends had been sending me care packages for months, and they never made it to Mosul. The orderly gave me a very pissed-off lecture about the package from Uncle Jay. He'd sent me a block of Limburger cheese some months ago, and it had been rotting in the desert heat ever since. The smell was still there, days after I claimed the package. They could have just thrown it away as far as I was concerned, but army regs tied their hands.

My mother's care package reminded me of a lie I'd told. Back in December, when I'd first shipped to Iraq, she cried uncontrollably while saying good-bye. She was beside herself, convinced I'd be killed. So when I got to Kuwait, I sent her an outrageous lie via e-mail. I'd hit it off with General Sanchez, I said, and he needed someone to look after his wife in Kuwait. So my assignment, I explained, was to drive Mrs. Sanchez around Kuwait City, translate for her, and tend to her garden. Mom was picturing me puttering around a garden with a watering can and speaking Arabic to this woman's servants. In Mom's care package were several envelopes of seeds—geraniums, daffodils, hyacinths. Now, what was I going to do with these at Abu Ghraib?

I'd been more honest in the rest of my e-mails. Back in my cell, I started opening packages and discovered that I had a little liquor cabinet on my hands. Friends and family had heard my desperate pleas and had hidden scotch in ginger ale bottles, vodka with a little food coloring in bottles of mouthwash, and gin in vitamin water bottles. Now that I'd managed to take an early vacation, the timing was absolutely perfect.

As desperate as I'd been for a shot of booze when I was in Mosul, I was surprised at how little I drank now that I had more than I could have ever hoped for. Somehow, I couldn't bring myself to get as thoroughly tanked as I wanted. Some of this was fear of getting caught—if Alpha figured out that I wasn't actually working for Bravo, and found me passed out drunk in my cell to boot, that would look pretty bad. Also, I was painfully aware that I was in a war zone, and that was a good reason to avoid getting completely blotto. Finally, I wanted to fill up my days with reading, and I knew I couldn't do that drunk.

For two weeks I read everything I could get my hands on: Hemingway, Wolfe, Twain, Orwell, and yet another failed attempt at Proust. Behind my bars, in self-imposed solitary confinement, I sipped my liquor slowly and absorbed novels rapidly. After midnight, when I knew that all of Alpha and Bravo companies had gone to bed, I'd venture out to the chow hall seeking provisions.

I'd become one of those slackers I'd grown to hate in Mosul. I felt I was entitled, having put in twelve-hour days for ten weeks, but mostly I was falling into despair. The mission was a failure. We were ruining the lives of thousands by the day. This institution was rife with incompetence, from top to bottom, and I couldn't escape the fact that this incompetence I hated was my own as well. In Mosul, I hadn't made the best decisions, chosen the right approaches, gotten good intelligence, done enough research, or made the right recommendations. I'd probably sent many innocent people to indefinite detention. They were here in this prison because of me. Besides my incompetence, I also knew I'd allowed myself to become a moral failure, but at this time, I still didn't fully recognize to what extent I needed to bear responsibility for my actions. That would come later.

There was a new strategy for interrogations, I found, when I got back to Abu Ghraib. No one was getting good intel, but the interrogators had to show they were getting something, so they focused on HCRs—Human Collection Requirements. These are questions, which could come from any agency, that are posted up on Sipranet for anyone else to try to answer. They presented an opportunity to show we were useful. So, I was told to look through the HCRs and get answers from our prisoners. Who's financing the insurgency? How do Iraqis feel about Sistani? What's the most popular mosque in Hit? There were thousands of questions, just waiting for answers.

And the beauty was that we didn't even have to get the right answer to file a report. We didn't even have to believe what the prisoner said. Some guys would offer prisoners packs of smokes or an extra meal to get an answer, and instead of probing a prisoner's statement or following it up with more questions, they'd just generate a report. If they did this enough times, they'd get a medal.

So this was my job now. Generate paperwork and post stuff up on Sipranet. As much as you possibly can. And don't worry, if it's wrong someone will figure it out. This was far from harmless. We were further constipating an already bloated intelligence network and making it harder to tell the good intel from the bad. Plus, you never knew how someone was going to use this stuff. An Iraqi prisoner might name an imam as a collaborator just to get a hot meal, and so our infantry would hit the imam's mosque. Now his congregation is pissed off at us, we're pissed off at them because they're ingrates, and it all started because someone was trying to meet a paperwork quota.

I didn't feel bad about hiding in my cell. I wasn't helping us win the war, but I knew I wasn't doing any harm in there.

✳   ✳   ✳

One thing made me eager to get back to Abu Ghraib, and that was finding out more about the scandal. Now, maybe that the word was out, we could talk about the "something bad" that had happened here. Those hopes were dashed quickly. By the time I got back, about three weeks after the story broke, no one wanted to talk about it, hear about it, or think about it. CNN was still pushing Abu Ghraib twenty-four hours a day, the hearings were still on, and there was the chance, however slight, that investigators would work their way up the chain of command. This was all very boring to everyone on base, who'd written this off as dumb hillbilly antics as quickly as they were able.

I kept waiting to hear something from our leadership. Maybe a morale booster about how the brass still believed in us? Maybe a stern lecture on how these sorts of shenanigans can undermine the whole war effort? Or maybe there was an officer who actually took this seriously, since of course it involved beating prisoners bloody, sodomy with chemical lights, and dogs attacking prisoners, not just naked pyramids and other "lighthearted" pranks. And maybe he'd pull us aside and tell us that if he ever heard about any of us doing anything remotely resembling this to any prisoner, no matter what the circumstances, he would personally make sure we were court-martialed to the hilt? Maybe?

Nothing. Not a word. It was just as silent as when I first arrived in Abu Ghraib, except for what I saw on CNN. Finally, one day, our sergeant major called a formation. I waited, wondering what form this long-awaited lecture would take, and then he launched into a stern series of orders on . . . uniform standards.

Actually, this had something to do with the scandal, though he didn't connect the dots for us. Senators and generals, in a rather public and embarrassing fashion, had complained that discipline was slipping at Abu Ghraib. How could they tell? People were out of uniform, and they weren't saluting officers.

Both of these observations were true. Interrogators never wore rank or name tapes in the booth. This was standard and sanctioned practice because it allowed us to deceive prisoners, let them think we were more important than a lowly specialist, and because we certainly didn't want prisoners actually knowing our family names. So going to and from interrogations, our uniforms weren't up to standard. And as for saluting, officers don't *want* to receive salutes in the middle of a war zone. It makes them a target for snipers.

The orders came down from on high. Interrogators now had to carry two uniforms around with them, one for the booth, one for the short walk to the booth. And we saluted every officer we saw, regardless of who might be watching.

There was obviously something simmering—a lot of resentment from interrogators, who felt they were now under a microscope—and this started to come out, finally, after the Nick Berg video hit the Internet. I watched it. I was horrified.

"Fuck them," I heard an interrogator say after being told he had to take a prisoner out of isolation. "Look what they did to Berg." There was general agreement and much nodding of heads around the JIDC. "Do you think they'd treat us as well," someone chimed in, "if we were captured? Fuck no. They'd cut our heads off."

I didn't engage. I didn't think the prisoners we had, by and large, had anything at all to do with Mr. Berg's murder, but I couldn't appear to defend any Iraqi in that room at that moment. There was too much anger.

I thought back to a day in Mosul when the guards crowded around a digital picture on a computer screen. They said the Humvee had rushed through a small crowd of Iraqis, and the Humvee's grille was splattered with brains and body parts. Soldiers jostled each other laughing and joking. I don't think those soldiers knew the context of that incident, and they didn't seem to care. An Iraqi torn and smashed to bits was good fun.

Then I remembered another video of a beheading that was passed around among soldiers via e-mail. There's an Iraqi man standing there one moment, and then the unmistakable sound of a .50 caliber opening up, and then, after a split-second explosion of red, the man's head is just gone. The headless torso crumples to the ground.

The terrorists' beheading videos, Abu Ghraib photos, and combat video shot by our soldiers and passed around for fun all attest to the most vicious, brutal war we've ever fought. These little digital slices of horror don't just document it, however. They feed the anger and feed the violence on both sides. They are both records and weapons, acts of violence and incitements to more violence. Combatants on both sides watch, and go into battle perfectly enraged and desensitized, where they create more corpses and shoot more video.

I was totally disgusted by the insurgents, by the behavior of my comrades, by the actions of my government, and by myself. I hadn't fully connected these still-compartmentalized and unfocused bits of disgust, but they were coming together. I was moving rapidly to a global sense of shame described by World War II veteran Glenn Gray: "I am ashamed not only of my own deeds, not only of my nation's deeds, but of human deeds as well. I am ashamed to be a man."[2]

I wasn't there yet, but going back to the United States on leave would bring me closer. The orders for my leave came up fast and I hopped a plane to Kuwait before I could contact friends or family and before I had time to think about what I was heading back to.

[2] J. Glenn Gray quote in Lt. Col. Dave Grossman, *On Killing: The Psychological Cost of Learning to Kill in War and Society* (Boston: Little, Brown, 1995), p. 38.

CHAPTER 16

Thanks, Soldier

The plane full of soldiers en route from Kuwait to Atlanta got a stern warning as we started our descent. "You are all still under General Order Number One until midnight tonight. There will be MPs patrolling the bars."

General Order Number One banned booze, pornography, and sex. It was widely ignored in Iraq, and I couldn't imagine any of the antsy soldiers on this plane exercising such restraint as they made their way home. I imagined one of my married colleagues arriving home and trying to explain to his wife that he couldn't have sex with her until after midnight. That would go over well.

I didn't have a wife or girlfriend to go home to, but I did feel I had a date with a beer, and that would definitely happen before midnight. After I got off the plane, I made for the nearest bar.

Walking through the airport in Atlanta, I stood out clearly as someone who had just returned from Iraq. I could feel the stares and discomfort from the civilians around me. Quite a few walked up to me with a quick "Thanks for your service," or "Thanks for what you're doing," and then walked away. I nodded back as they beat a hasty retreat. I didn't know what to say.

I couldn't be seen in my uniform in a bar, but with so many people saying thanks, I figured I should be able to work something out. I trapped one of my well-wishers before he made his escape and explained my situation to him. Was there an article of clothing in his suitcase I could have? All I needed was a pair of shorts and a T-shirt. "Sure, soldier. Here you go." And he slapped me on the shoulder, dug into his suitcase, and handed me a shirt with an

Abercrombie & Fitch logo. I appropriated a pair of shorts from the next guy, changed in the bathroom, and soon bellied up to the bar. The beer tasted sweet, but I realized that my endless grin and feelings of pure ecstasy came not from the cold pint glass but from being out of uniform for the first time in six months. When my flight was ready to leave, I was reluctant to don my combat fatigues again, but couldn't risk being recognized.

The cab moved slowly through Chicago toward the bar where my best friend worked. My beret sat in my lap and I tried to readjust to civilian life by looking out the window. I couldn't connect to what I saw. What was once normal now looked surreal. Well-dressed people carrying shopping bags and Prada purses, tourists leading their children through the streets, men in jackets and ties barking into cell phones, baggy-pants-wearing kids walking funny—they were all just a few hours away by plane from Baghdad. Did they know that? Did they know how close they were to the bloodletting and horror they had helped set in motion?

Pushing aside the surrealism of the moment as much as I could, I strode into my friend's bar wearing my uniform, still coated in Iraqi dust. Conversations stopped as I walked in. This was not a scene frequented by the military. Dave wasn't there. He had the day off. I had a few beers and talked to some of the waitresses. They were kind enough to ask me how I was doing, and kind enough to listen to an honest response.

I stayed for a few hours. When I got up to leave, I reflexively reached for my weapon. For six months, it was my most important possession, something I couldn't even go to the bathroom without. Even in the interrogation booth, I knew exactly where I'd left it. Fuck! Where was it? My body filled with panic before I remembered where I was; then I felt that joy again. I didn't need an assault rifle to walk down these streets. I was actually safe.

From there, my trip home phased into a steady blur. I had a full schedule of visits to friends and family, and still had to make sure I squeezed in plenty of drinks and as much sex as I could find. As the date of my return grew closer, I became aware of an increasing anger, slowly crowding out the joy and elation I initially felt when I stepped off the plane. I didn't expect it, and it wasn't welcome. It didn't have any aspect of self-righteousness or indignation that would have made it a guilty pleasure. It came to me as I realized how little people knew and cared. It was the kind of anger that stood as a flimsy bulwark, a last line of defense, between me and an oncoming helpless despair.

When people asked me about Iraq, which was rare, they often asked me if I'd killed anyone. This was an awful question. Of course I hadn't killed anyone, but if I had I'm sure I wouldn't want to tell some jerk I just met about it. But more than that, the casual and even enthusiastic way people expressed their morbid curiosity was a horrible, unbearable contrast to my despair over the tragic violence and suffering I'd witnessed, and in some measure caused. This wasn't stuff for light conversation.

When I joined or overheard political conversations, which was also rare, I found that few people, even among leftists, actually wanted to hold Bush and his administration accountable. When I watched news of Kerry's campaign, I saw no strong, discernible stance on the war—the war that he'd voted to support.

So even when there was discussion on Iraq, it seemed wildly off target. What was worse was how rare these conversations were. I heard more debate over *American Idol* than over the presidential election and the war combined, and absolutely nothing on our still-fresh Abu Ghraib scandal or treatment of prisoners. Maybe there was awareness that there was a war on, but minimal awareness on what that actually meant.

I wish I could have swept up these vaguely Republican frat boys, the apolitical sneering hipsters, the TV-absorbed working class, and the smug intellectuals, shaved their carefully quaffed hairdos, thrown away their shopping bags, and walked them through a prison facility while mortars fell. The best I could do, though, was get up in their faces, which I did almost every night toward the end of my leave. It did no good, of course. No one wants to argue with a combat veteran—nonveterans quickly grant you moral authority and the conversation's over. And they really didn't want to know about my world. They liked where they were.

My friend Paul, bookish-looking and pretty harmless, muttered, "That guy's an asshole," as we walked into a club, away from a minor altercation with a bouncer. We were quickly back on the sidewalk and denied entry. Paul wouldn't accept this, and the yelling escalated until the police showed up and started giving me orders. Something about the officer's manner and his bossiness reminded me of the army. So I lost it.

"Who the fuck are you to tell me what to do!"

"You're drunk and disorderly. You need to go home, sir."

"You can't tell me to go home!"

As they slapped the cuffs on, I yelled repeatedly about how I'd just gotten back from Iraq, how I'd been serving my country and had every right to be drunk on this sidewalk. I kept yelling from the back of the squad car all the way to the station.

These officers could have been a lot worse to us, and they really didn't deserve my tirade. Their night got even crummier when their sergeant, who was an army reservist, learned I was a veteran. As the officers tried to lecture me and book me, he buddied up to me for a little army talk—What's your MOS? What unit do you serve with? Where were you stationed? I talked to him, soldier to soldier, while occasionally yelling at his officers, who were booking us on minor charges that they knew would be thrown out of court. We were back on the streets at six thirty a.m.

A few days later I was back in uniform, beret on my lap, in the back of cab, stuck in traffic on my way to O'Hare Airport. It hadn't hit me until I put the uniform on that I had another six months left in Iraq. The first six months had seemed so long; I felt like I'd aged a lifetime. How would I ever make it through another six? Things were steadily getting worse, and Bush was determined to stay the course, which could only mean more mortars, more snipers, more RPGs, more chances to die, and more prisoners.

Looking out the window, it seemed to me like every other car had a yellow ribbon magnet on the back. Their brightness burned in the back of my head and the phrase "Support Our Troops" echoed through my hangover. Support Our Troops? That's nothing more than thinly veiled code for "Support George W. Bush and his suicidal foreign policy," and it also serves as a diabolical way to shut down dissent and debate. These yellow-ribbon folks are the people responsible for sending me to Iraq, and they're clearly proclaiming themselves while the antiwar public remains in hiding.

Support Our Troops? I'm the troops and I don't agree with you. Don't use me to support your political agenda.

I was in Atlanta once more, and this time I didn't want a beer. A man walked up to me and said, "Thanks for your service, soldier." I smiled and nodded, but I was thinking, *You don't know what I've done. You don't know what our policies are doing to tear the Middle East to shreds. I don't deserve your thanks and I don't want it.* An elderly woman made her way up to me slowly and said, "Thanks for keeping us safe." She walked away smiling.

They got to thank a soldier and get a warm glow inside, and then they got to go to their cars, slap a yellow ribbon on the fender, and feel good about themselves and their patriotic loyalty. Meanwhile, I got to go back to Iraq.

CHAPTER 17

Confession

When I got back to Abu Ghraib, I received a message through my first sergeant from a Special Agent Greene of the army's Criminal Investigation Division, and I imagined the prosecution of Specialist Lagouranis had begun. All the things I talked about with Tomas, how the Pentagon was gearing up to let us take the fall, were, I believed, coming to pass.

My appointment with Greene was for the next day at noon and I used the time before it to think about what I was going to do. I knew that many interrogators were being called in for routine interviews, but I couldn't help wondering if I was headed for a court-martial, and if my mug shot would soon be splashed across the screens of CNN and Fox above a caption that read "Spc. Anthony Lagouranis: The Face of Torture?" My mind replayed what I'd done in Mosul and fixated on the dogs. The dogs were a big concern during the Senate hearings, and the response, over and over, was that dogs were not being used in Iraq. This just a week or so after I'd sent up my interrogation report for Khalid, the Yazidi I'd tormented in the shipping container. As usual, I detailed everything I'd done to him, including the dogs. The paper trail I'd created to cover my ass was coming back to bite me in the same place.

I wrote a friend at home about my overwhelming "sense of doom" and I wrote a letter to a lawyer back in the States. Lying in my bunk, watching the lights flicker and listening to the diesel generator, I realized I'd done all I could and the rest was out of my hands. I resolved to come clean. I would give Special Agent Greene the full story, holding nothing back. There was no sense in trying to hide behind strained legalisms—the way Rumsfeld and his top generals were doing. It wouldn't work and it was dishonorable besides. So, I'd go down, but I'd also show CID where the bodies were buried. I'd make some noise while I was at it.

CID agents have lonely jobs. Soldiers generally despise them as a cop might despise an internal affairs investigator. I was expecting to find myself face-to-face with a tightly uniformed hard-ass who'd tear me apart with his probing questions. Instead, Agent Greene, looking relaxed, inviting, and the very picture of a guy you'd meet at your corner bar, smiled and invited me to sit. I remained guarded, trying to size him up. I was going to reveal all, but hadn't yet decided how and when. I watched and waited to see what he had. He started:

"Do you remember a prisoner named Ra'id?"

I did. During my first weeks at Abu Ghraib, when I was still doing right-seat rides, I'd watched Ra'id, exhausted and grievously ill, fall from the arms of two other prisoners when an interrogator ordered him to walk on his own. But why was Greene asking me about Ra'id? I hadn't even interrogated him. I told Greene what I saw.

"Where was he being kept?"

"Was he in the hard site?"

"When was he in the hard site?"

If Greene was going to go through this with every prisoner I'd brushed up against, this interview was going to take weeks. But stranger still, Greene never seemed accusatory or suspicious of my answers. He just wrote them down.

It didn't take long for us to finish with Ra'id. I'd had almost nothing to do with him and had little to say. Ra'id was accusing guards of torture, but that torture took place when he was housed in the hard site, and that was before I arrived.

"Sorry. I wish I could be more help." I shrugged at Greene.

"Don't worry. We just have to be thorough," he said and smiled again. He hit PRINT and we waited for the documents so I could sign them, making them sworn statements in an investigation. We were done. It wasn't about me at all, or even Mosul.

Greene and I bullshitted for a while about our jobs. He was frustrated about this case because no one would talk to him. I thought about all the work they were doing with the Abu Ghraib scandal.

"You guys must have your hands full right now," I offered lamely.

"Yeah, we only have a few guys handling that case. The rest of us have to cover the entire country."

He wanted to know about how I interrogated people. Like many, he believed that we interrogators had some magic powers that pulled truth from the very skulls of insurgents. I started to explain some things about approaches, but couldn't keep making myself out to be something special. I just kind of trailed off with "It's no different from what you're doing. . . ."

The sworn statements were ready for signatures. After I completed them, Greene said casually, "So, is there anything else you have to report?"

I waded in carefully: "We were doing things in Mosul, and I saw things, that I wasn't sure of the legality of."

Greene looked a little concerned, more serious. "So what happened?"

It took ten times as long to finish making and signing sworn statements for everything I told him about Mosul than it did for Ra'id, the case he'd originally contacted me for. I left nothing out—dogs, disco, stress positions, hypothermia, the special forces. My throat was dry and I grew increasingly nervous and angry, my foot tapping the floor rapidly and my hands slightly shaking. Greene spoke little, asked very few questions, and wrote everything down.

"I don't know what will happen," he told me as I signed the sworn statements, "but I promise you anything you tell us—there will be a report filed about it. This is my job, and I take it very seriously. I'm going to report this." I left the room dizzy with relief, fear, and release. I'd never been to confession before.

I believe that Special Agent Greene did what he promised. But I talked to CID several times after that—always with different agents—and there was no record of my sworn statements. No one ever contacted me, followed up, or started an investigation as far as I knew. Each time I talked to CID afterward, it was like starting all over again. I'll never know what happened to my sworn statements, but I figure Agent Greene sent them up through channels, and they got lost. CID is undermanned and overburdened. If an investigation hits a dead end because CID can't find a particular soldier or prisoner to interview, for instance, the case is closed. Once the case is closed, the army can say that it has been investigated and found to be unsubstantiated. But it seems that my sworn statements just disappeared.

I was soon sent back to al-Asad, which was now in the hands of the U.S. Marines. I'd seen the beginning of their transformation before I left back in February, five months ago, and now it was complete. The processes were streamlined, extraneous procedures and equipment were gone, and the base was much more Spartan, which was appropriate to a war zone, I suppose, but I missed my air-conditioning. When I remarked to our hosts that our quarters didn't even have electricity, they looked at me with the pity and contempt that marines often have for their pampered army counterparts, and their staff sergeant simply said, "That's right."

The marines wanted us for a field mission—the lack of A/C on base was nothing compared to the rough living we experienced next. We were attached to a marine unit that would stay out in the field. We would interrogate prisoners immediately on capture, generate our own intelligence, and then the marines would hit targets right away, which they hoped would generate more actionable intelligence. This was very smart, and totally alien to how our army unit was operating. It was usually hours or days before prisoners we captured were interrogated, maybe a few more days before whatever slim intel we got was processed and turned into actual targets. The marines had it right. To get a handle on the insurgency we had to act fast and keep moving. We started by establishing relationships with Iraqi police chiefs in two nearby towns.

At our first stop, the police chief was thrilled to see us and sent his deputies out to get lunch. We relaxed and exchanged pleasantries while eating deliciously spiced Iraqi food. The police chief gradually drifted from small talk to a thorough description of his town, and before we knew it, we were doing business.

The police chief gave us names of people who were possibly associated with insurgents and other troublemakers, and his officers went out to collect them. As they came in, I'd interrogate them in the police chief's office.

This, I thought, is the way it should be done. Instead of running off base in heavily armored convoys, hitting houses with maximum force, treating even those we just wanted for questioning as if they were al-Zarqawi himself, and detaining them for weeks, here we were doing things in a way that could make progress against the insurgency and build trust at the same time. We walked among the Iraqis, we treated them as if they actually had rights, and if we didn't have direct evidence against them, we learned what we could and then they were free to go. We were much more exposed; this operation was not without risks. But the marines accepted it without complaint.

Our next mission was in a nearby town, located on the Euphrates River. We set up in an abandoned farmhouse, and the marines established a minimalist perimeter. We slept on the ground next to our Humvees. During the day they were our only shade.

It was days before the marines arrested anyone—another positive sign. The units I'd been working with would *never* go out to make an arrest and return empty-handed, even if they had to arrest their target's son, cousin, or neighbor; they always arrested someone. The restraint and patience these marines showed was impressive.

The men finally returned with a subject for me to interrogate, and once again they brought him in "just for a few questions," sans ZipCuffs. He was also an Iraqi police chief, but very different from the one I'd met days before. At this point, I felt I was fairly good at telling when someone was lying, and this guy showed all the signs. As I discussed with him what we were trying to do and whom we had interest in, I could see him trying to walk a fine line.

He was clearly afraid of fingering insurgents and gangsters who had any kind of stature in this area, but knew he had to give us something. So he wildly exaggerated the power and influence of low-level thugs on our list—people who couldn't hurt him—and downplayed the importance of people we *knew* were important. As I kept track of who he wanted arrested and who he wanted protected, I began to see him as actually part of the web of criminality in this sector. Maybe he wasn't an insurgent, but he definitely was rubbing elbows and playing politics.

His lies were helpful and growing more so, but then I screwed up, probably the biggest mistake I made during an interrogation. I was reading names off a list of "persons of interest," and one name made him clearly uncomfortable. So did the next. He suddenly clammed up and even stopped spinning such elaborate lies. The sun was going down, and he realized, I figured, that he was in for a long night. But there was something about that name. . . .

Turned out I'd read this police chief his own name, and then the name of his father. Since the guy had been introduced to me by only his first name, I never knew his full proper name. I kicked myself for the rest of the year on this, though I'll never know if this particular interrogation would have gone anywhere.

Our "take" from this three-week operation was not as strong as we would have liked, and maybe that was partially my fault. But I left these marines with a new hope for our mission in Iraq. There was a way to get this job done. It was dangerous, time-consuming, and unglamorous, but the right people could make it work.

Getting off base, living among Iraqis, and working with men I respected lifted the despair that had been building since my days in Mosul. The Abu Ghraib scandal was forcing people to clean up their acts, I'd come clean to CID about my own actions, and I'd resolved to never again stray into the dark enhancements during my interrogations, even if that meant disobeying a direct order.

As we stopped off at al-Asad, I ran into an interpreter I knew from my first mission there. She was an older, short-statured Lebanese woman. I asked her about rumors I'd heard about serious abuse of detainees by the army. She didn't pause: "I can't talk about it." That was all I needed to know. Something was happening—someone was being investigated. CID was doing its job and maybe now the nonsense would stop.

Returning to al-Asad was a harrowing experience. We staged our convoy at Haditha Dam and the marines told us that we were going to drive back after dark using no headlights, only night-vision goggles. Sergeant Jones drove our Humvee and I rode on a bench in the back, totally blind as we sailed through the desert. I'll take mortars and snipers over a ride like that any day.

When I rejoined my unit, I had another message from CID. I figured this was a follow-up to my previous abuse reports and confessions, but it was a new agent and a new topic. I told him right off the bat that I'd spoken to Agent Greene and gave sworn statements on abuse in Mosul, but he had never seen or heard of my previous reports. That was strange, because I knew these should have been entered in a database with my name attached, and should have been at his fingertips. But maybe he was busy.

This was a much more serious interview than before. Special Agent Porter was investigating a homicide—probably the same one I'd heard rumors about in Mosul. I'd never been near the SEALs' compound that he was interested in, so I was little help. I repeated some of my previous reports, but seemed to have just confused Porter, because now he had two "discotheques" to deal with—ours and the SEALs'. I gave him the name of a guard who had told me about what they were doing, but this was little help. Even though he had his name, unit, and even a description of the patch he wore, Porter still called me for weeks trying to get me to find the guard for him. It didn't seem like it should have been so hard for a special agent to find out what unit was guarding the detention facility in Mosul in April and who was in the unit and where they were now. I have to think that CID didn't have the access or resources they needed. (Though, reflecting on it now, I wonder why the army was investigating the actions of the navy. The navy has its own investigative body.) I gave Porter what I could, though, and filed a sworn statement about what I had heard, secondhand, about the SEALs' activities.

Another disturbing thing about this interview was the inclusion of Jafar Ali Abdul Naser. He'd claimed a series of abuses by the SEALs and by me, but he'd evidently padded out his complaint. Special Agent Porter read from his sworn statement that an interrogator had pissed on the floor of the discotheque, and then we forced Jafar's face into it. This was a lie. He did wet his pants when we got the dogs to act up, and we taunted him about that, but we never got so physical with him or pushed his face in the puddle he left on the ground. We certainly didn't piss on the floor ourselves. I explained to Special Agent Porter exactly what we had done, which was bad enough in itself. Porter said that that investigation was going to be conducted in the near future. I expected to hear from him again about it, but I never did.

My unit was no longer based at Abu Ghraib. Rumor had it that our battalion commander didn't want his name associated with that infamous prison, so now we were at Camp Slayer. We left Alpha Company, which comprised the interrogators and analysts back at Abu Ghraib, and all the support personnel came with the command and the mobile interrogation teams to Slayer. This base, set up on the grounds of one of Saddam's palaces, was deluxe. We had a swimming pool, great food and A/C, and, oddly enough, a man-made lake where we could fish.

Problem was, we had no prisoners to interrogate. Our intelligence people were either sitting on their hands or were on loan to other units in other locations. This meant that our support and logistics personnel were essentially doing logistics not to support our mission but merely to support themselves. This was wasteful and absurd and everyone knew it.

Still, it was an opportunity for a guilt-free mini-vacation. I raced through novels, exercised, and went fishing. Finally, bored out of my mind, I found an opportunity to make trouble.

Matt was a buddy from back at DLI, and may have been the mellowest person in the U.S. Army. He'd also been serving on mobile interrogation teams, but like me was on a little vacation. So we were jogging around this lake one day and I noticed a boat, totally submerged in the water.

We were expressly and repeatedly forbidden to go in the lake. For some reason, this rule was taken very seriously (much more so than the prohibitions on alcohol, drugs, pornography, and sex). No one *ever* went in the lake. It may as well have been full of battery acid.

We realized that we'd found a loophole. No one had thought to put a ban on getting in a boat and paddling around the lake. So, having found an activity that wasn't tightly regulated by the army, we had no choice but to do it.

It took us at least five hours to surface this boat. Since we couldn't go in the water to get it, we had to make a very short human chain so I could lean out over the water and try to drag this leaky vessel to shore. A sergeant walked by and stopped dead in his tracks. "Hey, you guys can't do that." We gave him a polite glance, and then ignored him. He watched us for a minute, and then walked away, deeply troubled by what he saw.

A sergeant from our unit walked by, assessed the situation, and walked away, shaking his head. "I don't even want to know about this."

You'd have thought we were burying a body. Everyone who passed not only refused our requests for help but walked away, saying, "I know nothing. I see nothing." Iraq's Sergeant Schultz.

Once we got the boat up, I went directly to the company commander and asked him if there were any orders prohibiting me from paddling around in a boat. After a nervous laugh he said, "I'll check on that." That clearly meant "I'm too scared to make a decision, even about something so insignificant, so I'll just indefinitely delay giving you an answer." That was fine. It just meant we'd have to do it at night and not tell the commander. I'm sure that's how he preferred it.

I'm not exactly sure why this was such an obsession for us. Once we were out on the lake, there was nothing really to see or do, and not very far to go. Matt paddled with a broom as I sang Mozart's *Don Giovanni*. The boat was steadily taking on water, so we had to keep bailing. It was really more trouble than it was worth.

I suppose one attraction was that we got to assert our independence while breaking up the awful, mind-numbing tedium of this base. We got to operate outside the rules for a short time. That dumb little ride was the best time I had in Iraq. I was happy.

PART IV

NORTH BABEL
SEPTEMBER 2004 TO JANUARY 2005

*On the ground, the physical reaction—or overreaction—
was predictable . . . because this is the way an administration caught
with its pants down habitually reacts under such circumstances;
whether it be the British in Palestine, Cyprus or Northern Ireland, the
Portuguese in Mozambique, or the French in Indo-China. First comes
the mass indiscriminate round-up of suspects, most of them innocent
but converted into ardent militants by the fact of their imprisonment.*

—Alistair Horne, A *Savage War of Peace: Algeria 1954–1962*

CHAPTER 18

Image

watched the DVD that came in with the prisoner—they'd found it in his car. It was the most amazing video clip I'd seen in Iraq. Here the prisoner was, unmistakably recognizable, standing in a field and dropping big, juicy mortars into a tube. Puffs of smoke emerged as the shells shot out from the makeshift launcher. After a while, the video cut to the carnage of an IED attack. *"Hatha demihoom, hatha lehoomihoom, AlHamduallah"* (This is their blood, this is their flesh, praise God), an off-screen voice narrated as the camera panned across a road covered with gore. I was disgusted by what I saw, furious, and so ready for this interrogation. At the same time, I felt a touch of gratitude toward this guy. His attempt to become a jihadist movie star had handed me the most clear-cut case I'd yet seen. It was nice to be in a situation where I could clearly tell black from white and not have to worry about any shades of gray.

The prisoner had been caught red-handed carrying a Kalashnikov and standing next to a mortar tube that was still warm. His two buddies had made their escape. I wanted this guy, Mumtaz, to tell me where they were. To get him talking, I gave him a chance to justify himself.

"Why did you attack the Americans?"

"No, no, *sadigini* [believe me]. I never wanted to hurt the Americans. The two men who got away *kidnapped* me, and made me do it. They *made* me fire the bombs." His eyes were huge as he tried to affect fear and dismay.

I tried not to smile. "You were caught carrying an AK-47."

"When the Americans came, the bad men *pushed* the rifle into my hands! I never wanted to attack you Americans, please!"

"So this was just a misunderstanding," I said with a small measure of disbelief.

"Yes, yes, please, believe me, *saidi*."

"No, I don't believe you," I continued, growing more stern. "There was a video in your car showing you firing mortars. No one made you do it. Now, who was with you?"

"*Min fudhlik*." Please.

I shuddered to think what we would have done to this guy if we'd caught him in Mosul a few months before. If we'd tortured and tormented people on flimsy, highly suspect evidence, what would Mr. Mumtaz have faced? What new schemes would we have developed for this joker?

I was done with all enhancements or torture lite treatments. If it wasn't in the army manual that I'd been trained on, it wasn't in my toolbox. I was now on a new mission, serving with marines in North Babel. At this new site I didn't even ask to see the interrogation rules of engagement. I didn't want to know what was going on there.

I ran approaches across the spectrum, from those that tried to establish a relationship to harsh (but noncoercive) attempts to create fear. Mumtaz got Fear Up Mild. Fear Up Mild doesn't involve physical intimidation or yelling, but rather merely pointing out that the detainee might have something serious to worry about unless he cooperates.

"You're screwed, Mumtaz. You'll be rotting in a cell the rest of your life if you don't get straight with me. Believe it or not, I'm here to help you out."

At this point he started to cry, shaking his head and repeating through his sobs, "*La, la, la!*" No, no, no!

These were crocodile tears. Although he could cry at will, Mumtaz was a terrible actor. All he did was manage to piss me off more. I wrapped the interrogation up quickly. I'd not expected him to cave on my first try, but he was going to get to know me very well. This would take time and patience, but Mumtaz was going to be very useful to us.

* * *

This mission was going to work out. My ridiculous vacation at Camp Slayer had left me rested, the Abu Ghraib scandal had given me leverage if anyone ever again tried to get me to enhance my interrogations with brutality, and I would once more be serving with marines. My last experience with the jarheads, even though they sometimes talked to me like I was a spoiled army brat, was pretty much bullshit-free. They got down to business without wading through incessant paperwork, worked as a team but respected individual initiative, and didn't use more force than was necessary.

Our team—Jones; Specialist Brian Reilly, a short, understated but very funny guy; and Specialist Wayne Tascun, a towheaded, six-foot-plus, all-American quarterback type—convoyed the short distance to North Babel where the marines operated a small but very busy forward operating base. It was brand-new and they had slim to no interrogation system, and, instead of simply sending all prisoners to Abu Ghraib straightaway, they wanted to generate new targets here. This made perfect sense to me, and was similar to what'd I'd done with the marines around al-Asad. They planned to ramp up the pace of their operations, so we knew we'd be very busy.

The base sat near a highway crossroads that could take you to the heart of Baghdad or the airport, south toward Najaf, or west into the always-unstable al-Anbar province. These routes were valued supply lines for both Americans and insurgents, so the base was here to protect our shipments and interfere with theirs. Unlike Abu Ghraib, this base did not butt up against a town, but there were small, scattered villages dotting the countryside. Mostly what we saw were farms.

I learned through research that this was a very mixed area, with Sunni and Shia living cheek by jowl before the invasion and now pulling apart slowly and painfully. We could expect to see a lot of sectarian violence here, and the fact that it was sparsely populated, lightly patrolled, and so close to major highways meant that a substantial criminal element had taken root here as well. So. Gangs of street thugs, budding sectarian militias, and a steady supply of virulent anti-American insurgents. This sector was a serious mess.

Some of our bases were set up on airports or palaces—because there was something there we could use. This base was set up to be close to the roads, and there were just a few small hard buildings. The rest of the sprawling, ugly compound was trailers and tents, some of them protected from mortars by the tall, portable concrete barriers known as Bremer walls. The perimeter was wire.

As we got a tour of this primitive and miserable-looking base from Major Fritz, he kept talking about how many improvements they'd made. I suppose to marines this was the lap of luxury. I believed him, though, when he said that what they inherited from the army reservists they replaced was much worse. As we walked together he editorialized a little. Their intelligence system was understaffed, they only had one intelligence man in the detention facility, and he was leaving. They'd only just recently gotten interested in keeping detainees for any length of time, so the prison facility was all new. The pace of operations was increasing steadily, so we should expect to see lots of work. The pressure was on, and the commander in charge was on a tear. "Nothing's going to keep Colonel Maxwell from getting his star," he said. He made it clear that our mission was to help make Maxwell's promotion happen. We rarely saw Major Fritz after that day.

The prison facility was on a lightly traveled corner of the base, butting up directly against the perimeter. We lived inside the wire of the prison, which had its benefits. Few officers ventured inside the prison, so we were left pretty well alone. We didn't have to carry our weapons with us or wear our full uniform and armor everywhere, which was truly a blessing. We lived in shipping containers that doubled as interrogation booths. Our office was a blue-and-white-striped tent that looked like it belonged in a circus. We didn't have running water, but we had a water tank that got filled up every day, and it had an improvised showerhead. By the end of the day, the water in the tank was warm enough from the sun to remind us what a hot shower was like.

An efficient, likable staff sergeant named Lobos ran the prison and issued direct orders about how he wanted things done. "No prisoner will get killed in this prison," he made sure everyone knew. "There's no excuse for a dead prisoner—there are too many nonlethal ways to take someone down. No abuse will be tolerated in this prison. We are here to guard them and maintain their welfare." We liked him; he liked us. We let him do his job, and we did ours. That was one part of the operation we didn't have to worry about. There were just two problems with this facility, and neither was this staff sergeant's fault. One, the prisoners were kept in individual, very small plywood cells. In other prisons, isolation was there for punishment, but here it was a matter of course. Two, none of the cells had toilet facilities. Guards spent their days escorting prisoners to the bathroom—or not, if they didn't like someone. This facility was run very well and it was due to Staff Sergeant Lobos's leadership. He was the only person I met in the military who was actually trained by the military in prison operations. I don't understand why the Pentagon wouldn't institute a broad program for that purpose. Clearly detention facilities require leaders who know what they are doing, especially in Iraq, where detention operations became a central part of the whole mission.

We reported to a chief warrant officer named Polk. When we first met him, he was frantic, pacing and shuffling papers as fast as his short limbs would allow. Although he was clearly glad to see us, he was not one for formalities. He made sure we knew where the prison and interrogation booths were, and rattled off the names of five prisoners. "You can start with them. Right away." We'd been on base for less than an hour, but this is how it would be for the next eight weeks. At least five interrogations a day, as many screenings as there were new prisoners, multiple reports, and as much research as we could squeeze in. Rarely did a workday last fewer than sixteen hours.

They had about thirty prisoners in custody (by the time we left we'd processed over four hundred), and as I ran through my first set of interrogations, it seemed like these were "good" prisoners. If they weren't insurgents themselves, they at least had some intelligence or there was a legitimate reason for picking them up. Two Shia brothers I interrogated, for example, had been accused of giving gas to insurgent groups. They both admitted this freely. "Sure we gave them gas. They had guns. We don't want to be killed. What do you want to know about them?"

From these brothers, I got names, places, and past activities. Since we had direct and ready access to the marine analysts, I could check their stories. Yes, the names were suspected insurgents, and the additional information gave us a more complete picture of their group. Even better, when I came to the point where I believed these two brothers had told me everything they knew and I recommended release, they were let go without delay. Now, that *never* happened in Mosul.

The prison population doubled within a few days as patrols ramped up their arrests. It was like they'd been just waiting for us to arrive, and now that we interrogators were on duty, we had to be kept busy. This was fine with me, so long as we kept getting good prisoners. I'm sure there were enough bad guys out there to fill up this prison several times over. At the same time, I really wanted to focus on the ones who were most directly responsible for the ordnance on the roadsides and lobbed over the walls. Especially that guy who'd been caught with the DVD. He deserved special attention.

As night fell after my first interrogation of Mumtaz, and as I collapsed into my bunk, the mortars started falling. As usual, I didn't start worrying until after the third or fourth one fell. North Babel got hit just about as often as Abu Ghraib—a lot. Normally we'd get just a few mortars per attack, and then the insurgents would bolt before we could respond. This attack, however, wouldn't stop. The insurgents were feeling cocky tonight. I should have rolled under my bunk or gone outside to look for better cover, but I was exhausted and remained in a long pause of indecision.

Polk suddenly marched in and told me to get up. Get that guy with the DVD, get him into the booth, and break him, now. I jumped up without complaint. Polk was clearly in a moment of fury about this attack and wanted to do something (the feeling of helplessness was the worst part of these mortars), but it was actually a good idea. Mumtaz would be shaken up by the attack too. It might give me a way in.

I suited up and ran toward his cell as the shells dropped ever closer to the prison. Were they targeting the prison in particular? Not so good if they were. The prisoners were in little plywood shacks. Unlike us, they had no Kevlar. I pulled Mumtaz from his cell and brought him into the yard.

Mumtaz was afraid, and more so when I started yelling at him. "Who's doing this? Where are they?" Another mortar, a big one, landed just outside the prison perimeter.

Mumtaz started his waterworks, just like he'd turned on a faucet. His crying and sobbing filled me with disgust. Not only was he trying to play me for a fool, but he was clearly not going to cave in tonight. I gave him a few hints about his dark and lonely future, just a few things to think about, and put him back in his hole. I'd come back to him tomorrow with a new approach. I'd have to think about what would get him talking.

I saw Polk in the office in the morning. I reported to him on my lack of success with Mumtaz and mentioned a plan for continuing. No, he replied, there were new prisoners who were more important right now. Five brothers had been caught with a mortar sighting instrument, and a schoolteacher had a younger brother we wanted to target. They were now priority.

The marines were using a tactic called cordon and search. They'd roll into town, define a perimeter, and search every house. They should have been doing this on specific intelligence, but seemed to simply target areas where there had been a lot of suspected activity. So that's how these guys with the "mortar sight" got picked up. I took a look at their instrument before I went into the booth. It was a long wooden pole, about five feet, with red and white horizontal stripes on it. Pretty unremarkable. I checked the sworn statement that was filed from the field. No weapons in the house.

"Okay, what is this pole for?" I asked the first guy, Adel. I showed him a picture.

He seemed a little confused while he explained it to me, like he didn't actually know that this pole was the sole reason he'd been picked up. "It's for measuring the depth of the canal. For farming. We got it from my brother who works in the Department of Agriculture." I gathered some more details and went to see one of Adel's brothers. Same story. Same recall of details. This was a waste of my time. After spending most of the day on this, I got the same story from all of the brothers. I wrote my reports—no intelligence value, showing no signs of deception, no reason to hold these guys.

On to the teacher. This gentleman had been picked up in lieu of his half brother, who was suspected of running with insurgents. The half brother was in his early twenties, and our prisoner, Hakeem, was middle-aged. Like many educated Iraqis, he held himself with an immense pride, but seemed accessible at the same time. The interrogation took all of thirty minutes.

"He's a bad kid, associates with bad people, but I barely know him." The father had two wives and the detainee had a different mother from the target. They were twenty years apart and Hakeem had never lived in the same house as the target. "He lives with my father, but I don't know if he's still there." He then proceeded to tell me where his father lived, which was remarkable. He must have known we'd hit that house next.

I ran out of questions quickly; Hakeem had answered every one. He wanted to get back to work—he had a classroom depending on him. I told him he was not being charged, and would not be here long.

I would not get another shot at Mumtaz today. I'd not get another shot at Mumtaz ever. His buddies, who ran when the Americans came upon them in mid–mortar attack, were getting farther and farther away, but each day for the next five days I followed orders to interrogate Adel and his brothers, every day. I got and followed orders to continue to put pressure on Hakeem, every day. I asked Jones about this, and he went to talk to Polk.

Jones and I talked later that night. "The prisoner with the DVD—Mumtaz? He's clearly guilty and slated for transfer to Abu Ghraib. They consider that case closed. The other guys—basically, they want confessions. Polk told me to keep the pressure up and see that they break."

Both of us remembered a point of time back in Mosul when our jobs became more about securing confessions and less about gathering intelligence. Along with that fundamental shift in purpose came a fundamental shift in tactics. That's about when we started torturing people. If it was happening here already, this was going to be bad.

"Do you know where you are?" Hakeem asked me, with more force than any prisoner had ever dared to use with me. Hakeem didn't have a problem talking to me as an equal. He wasn't trying to intimidate me, but he felt passionately about what he was trying to explain. It was very important to him that I understand.

I had to show that I'd made an effort to further interrogate Hakeem, but I wasn't going to put the screws on him. I'd ask him a couple questions, and then we'd just talk. It was a pain, because I had so much work to do, but it made the paperwork complete, and it got Hakeem out of solitary confinement.

"I'm in North Babel," I answered.

He reminded me that this was the site of eight thousand years of civilization, the legendary site of the Tower of Babel, the birthplace of the written word and written law, the locale of Babylon, Ur, and Sammara. "I wonder if Americans can even imagine a history that long. Can you?"

I wasn't sure. I had to admit it was a stretch. I could see that at the very least there was a huge cultural chasm between Americans and Iraqis, and maybe our distinctive concepts of history were part of it. We were living in timescales that were different by several orders of magnitude.

"We have long-established customs. Some of the peoples here have been living this way since the very beginning," he continued. I could see this whenever I got off base. The farmers lived in mud huts and had little more than the average Babylonian would have had (aside from a Kalashnikov), and worked the land in much the same way. The berms, these high walls of dirt that contained the canals—how long had they been there? I recalled my early difficulty with the Iraqi word for "canal." *Bezel* is definitely not Arabic. I wonder if, like the canals themselves, it predates the Arab conquest. Iraqi Arabic has a number of words like that. Words of ancient empires and long-dead languages still fall from Iraqi lips.

Hakeem told me of how Christians once lived here in peace, how Jews once lived here in peace. Iraqis knew this. They weren't afraid of other peoples. They are ready to accept outsiders, to a point. "We welcomed you when you first came here, but you don't understand Iraqis, the way Iraqis are, our customs, our history."

"Why does your history matter?" I could see that we were different, but what would knowing Iraqi history have taught us about how to treat Iraqis?

"We've seen empires come and go—so many empires. And the Iraqis stay. What does their power mean to us?" he asked. It was quite an image he was giving me. With his flowery, prideful poetics, I saw the Iraqis standing fast as empires washed over them like waves. So what did military power mean to a people like that? Was that power really strength?

He continued. "You come out of your bases in armored cars and guns pointed at our children. You arrest us and run back to your base. This isn't strength. We see this as fear."

That was a terrible outcome, if true. It seemed to me like everything we were doing here went back to that perception of the "Arab mind," and the notion that all they understand is force. Here, our display of force made us look weak.

Next to my bunk was a small stack of books I'd been trying to read in the few moments I had between lying down and passing out from exhaustion. One of these was a collection of Orwell's essays I'd picked up at Camp Slayer. In the famous essay "Shooting an Elephant," I'd been faced with ideas similar to the ones Hakeem so desperately wanted me to understand.

In the essay, the local population hates Orwell, then a police officer in colonial Burma, but he still walks among them. One day, he shoots an elephant that doesn't need to be shot, solely because he believes the natives expect him to, and will think him a weak man if he doesn't.

> I perceived in that moment that when the white man turns tyrant it is his own freedom that he destroys. He becomes a sort of hollow, posing dummy. . . . For it is the condition of his rule that he shall spend his life in trying to impress the "natives." . . . He wears a mask, and his face grows to fit it.

What mask were we wearing here in Iraq? As we tried our hand at an American Empire, were we just falling into historically assigned roles? In trying to impress the Iraqis—from our Shock and Awe bombings to our cruel interrogations—were we being actually more brutal than our society had capacity for? If so, and if Orwell was right, we'd develop that capacity for brutality the longer we held this aggressive pose. Our face would grow to fit this mask. It had already happened to me in Mosul.

Hakeem was released after two weeks, but it caused a lot of friction between Polk and me. His superior wanted to send the schoolteacher to Abu Ghraib.

Abu Ghraib is, however, where they sent the brothers with the striped pole. If there's a picture of a mysterious object like that in a prisoner's file, with a label that identifies it as an object used to kill Americans, who'd let a prisoner like that go? Who'd risk being labeled soft on Iraqis? No, these poor guys, their fates were sealed when a young marine picked up their striped pole and thought, *Hmmm, looks like you could use this to fire mortars!*

CHAPTER 19

A Wide Net

The marines in North Babel had intelligence guys working in the field, and one of them brought some prisoners in to our facility for me to help interrogate. The prisoners were a small group of insurgents who had been involved in looting an American supply truck and instigating a minor riot. One of them, he said, was talking and I should focus on him. He had interrogated the prisoner and broke him in a location in Mahmoodia before he brought him to us. I was very interested in how he got the prisoner to talk.

It was very simple, he claimed. He just put a cloth over the prisoner's mouth and nose and poured water over it until he started gagging. He did that a few more times, and the prisoner broke. Easy.

I'd never heard of this technique before, but it's a CIA classic that evidently migrated to Guantánamo for use on special, high-value prisoners. People who have experienced it describe it as unbearable. The feeling of drowning and imminent death is overwhelming.

The marine clearly assumed that I would be on his side with this. I wasn't. It made me very uncomfortable just knowing about it.

As soon as I got a chance, I reported to Jones what I'd heard. We were in our office/shipping container with Wayne and Azzi, our new interpreter. We tried to absorb this new knowledge. Azzi had something to add. He'd been in the booth on a different interrogation with this same sergeant. When the prisoner failed to cooperate, the sergeant dragged the prisoner out of the booth, put him on his knees, pulled his sidearm, chambered a round, and held it to the prisoner's head. A mock execution.

We were pissed. He shouldn't have been doing this at all, but especially not in our facility and with our interpreter. This guy was out of control, we decided, but felt that, as far as direct action, there was little we could do. He was well liked and respected on this base, while we were a small group of outsiders on a remote corner. We were in a situation where it was probably wise to make friends before making enemies.

We took a less direct and, I'm ashamed to say, more cowardly route. We resolved to quietly ban him from the booths and interrogations, and told our interpreter to refuse any order to accompany him on an interrogation. The sergeant was leaving soon anyway. We'd just wait it out.

The prisoner he'd broken started backpedaling on his confession when I interrogated him. We did get some names and descriptions of tactics from him that confirmed intelligence we already had, however. He also confirmed that he'd been subjected to simulated drowning. I was amazed that this prisoner broke. There was clearly something to this technique, and I could see no signs of lasting permanent damage—no bruises, marks, or broken bones. If there were psychological scars, they were buried pretty deep. Reflecting now, however, I can see that what we got out of him was primarily a confession, which would help keep him in prison, but little intelligence. I wonder if we had broken him through other means if we might have gotten some extensive information that could have been acted on in a positive way.

Something about the guy who'd tortured him reminded me of a pop culture reference I'd heard all over Iraq, but especially on this base. In the chow hall, Internet tent, or just in bullshit conversation, a lot of guys found ways to work in the quote, "The truth? You can't handle the truth!" Everyone knew what it meant.

It was from the movie A Few Good Men, from a long speech by Jack Nicholson's character, a marine general in a witness box. "You can't handle the truth" sums up a very specific worldview. There are men who go out into the wilds and down the dark alleys of the world so the rest of America can shop, fuck, and watch TV. In these dangerous places, these brave men break laws and do immoral things, both of which are necessary to preserve the freedoms of the weak citizenry back home. Morality and laws are for those who live in

safety—not for the warrior caste. As far as what they actually do in their struggle against evil, it's just better that civilians don't know. I hated this view of
the military's role, but it was pervasive.

We were awoken to do intake and interrogation for fifteen prisoners fresh off
a farm that had just been raided. We got no paperwork on these prisoners,
which was becoming the norm. All we got was the most damning evidence—
pictures of weapons. Tons of weapons. They'd been found buried on the farm.

It took most of the night for me to figure out that the fifteen captives were
from three different farms and to determine who belonged to what family
and what their relations to each other were. Slowly, I pieced together what
happened. The marines hit the target house, and the owner resisted. There
was a firefight, and the farmer finally gave in after being burned pretty badly
by explosives the marines threw at him. They searched the farm and uncov-
ered the weapons. They did well.

Then, it seemed, they didn't stop. There were two other farmhouses in
view—not at all close, but still in view. The marines decided to hit those too.
In one of them, a little girl was standing too close to a window when it was
blown out during the raid, and the flying glass killed her.

Once I had this sorted out, I closely interrogated the original target.
"Yes. All those weapons were on my farm. I looted them," he stated matter-
of-factly. He denied he was an insurgent, but after shooting at the marines
and being in possession of so many rockets, mortars, and artillery shells, he
gave me little reason to have faith in his story. I focused on where he got the
weapons.

We were in very close proximity to Qaqaa, an Iraqi weapons depot that
made it into the news in the aftermath of the invasion. In one of the biggest
screwups of the war, the base had been left unsecured as the invading force
focused on Baghdad. Iraqis picked the place clean, and we were still feeling
the effects. These mortars, RPGs, and artillery shells that now served as
deadly roadside bombs were once the tightly held property of the Iraqi army.
Now they were in the hands of farmers like this, people who'd either use
them, if they were in that frame of mind, or sell them to someone more diabolical.

Anyway, if he was lying, maybe the ground where the weapons were buried would be soft and recently turned. In that case, he might have gotten the weapons from someone else, and I'd have a trail to follow. Either way, he was going to jail, but there was intelligence here, maybe. I put in requests for descriptions of the ground at the site. They must have thought I was crazy. Nothing came back from that.

I focused instead on the other two families. Why were they arrested? Why was a raid even conducted? One of the families had a teenager; kids are often talkative and, of course, easier to intimidate if it came to that. I'd start with him.

Ahmed's face was swollen and lacerated. He calmly submitted to the medical exam required prior to interrogation. The navy corpsman who examined him was a very young, very cocky teenager who tried to get us to call him "Iceman," and tried to act as cool as his chosen moniker would suggest. As Ahmed removed his shirt, Iceman winced. "Jesus. They're really fucking people up," he whispered. Ahmed's torso was spotted with deep purple bruises. The corpsman said he'd seen a number of others from this raid in similar condition, but this kid got the brunt of it.

Ahmed said he didn't know who lived on the other farms. His family kept to itself. But he heard the gun battle on that night. When the marines came to his house and kicked in the door, they arrested his parents and took them outside. He was suddenly the man of the house. The interpreter asked him where the weapons were. Before he could answer, someone punched him in the face while yelling something in English. He fell and tried to cover his head while yelling in Arabic that the weapons were under the bed.

And that's where they found them. Each family in occupied Iraq is allowed to keep one AK-47. This family had three. The marines were pissed. Ahmed said he took more beatings while denying repeatedly that there were other weapons in this house. When the marines were done searching, he said, the beating stopped.

The kid was incredibly collected and cooperative. Once he saw that I wasn't going to beat him, he relaxed. I suppose he considered himself lucky to have all his fingers and toes.

Every angle I tried on these other two families that had been swept up with the original target pointed to the same thing—there was no reason to keep them in jail. Within a few days, I was resolved to get them out so they could go home to their ransacked homes and try to pick up the pieces. I thought I had a shot with Ahmed's family, but the other family got screwed by one of their own.

They also had a teenage kid, Umar, but something was not right about him. When I asked him if he knew anything about the hidden weapons, he launched into a wild tale about how insurgents had come to him and asked to hide weapons in one of his canals. At first, I thought I was actually onto something, so I pushed ahead. Then the insurgents told him, he said, to go to the town of Abu Ghraib and pick up money from their contact. Okay, maybe there was something here.

I interviewed Umar's brothers separately and they were totally confused. He was never home alone—no one came and talked to him. He's never been to Abu Ghraib. And yes, he's a little slow. The kid's brothers' stories matched up. Time to go back to Umar and see what he'd do with this contradiction.

With each moment we talked, Umar's story got wilder and more elaborate. Now the insurgents were asking him to buy missiles and Umar was valiantly refusing, then Umar was asked to steal an American tank. As he went completely around the bend, I realized that he was probably very disturbed. But I would have to report everything he said, and that would be enough to send his entire family to Abu Ghraib, no matter how many times I also wrote on my report that this kid was crazy. As he prattled on, I couldn't take it anymore, and swiped him across the head with my file folder, just enough to get his attention. It was the only time in Iraq I'd ever "hit" a prisoner.

Trying to get these two families released was a fool's errand. Each one of them, even Ahmed, had a file, and each file had photos of those weapons turned up in the raid of someone else's farm. Those images were more powerful than anything I could write on an interrogation report. Looking at the file, it seemed like these prisoners were captured in a raid that turned up enough weapons to kill a few dozen Americans. They simply had no chance of release.

Everyone on our team noticed the beatings these families got, and everyone on our team was pissed. It wasn't unusual for prisoners to show up with bruises and lacerations, and most didn't warrant a lot of concern, but this was egregious and was done to children. Jones took our concerns to Chief Polk, along with a few other related issues, the most important being that we weren't getting any paperwork with these prisoners. All the sworn statements (each arrest required two) were going up to the lieutenant colonel, where they were held tightly, so we rarely got a look. This left us interrogating with one hand behind our backs. Without knowing why these other two farmhouses were raided, for example, what could we do with these prisoners? Or if the marines had a good reason to beat the shit out of this fifteen-year-old boy, let us know so we don't have to come back and report possible abuse. Jones came back assuring us that Polk would send our concerns up the chain of command. But this complaint was just the first.

I was writing an interrogation report when Chief Polk burst in and said he needed an interrogator and interpreter at the hospital. Now. I got Waleed and we met Polk at the hospital, where he gave us the briefest of briefs. Two Iraqis were being treated. They'd opened fire on marines, and the marines took them out. I had to interrogate them before they either died or went unconscious.

In the first room was Sadir, who'd been shot six times. The navy doctors were frantically working on him in the middle of a mess of tubes, trays of medical equipment, and blood, which was still flowing freely from Sadir's body. One of them looked up at me as I came in. "Doctor," I blurted, "is this prisoner fit to be interrogated?"

"Sure, go ahead," he replied casually, turning back to the bloody mess on the table. This wasn't the answer I expected or hoped for. Sadir wasn't even stabilized. They were still trying to stop him from bleeding out. I turned away to check on the other prisoner, followed by Polk and Iceman, who looked a little queasy.

Naji had only been shot once in the thigh. The activity in his room was much lower and he was completely cognizant. He lay back, blindfolded, as a doctor worked on his leg. I started with the standard question: "Tell me exactly what happened when you were arrested."

"It was me and my uncle. We were driving not far from here. We had just taken milk to market. We came to a group of soldiers who yelled 'Stop!' in Arabic. And we stopped. Then they started shooting."

He said he and his uncle came out of the car with their hands up, but the shooting continued. They scurried to the back of the car to take cover, and that's when they were hit. I took this down carefully, and then backed up and got close details about his association with his uncle, what business they do together, and what they did that day, step by step, up to the point where they were shot. Naji was one of those Iraqis who'd disprove that assertion we got in the Arab mind lecture about Arabs not being able to construct a timeline. He put one together effortlessly.

I returned to Sadir, who was still being worked on. Amazingly, he was actually going to survive being shot six times by marines. I don't know if he had been given painkillers, but he was lucid. I ran through the same list of questions and got the same answers, with a level of detail impressive for someone with six bullet holes in him. He was also blindfolded, which was frustrating because I wanted to see his eyes as he told me his stories, but probably better for him because the doctors were in the process of sticking a tube in his chest and a catheter in his dick. Sadir groaned as they did so, and at that point Iceman's eyes drifted back into his skull and he passed out cold.

Sadir had offered some new details, and I took these back to see if Naji would get tripped up here or if he'd match what his uncle had said. Polk was in the hallway, looking impatient and talking to an Iraqi translator for the hospital who'd inserted himself into the scene. "He's from Fallujah!" the Iraqi whispered. Polk asked him how he could tell. "His goatee. That's what they wear in Fallujah!" Now, I'd been following the news in Fallujah closely, thinking I'd be sent there as soon as the next offensive started. I couldn't re-member seeing any goatees on the faces of the angry demonstrators. My first impression was that this Iraqi contractor was trying to impress us.

Polk was game. When the Iraqi said he thought he might even recognize the man lying there on the bed with a wounded leg, Polk arranged to have his blindfold removed so the Iraqi could have a closer look. He ordered the corpsman to lift the bandage, but not before he ordered the marine standing guard to point his M16 in Naji's face, so that the first thing he saw when the blindfold lifted was the long barrel of a rifle and a marine drawing a bead. The Iraqi hospital worker didn't recognize him.

I pushed these prisoners' stories as hard as I could, and found no inconsistencies to exploit. After about twenty minutes of this, Chief Polk took over and was yelling at these guys. He was intent on catching them on something. I was confused about what he was after. They had no weapons and their stories checked out. They were obviously stopped and shot by mistake. "What else do we have on them?" I asked. I still hadn't seen any sworn statements. "Any weapons in the car?" No, nothing but milk.

I told Polk that they appeared to be clean, and he looked like I'd just told him his dog died. He wouldn't accept it, and latched on to the only inconsistency I'd found. One of them thought the marines yelled "Stop" several times, one thought they only yelled once. He took over the interrogation, and went back to Fear Up Harsh. *"Kathab! Kathab!"* he shouted at them. *Lies! Lies!* He knew a handful of Arabic words, and this was one of them. Sadir was stable, but still moaning as he tried to answer Polk's rapid questioning. For another twenty minutes Polk raged at them, going from room to room, pointing his finger and never lowering his voice. I'd never seen him like this. I couldn't figure out why this was so important.

Polk finally agreed that there was no more story to squeeze from these two, and we left. He went to his office and I went to mine.

I had a chance to clear the interrogation roster I had for that day, I thought, until I got the note that a new prisoner was waiting for me, and he was of the highest priority. He must have been—there was actually a sworn statement on my desk describing his arrest. I read it carefully, and found that sometimes having a sworn statement is just the same as not having anything. From this piece of paper, I couldn't figure out why Latif was in our custody and care.

The sworn statement simply told me that Latif was arrested in a truck he was driving after he pulled it to the side of the road. And he tested positive for gunpowder residue. I knew about this test—it never gave a negative result. It reacted strongly to fertilizer and even to dirt, so anyone who'd been near a farm (which was just about everyone in Iraq) was sure to get a positive result. I tried it on myself and got a strong positive despite the fact that I hadn't fired a weapon in months. So did the corpsman, who gave himself the test.

Wearily, I asked Latif to tell me what happened at the time of his arrest. It was consistent with the sworn statement, only much more detailed. Latif came upon a group of our marines while driving, and heard some gunfire at the same time. The marines waved him off the road and pointed him to a side road. As he drove, he could see marines in a flurry of activity—it seemed like they were suddenly everywhere and their weapons were raised. He was very worried what would happen to him if he kept driving, so he pulled over and waved a white shirt out his window. He climbed out of his truck, still waving the white shirt over his head. The marines surrounded him, arrested him, and searched through the produce in the back of his truck.

As I left the booth, the obvious question—why Latif was in prison—fell by the wayside as I pondered why he was considered high-priority. I reported to Polk: "Sir, this truck driver doesn't appear to have any information."

"Bullshit. He has something," Polk shot back. Now this was even stranger. Polk must have learned about this prisoner about the same time I did. He didn't have any more information than I did. What was this?

Maybe if I were smarter it would have hit me sooner. Latif was arrested near the same site where Sadir and Naji were shot. The gunfire he heard was from that same incident.

"He must know something," Polk continued. "He was right there when our marines took fire. He must have seen something." This statement gave me the last piece of information I was missing before. The marines were claiming that they'd been fired on—that's why they shot up Sadir and Naji. But these two unfortunate souls had no weapon. So someone else must have done the shooting.

"If he did see something," I asked Polk, "why won't he tell us?"

Polk looked at me like he was explaining something to a third-grader. "If he won't say who shot at our guys, he must have been shooting at our guys. There was no one else out there."

Something stunk here. No one found a weapon on Latif, no one saw him open fire, and no one had any additional information. And yet Polk expected me to go in there and break this guy down—with what? I had no leverage, no contradictions, no eyewitness accounts.

Sadir and Naji, we found out the next day, were connected to a local Shia cleric who had some pull. His people came around and convinced someone that it would be better for all concerned if they were released as soon as they were able to walk. But Latif had no one pulling for him. Every day for the next two weeks, I received new questions to ask him.

What kind of truck were you driving?

Where'd you get it? Who sold it to you?

What were you hauling?

Where did you get it? Where were you going to sell it?

You could go on forever like this, and it must have seemed to Latif, as he sat in isolation, that this *was* going to go on forever. He grew sick of the sight of me, sick of my promises that he'd be released soon, and sick of my incessant questions.

This case was eating into my time—time I could have spent interrogating someone who actually had intelligence. Even worse, I realized as I sent up a report that detailed where he bought the truck, I was generating bad intelligence. The man who sold Latif this truck was now in the system. He was now an associate of someone who'd allegedly fired on American troops. Our net was spreading wider, scooping up fish big and small, and refusing to let go.

CHAPTER 20

Evidence

The U.S. death toll was now over one thousand, and across Iraq we were dealing with an average of eighty-seven attacks per day. Our chow hall was a highly desired target, and their mortars had been getting closer. We now had to wear all our gear, including helmets, while we ate. A little archipelago of cement bunkers sprung up around the sheet metal trailer that served as our chow hall. That was great, but the first shell almost always falls without warning.

One day in October they finally hit our chow hall. The first shell exploded on the corner of an outdoor refrigeration unit, a few yards from where I was standing in line, bullshitting with some Iraqi national guardsmen. The explosion sprayed the chow line with shrapnel and we disintegrated into a controlled panic as we dove for the bunkers. I had two guardsmen land on me, just as the second one hit. There was a brief pause, and I wormed my way to the top of the pile to see what was going on. More mortars were falling, people ran, some fell, and some were covered in blood. Nine guardsmen were seriously wounded that day. I was untouched. If I'd been three paces forward in line, it would have been a different story.

I often thought that the prison compound was also a target, but could never figure out why. It sucked especially badly if they started shelling in the middle of an interrogation, because it was often way too risky to grab the prisoner and make a run for the bunker in the middle of the prison compound two hundred yards away. We'd just hit the floor, shielded only by the walls of the shipping container, and I'd try to shield the prisoner with my body if I was wearing armor.

It happened one time with a prisoner I was fairly confident had dealings with insurgents, and this time the hits were right outside, one right after the other in tight little patterns. My interpreter was on the floor before I could react, and when my prisoner saw this he went prone with his hands over his head. Before I lay down next to him, I unfastened the front of my body armor and arranged myself so I could place it over his back. We lay side by side, and looked at each other. He was shaking, his lips were quivering, and the color had drained from his face. He was looking directly at me, his eyes wide with fear. I asked him, "So, are those your buddies out there?" He said, "If my friends did this, I'll kill them myself."

Twelve mortars fell that time, in the space of about four minutes, which of course seemed much longer. They were close enough to shake me to my bowels. Whenever there are so many, so close, you can't help but think that the next one is for you.

I was once again alternating between utter despair and blinding anger. Out of every ten prisoners I interrogated, I'd maybe encounter one who I suspected was either actually guilty or actually had information. I kept staring into bruised faces that were full of either fear or hate, and when I couldn't salvage what was left of my compassion and humanity, I would hate them back. I was making enemies on base. My complaints had gotten around, my efforts to keep prisoners from being sent to Abu Ghraib were widely known, and it didn't help that I'd written "Vote Kerry" on my helmet's cammo band.

Jones was a saving grace, always willing to run interference with Polk and work extra hours to make sure we got our admin taken care of. Specialist Wayne Tascun, my partner, was a huge help, and really deserves credit for keeping me on an even keel during this very dark time. The man was unflappable and unstoppable, a great pal to have in that place. He knew how horrible things were here, and he wouldn't let it get to him. "There's nothing you can do," he told me at the end of an especially bad day, "except to keep doing your job. Write your reports, and know that if it wasn't you it would probably be someone who didn't care." We did a lot of interrogations together and especially enjoyed doing screenings together.

Still, our discipline suffered a little and we started goofing off in the course of doing our jobs. Since just about every prisoner we got was likely completely innocent, we tried to break the ice and calm fears during screening. As Wayne lined up the camera for the prisoners' mug shots, he'd say, in Arabic, "Smile!" About half of them did—unable to resist Wayne's big goofy grin. If they didn't smile, I'd step around and tickle them in the ribs.

We added a few items to the standard list of screening questions, and delivered them in the same dry, half-bored, bureaucratic voice we used for the "real" questions, and dutifully wrote down their confused replies.

Where do you live?

Who do you live with?

Are you married?

Where is Osama bin Laden?

What is your favorite color?

If you could be any animal, what animal would you be?

Do you know any good jokes? (No one ever did.)

Wayne was right, there was nothing I could do. The prisoners just kept coming, and the absurdities surrounding their arrests seemed to grow more preposterous. This came to a head one day when we finally got around to working on a group of six prisoners, who we loaded up in a shipping container so Wayne could pull them out and quickly screen them while I guarded the others in the container.

The prisoners were bound, but not blindfolded, and looked like they'd come from some miscellaneous grab bag of hapless Iraqis. We had a huge man, midthirties, with a round head and a thin mustache; an old bearded man, about seventy, who was hunched over and moved only with great effort; a cowering fifteen-year-old with straight black hair; an average-looking young man with no facial hair; a very small, skinny, and frenetic middle-aged man who immediately smiled when we came in; and a sullen guy in his midtwenties who sported a few bruises and shifted uncomfortably where he sat. Wayne took the big man away for screening, and I stood guard.

I explained to the remaining five that we were going to ask them a few questions and then they could get some sleep. For now, just sit tight and be quiet. This situation worried me. Even with hands bound, these five could quickly overpower me or at least create trouble. But they went back to staring at the wall or staring at the floor or staring at me. Except for the little guy, who kept motioning at me with his chin. When he finally got my attention he looked down at his hands, which were cuffed in front. I guess they'd run out of handcuffs that day because he was bound with leg irons. As I watched, he pulled one of the cuffs clear off his slender wrist, then put it back, lifted it off, put it back, and flashed me a huge grin. I laughed and shrugged and said, "Okay, I see. Just don't do that anymore." None of the others paid attention.

Wayne returned in minutes with the jolly Iraqi giant, and they seemed to be in a good mood. As he prepared to take his next prisoner, I stopped him. "Look, you have to take him to the prison—I don't want to be in the same room with him." Wayne laughed and said, "This guy? You don't have to worry about him at all," then slapped him on the shoulder. It was true. No one on this base—in all of Iraq for that matter—had to worry about this guy.

Wayne had learned why this man, Mahdi, was in our company. At a routine checkpoint stop, a search revealed that he had a cell phone and a shovel. The sworn statement said that the arresting infantry suspected the shovel would be used to bury a roadside bomb, and the cell phone would be used to detonate it. This was so far-fetched that even Mahdi had to laugh about it.

As we worked our way through this group of prisoners, we found it was a good day for arbitrary arrests. The old man, Akram, owned a small roadside restaurant. He was arrested because someone, somewhere, asserted that insurgents ate lunch there.

The fifteen-year-old kid, Taslim, was arrested in a cordon search. When the infantry tossed his father's house, they found $3,000 cash. The kid explained that his father and uncle were trying to expand their small trucking company. The money was their savings for a new truck. No adults were home, so they arrested the kid.

The average-looking young guy, Isam, had been arrested at a checkpoint. His car had no backseats, so the arresting infantry decided he was building a car bomb. No other evidence supported this.

Abbas, the little guy wearing the leg irons on his wrists, was another checkpoint arrest. His tribal name was the same as that of a man on the blacklist. I'd seen this many times before. Abbas turned out to be a real pleasure. He was certain it was all just a mistake that we'd sort out soon, and we did, but this was pure luck. I'd seen another case like his result in a two-week detention.

Finally, we had Hanbal, the sullen man from this group. His angular features gave him a sinister air, and his attitude during screening didn't help. As we went through the standard questions, he seethed both fear and contempt. On this guy, we had some actual intelligence—a source that I trusted—but no physical evidence.

So if Hanbal turned out to be an actual insurgent and/or could provide some intelligence, then the ratio of "good" prisoners to worthless (probably innocent) prisoners in this microcosm was one to six. As bad as that was, it was far better than usual. If this was acceptable, I had to wonder, why bother with coming up with ridiculous reasons—cell phones, shovels, lack of backseats, or possession of money—to detain someone? Why not just do mass random arrests and see what we get? There was sure to be a terrorist in there somewhere.

I was relieved when they let Abbas walk after holding him just a few days. The rest of this crowd was not so lucky. We sent up a report about Mahdi and his cell phone. It belonged to his boss, and we used the phone to call him. The story Mahdi gave us checked out, everything about what he did the day he was arrested and what he planned to do next was plausible and confirmed. He had the shovel because he had recently bought it used to give to his father, who was a farmer and needed a new one. Such was our report, but this unit's officers turned it around immediately. They sent us back into the booth to get more information and demanded we ask questions like "Does the prisoner have a receipt for the shovel?" "Why was there dirt on the shovel?" "Why would the prisoner have the shovel in his trunk?" We interrogated Mahdi six times, long enough for him and Wayne to become great friends. After Mahdi spent two weeks with us living in a plywood box, they let him go.

Akram, the restaurant owner, told me that insurgents probably did eat at his restaurant, but he couldn't tell an insurgent from an average Iraqi, so how would he know? He wasn't running a community business—it was more a roadhouse, just a stop on the way north—so it wasn't like he had his finger on the pulse of the local situation by virtue of running this restaurant. He just sold people food.

Akram was forthcoming and easygoing, and could have been a source if we'd gone about this the right way—that is, if we'd gone to him and asked him questions or asked him to watch out for particular people, instead of arresting him and interrogating him repeatedly. At least five times Wayne and I went through the same questions with Akram, and it soon dawned on this seventy-year-old man that we weren't going to let him go. I finally confirmed, two weeks after his arrest, that he was being sent to Abu Ghraib. For the first time, he looked like he was about to cry as he stated what was now obvious: "So I'm going to die in an American prison."

Isam's car, the one with no backseat, had been hauled to the base as a suspected future vehicle-borne improvised explosive device. We took Isam to his car so he could show us all the work he'd had done on it since it had been hit by another car. He had receipts for the bodywork, a new back window, and two side windows. He showed us where the frame was bent and explained that the backseats would go back in once he got the frame torqued. We wrote on the report, in a slightly sarcastic tone, that it was clear no one would have so much work done on a car if they were just going to blow it up. But there was no way, we should have known, they were going to take that kind of shit from two dumb army guys. Isam stayed with us for two weeks, and we interrogated him repeatedly.

As for Taslim, I felt there were cases where a big wad of money could be pretty damning evidence. Like if we had any other shred of evidence, such as weapons or a tip from an informant or anything. But if they were going to arrest everyone in a cordon search who has some cash stashed away, I'd at least hope they'd arrest the man who owned the house and not just the fifteen-year-old kid who happened to be there.

The analysts really wanted me to hammer this kid, sending me one request for information (RFI) after another. On one report I dutifully noted that someone in his family owned a farm and his dad sometimes helped haul the potatoes in his truck. So an analyst got ahold of that in the middle of the night and sent me an urgent RFI. I had to wake the kid up, pull him into the booth, and ask him about those stupid potatoes. They'd decided up at the command and control center (the CoC, or "cock") that potatoes was code for hand grenades, and lettuce was code for money to buy weapons, and so on. (I don't know why the analysts would imagine that Taslim would be telling me about his insurgent activity in code.) Taslim had been with us for almost two weeks and I knew what was going to happen next. When he asked me that night about his fate, I told him sorry, he was probably going to Abu Ghraib, at which point he started to cry. I felt myself going completely numb. I couldn't do this anymore.

I was getting nowhere with Hanbal, but I was also growing more convinced that he was up to something. I begged the counterintelligence teams for more information I could use to hang him and got nothing. We just had these vague statements from an informant.

The marines had a decent-sized firing range on base, right next to the prison, that they used irregularly for training Iraqi national guardsmen. Groups of them would line up, fire a clip, check their targets, and fire again. If this was going on while I pulled a prisoner from a booth, I'd be sure to let him know, right off the bat, that this wasn't a firing squad. *"La tkhaaf. Ymarisoon itlaq annaar."* "Don't worry. They're practicing shooting."

My mind was elsewhere when I pulled Hanbal from his cell, or I would have read the fear in his eyes. I cuffed him and placed blacked-out goggles over his eyes, and led him by the shoulder out into the compound. We were walking in the direction of the firing range when the sound of rifle fire crackled toward us. Hanbal went limp under my hand, his knees buckled, and he tried to resist forward motion. In a moment of cruelty, I didn't try to calm him. If he was going to think I was leading him to his execution, I'd let him. I gathered up the fabric of his jumpsuit in my hand and pushed him forward.

A pair of Iraqi policemen conducted our last interrogation of Hanbal, with me observing. I quickly lost track as their Arabic moved ever more quickly and colloquially. The policemen agreed with me that he was probably up to something, and there was no way we could prove it. Hanbal was released.

So, what was the score here? Out of six prisoners, one case of mistaken identity, released very quickly. Two cases of our soldiers' imaginations running wild, released after two weeks of solitary confinement. A teenager and an old man on death's door, both held for God knows what reasons, both sent to Abu Ghraib for indefinite detention and further interrogation. And one guy walks free because even though we think he's an insurgent, we can't prove it. I know that war is fundamentally irrational, but that didn't mean we had to be irrational and arbitrary in every decision we made.

I loved Sergeant Jones like a brother, but maybe he wasn't being assertive enough. Catching Chief Polk alone, I complained about having to go back for repeated interrogations of Iraqis who should be let go. I focused on Mahdi with his cell phone, and Taslim with his dad's cash. Polk was a good political operator. He didn't rip into me for questioning his judgment, but gave me a patient and slightly patronizing little lecture on counterinsurgency:

> Look, maybe not everyone's guilty, but they know something. We're casting a wide net. We're going to get everyone we can, and if you can't handle the interrogations here, we'll send them to Abu Ghraib, where they have a bigger facility. I'm not concerned about whether we have "evidence" or not. We're trying to stop an insurgency.

When Taslim got to Abu Ghraib, the chief warrant officer in charge of screenings there, Chief Warrant Officer Parker, who was a very sane and reasonable man, not given to knee-jerk reactions, sent the marines an angry e-mail: "Stop sending us these prisoners." For one thing, there were too many, and for another, they had no intelligence value and posed no threat to the occupation. "They need to be released at North Babel." That's what we heard from Staff Sergeant Lobos, who often gave us information from the marines, since Polk liked to keep us out of the loop on some things.

We didn't bring up this e-mail to Polk or anyone else, but we continued to complain. Polk brought a response from the lieutenant colonel who had the sole responsibility of determining the detainees' fates. "Anyone who comes into this prison is guilty, and if I let them out it's because of overwhelming evidence of innocence."

I was absolutely floored. We'd come here to spread democracy and the rule of law, but ended up inverting our own values.

Even the Iraqi police interrogators with whom we worked were appalled at our system of justice, or lack of it, and they ridiculed the lectures from the marines about how fair, humane, and just the Americans were. "We won't tolerate any Iraqi-style interrogations," they were told. Well, it was clear to them now that we would tolerate a lot of very flimsy evidence.

Do your job, Wayne kept telling me. Write your reports. Someone at Abu Ghraib will catch it. I did so, trying to keep myself from total despair, only to find out later that my reports weren't leaving Polk's desk. Once the Abu Ghraib screeners complained about the steady stream of innocent prisoners we were sending them, prisoners started arriving at Abu Ghraib without our interrogation reports—without the nagging opinions of a ticked-off interrogator to cast doubt on the whole case. We confronted Polk about this and he said, yeah, he was behind on his paperwork.

CHAPTER 21

Pride and Ego Down

The worst thing about my anger—which I carried from my first waking moments, through my long days, and into my dreams—was that it had no single focus. I couldn't blame it all on one person, like Chief Polk, as much as I wanted to. I couldn't, and didn't want to, pin it on the infantry or marines, who went out every day to face hostile fire and possible death. I would have loved to have a serious talk with the guys who beat up Taslim, the fifteen-year-old kid caught up in a pointless raid, but I would never find out who was doing these beatings. I only saw the results. I'd have loved to blame the Iraqis. After all, a good number of them were trying to kill me; I just didn't know which ones.

The brass here was very blamable, but when it came to the number of Iraqis detained on flimsy "evidence," or when it came to the beatings we saw, the officers would say, "Well, we have to trust and have faith in our men." That sounds really good, and I wanted to believe that, but it's also a way for the officers to dodge responsibility for patterns of wrongful arrest and abuse. The men respond to orders and signals from above, and generally act in ways they think will further the mission, which is largely defined by these officers.

If someone wanted to stop the absurd detentions and beatings, all they had to do was make it clear and simple: we will not stand for this. I looked to Staff Sergeant Lobos, who ran our prison compound in North Babel, for an example. He ran it professionally and by the book. No prisoner was ever abused or killed here, because the sergeant put down the law right from the start and *then* had faith in his men.

Further blurring my ability to really focus my anger was my own self-doubt. I was painfully aware of how incompatible my training was with the actual situations I faced. I wondered constantly whether my reports had sent an innocent man to Abu Ghraib or set an insurgent free. I knew the marines saw me as a softy and a terrible interrogator, and I wondered how much of that was true. Finally, and worst of all, I knew that I'd brutalized prisoners in Mosul. In getting all worked up about these beatings and unnecessary detentions, wasn't I being the worst kind of hypocrite?

Abdul-Aziz was a local imam, a minor but not-insignificant figure in the area, and I royally screwed him over. The infantry searched his house on a tip that he was inciting Iraqis to violence, and felt their suspicions were confirmed when they found stacks of anti-American flyers. I got a good, thick file on this guy from Polk, who labeled him a "dirtbag," and with all this information was able to put together an effective plan.

I introduced myself as an army public relations man. He never knew that I was an interrogator. "I'm sorry about your conditions and your arrest," I started, immediately after sitting him down and removing his cuffs. "I know you are an important man."

My way in, which never wavered and which he totally believed, was to ask him for help. "My job is to build relationships between America and Iraq," I explained, and asked him to help us by building bridges between Shia and Sunni. I knew this is where his heart was. He was Shia; his wife was Sunni. Among the anti-American propaganda in his house was a wealth of literature on national unity. Iraqi Nationalism as opposed to sectarianism was rare and was the kind of force we needed to foster and protect. Nationalism isn't necessarily pro-American, but it is a stabilizing influence. I convinced him I was willing to look past the anti-American stuff and help him build a new Iraq. "I'm going to get you out of prison," I falsely promised.

He was not a humble man, and easily believed that the army would take an interest in him. He was further won over by the fact that I spoke Arabic and could talk at length about religion. I told him I was interested in Islam and let him try to convert me. We built a strong relationship based on shared interests and mutual understanding, helped along by the fact that I kept asking him what he needed for his mosque and wrote down every request.

I visited Abdul-Aziz every day to feed him false updates on his case, and in his mind, every day it seemed like he was getting closer to release. The only problem, I finally let him know, was that some people were worried about the flyers found in his house. What was that all about?

"Yes, the militia put those up, and I know it causes problems for you. I take it down whenever I see it. Iraqis don't need to fight the Americans." He continued by explaining that the flyers in his home were the same ones he'd taken down. He didn't plan to distribute them, but his daughter used the blank backsides to color on.

That could have been true. There were a lot of these posters and pamphlets in his house, but only one copy of each. Some of them had a child's drawings on the back. If this imam was creating them, maybe he'd have multiple copies. But it didn't matter. This whole charade was just for one thing:

"Who's putting up the flyers?"

Abdul-Aziz listed some possible names, organizations, places, and businesses where the material was printed. He also gave me locations of people he thought might be involved in active recruitment of anti-American forces.

We met a few times after that. I had some minor follow-up questions for him, which I worked into our wide-ranging conversations about religion, Arabic, mathematics, and philosophy (which he thought was "dangerous"), and how to fix Iraq. Polk was thrilled. "Good job on this guy." Within two weeks we felt we had all we could get, and Abdul-Aziz was processed for transfer to Abu Ghraib. He must have wondered, as he was shipped off for indefinite detention, why I didn't stop in to say good-bye.

I'd done my job and gotten actionable intelligence without using torture or Fear Up Harsh, and yet I couldn't take even a sliver of pride in what I'd done. I didn't especially like this guy—he was rather arrogant and sanctimonious—but still, I'd thoroughly betrayed him. As Polk congratulated me on running such a number on this "dirtbag," I had to wonder why he deserved prison. That anti-American literature we'd found? I read it closely, and although it was clearly propaganda, it didn't encourage Iraqis to take up

202 ■ TONY LAGOURANIS

arms. It wasn't really any worse than what you'd find posted around an American college campus. Anyway, if he was so responsive to flattery (or Pride and Ego Up, as they'd call it in the army field manual), couldn't we have accomplished just as much without the arrest? Or did he need to be confined and humiliated first? Finally, I had to wonder, what would he think of Americans now that one had royally fucked him?

Wayne and I looked down at the gadget brought in with five detainees and decided it *had* to be a bomb. What else could it be? There were a mess of wires coming out of a car battery, and the battery poles were attached to two big capacitors and from there to two long rods. What kind of bomb, we had no idea. The only thing the contraption seemed to lack was an artillery shell or a pound of C-4.

So we asked each of these guys separately what it was all about, and we learned that this is one way to fish in Iraq. They go out in a boat, stick these two rods into the water, flick a switch, and a current arcs between the rods, stunning the fish. Not very sporting, but plausible and possibly effective. Wayne and I were still suspicious and still ready to label these guys as mad bombers, so we put in a call to EOD (Explosive Ordnance Disposal) to send out an expert. This takes a couple days. The fishermen waited it out patiently.

Meanwhile, we got another pair of prisoners, and the evidence against them was a motorcycle battery. This one had a wire soldered onto it on one end, and someone in the field said it was an IED detonator. Wayne and I figured "Here we go again," and he took the first one into the booth. I guarded the other one, just outside the booth, as he waited his turn.

I was bored and tired. We both sat on a berm, and I casually chucked rocks down the side. He was very nervous, and I told him to relax—"*La taqluq.*"

Wayne got both of their stories, which matched up fairly well. They said they had a motorcycle with a damaged terminal, and they came to Baghdad to have the battery permanently wired to the bike and that was the only way it could run. Again, this was plausible—actually more plausible than the fishing machine. I was ready to give up on these two, but we had the explosives expert coming in to look at the fish killer, so why not have him examine this motorcycle battery as well?

Soon he arrived. I'd seen these demolitions guys at work before. When a convoy spots a suspected roadside bomb, they stay back and wait for the EOD. Then the explosives experts pull up and fearlessly walk right up to the bomb, every time. They're insanely brave.

This one was friendly, but in a big hurry. Probably had a lot of business. So we showed him the two contraptions.

"That"—he pointed to the device with the two poles—"is a fishing machine. Very common." He proceeded at that point to tell us the same thing these two detainees had told us about how it works.

"That"—now pointing to the motorcycle battery—"is for an IED. This is how they do it." And he proceeded to give us a detailed and very helpful lecture on how to hook up this thing to an artillery shell.

I knew, from training, about a wide array of Soviet weapons and tactics, but I didn't know the difference between a fishing machine and an IED detonator. We were about to recommend that two insurgents be released (with their detonator) and that five fishermen be detained until we could confirm their story. All because the army had somehow not managed to squeeze in a PowerPoint presentation on insurgent weapons and tactics, even as we got endless training on the dangers of drunk driving or discrimination in the workplace.

These cases started to swirl around in my head, reminding me of other cases that maybe weren't so clear-cut. These two who'd been picked up with a wad of cash in their car . . . now that I think about it, they were lying to me. And that was one of the few cases where I got them out on the same day. Now, were they actually lying, or am I just thinking now that they were lying? These and other cases—there were so many—started to haunt me. I'd always tried to be skeptical of both the sworn statements and the prisoners' statements, but now I was second-guessing my own second-guessing, and it wasn't healthy.

It was during this time that I came to two conclusions, equally depressing. One, we were going to lose this war. We would withdraw in such a way that

204 ■ TONY LAGOURANIS

would guarantee our humiliation. Two, it wasn't just the fault of Bush, Cheney, and Rumsfeld.

I read *War and Peace* twice while I was in Iraq. Usually, I just escape into the novel (I'm in love with Natasha Rostov) and ignore Tolstoy's little treatise on history and the course of nations at the end, but this time I followed it closely because I was thinking about Napoleon's humiliating retreat from Moscow, after he'd "conquered" it, and our own impending retreat from Baghdad.

What forces produce events? Not, in the view of some historians, the Napoleons or Alexanders: "In describing a war on the subjugation of a people, the writer of general history seeks the cause of the event, not in the power of one person, but in the mutual action on one another of many persons connected with the event."

My actions on Khalid (whom I tortured) and on Abdul-Aziz (whom I betrayed), combined with the actions of the arresting infantry who left bruises on their prisoners and the actions of the officers who wanted to get promotions, repeated in microcosm all over this country, had a cumulative effect. They were leading us from one event—the invasion of Iraq—to another event—our retreat from Iraq—with the certainty and inevitability of an oncoming train. I could blame Bush and Rumsfeld, but I would always have to also blame myself. The project in Iraq would die, not of a single blow, but of a thousand cuts.

CHAPTER 22

Oil

At the CoC, they showed us the best PowerPoint presentation I'd seen in the military and delivered the best briefing I'd received as an interrogator. Finally, about six weeks into our time in North Babel, we were seeing a serious, concentrated, and coordinated effort against a hard target.

The aerial photography showed us a terrorist training camp, which the enemy had the gall to set up on the site of an abandoned U.S. Army forward operating base. In the amazingly high-resolution photos, we could see the insurgents openly carrying arms, standing on rooftops, and going through what our briefer described as "martial movements." They'd watched this camp for some time, from the ground and from the air, and noticed the same car visiting each day. By air, they followed the car back to a particular house in town, one that was firmly middle-class by Iraqi standards. From our eye in the sky, we could see the driver of the car meeting in a circle with his deputies. They sat in a circle for a time and then quickly dispersed.

The owner of this house had some connections to the owner of another car who made visits to the training camp. One of them even had a piece of property (the nature of which is still classified and should not be divulged here) that had, analysts determined, once belonged to someone who had contact with a known insurgent. This innocent-looking middle-class house, they determined, contained the leadership of the insurgency for the entire al-Anbar province.

It was an awesome piece of multisource collection and analysis, just the sort of thing that would finally break the back of this insurgency, and just the sort of thing that I'd always wanted to be a part of. Finally, we were moving from picking up suspicious people at checkpoints to hitting an entire camp of bad guys. As an added bonus, the photography, the involvement of special forces units, and the simultaneous coordinated raids (which were happening that night) gave the whole operation a fast-paced cinematic feel. They even gave movie-star code names to the two guys spotted driving to and from the camp. It was all very exciting.

They were hitting the camp and the two houses in a matter of hours, so we got the interrogation booths ready, discussed our plans, and got ready to stay up all night. We intended to screen and interrogate the main targets right away, trying to preserve the "shock of capture." They were certain to be surprised and off guard, and we were excited about the possibility of getting even bigger fish from interrogations of these insurgent leaders.

The first wave of prisoners came in around midnight, and we wanted to move fast. Sergeant Jones grabbed prisoners the moment they'd been medically screened, but sometimes he had to walk with them very slowly. These prisoners had been roughed up quite a bit more than normal. Fine. I didn't have time to take pity on them, and my overtaxed compassion hardly had room for known insurgents at this point. We launched our interrogations.

The first group was from the second house, targeted because a car from that house made occasional stops at the training camp. We had about seven prisoners, and it was soon clear that we were dealing with a family and a houseguest. We interrogated them one by one, focusing on the father, Ghanim. With his sons and comrades quickly available to confirm or deny his stories, he was going to have a difficult time lying to us.

Ghanim looked tired and deeply concerned, with just a hint of confusion in his eyes as I started peppering him with questions. As soon as he spoke, I could tell he was an educated man who held himself with pride. He had hair neatly parted to the side and a carefully trimmed beard flecked with gray, looking very much like George Clooney in *Syriana*. The corpsman told me that he may have a few broken ribs, and his breathing was laborious. He winced in pain each time he shifted in his seat. His hands were bruised and visibly swollen, and something was wrong with his feet. I never got a good look at them, but he clearly had trouble walking. His face was spotted with a few bruises, but unlike other prisoners who'd been beaten up, he sported no black eye. He gazed at me with eyes wide open.

I'd already spent a little time with his sons, asking them all the same question: "Do you visit the compound outside of town?" I was fishing, not letting on all I knew. I wanted them to lie, and they obliged. "No! Father tells us to never go there." Well, someone in that house drove a car to the compound, so my first job was to find out who.

Ghanim looked me straight in the eye and said he had no idea what I was talking about. I pushed him further. "A former military compound," I hinted, assuming he'd have known that the U.S. Army had once operated a base there.

"No, no." His pleading voice let me know that I'd touched a nerve. "I know people who go there, but I've never been there."

The prisoners from the other raid arrived. Ghanim would have to wait while I helped process them. Soon I'd have a new set of lies and new leverage to use on Ghanim.

Once again, we clearly had a family. Most of them sported bruises. One of them had a foot that had swollen to twice its size, and which was marked with a rectangular impression that was surrounded by broken skin. He said that one of the marines smashed his foot with the back of an axe head. The impression was about that size.

Some of these children were too young, I felt, to be really active insurgents, but that didn't rule out the fathers, or make those young ones useless to our interrogations. Of course, everyone from this group also denied going to the compound, but one of them mentioned the compound being to the south of their town. That gave me pause, as we knew the terrorist training camp was to the north. "What happens there?" I asked him, totally fishing. He replied in a state of bafflement, as if I should know, "People sometimes go there to steal. But I've never been."

Okay, I'd made a mess of this and wasted valuable time. When I started asking about a compound, each of these people thought I was talking about Qaqaa, the large and infamous former Iraqi base that was the source of looted weapons now used against U.S. forces.

I went back to the head of the next family, As'ad, to ask him about visits to the *terrorist* compound. I described where it was located. He again seemed surprised, but fully admitted going there. "Yes, I drive there to deliver money, and sometimes to take people to work." A pit started forming in the bottom of my stomach. "Who do you work for?" He didn't pause, but didn't seem any less confused. "The Ministry of Oil." Shit.

Okay, back to Ghanim. I explained that now I was interested in the compound north of town—and don't lie to me, we know you've been there. Again, no pause: "Yes, one of my sons is a security guard there, so I do drive him sometimes, or one of my other sons might drive him." At this point the pit in my stomach came to feel like a burning hole and my head felt light. "Who does your son work for?" I asked, and I knew what Ghanim was going to say. "The Ministry of Oil." A realization, that this whole operation was an incredible fiasco, washed over me all at once.

I talked with Wayne and Sergeant Jones. After a few quick questions, we felt we'd cracked this case. As'ad was a security director for the Iraqi Ministry of Oil. He supervised the men we'd seen in the photos carrying AK-47s. But why was the Ministry of Oil set up at this site? By coincidence, Jones had served briefly at this site during his first tour in Iraq, when it was an army base. He now remembered the base being dotted with oil tanks and oil pipes, pieces of infrastructure valuable enough to protect with a forward operating base. He was only there for a few weeks, but it appeared now that the army had left the base in the hands of the Iraqi Ministry of Oil.

At that point, about four a.m., the final wave of prisoners, all from the "terrorist training camp," arrived. After we processed them, I volunteered to finish up here, so Wayne and Jones went to bed. I knew, as the anger started to fill my head, that I wasn't going to be able to sleep that night. I couldn't wait to get this cleared up and get these people out of jail.

The final wave of prisoners were all security guards at the Ministry of Oil compound. Most of them carried ID that described them as such. The arresting infantry was thorough enough to bring in all the paperwork they could find, and I quickly fished out payroll rosters that matched up with the IDs, memos from the ministry, time cards, schedules, and everything else you'd expect to find at a government site. I felt my job here was done.

I went to Polk and explained the whole situation. The only thing left to do was call the Ministry of Oil and get final confirmation. That could wait until the morning, and for now I'd just make sure the prisoners were comfortable and got medical attention. So I was going to call it a night. No, Polk insisted, we're going to keep interrogating.

I guess it didn't sink into Polk's skull that this was a huge mistake and there was no information to be gleaned from interrogation. Probably, he was at this point very suspicious of me and ready to have a knee-jerk reaction against any assertion of innocence that I made. But the scale of this snafu was so mind-boggling that maybe he just couldn't believe it. He accompanied me back to the booth, where we interrogated a few of the guards.

These guys were not just sympathetic to the Americans; they were actively fighting the insurgents. A couple of them described getting attacked all the time, and another was full of elaborate ideas of what we should do to break the insurgency. It was so convincing it convinced Polk. After just an hour, he said, "Okay, go to bed. We'll make the call tomorrow."

I woke up from a very fitful sleep, and the first thing that went through my mind was the fact that we had thirty people, including all the male members of two families, in prison for no reason. I made a beeline for Chief Polk, who, true to his word, had already been to the CoC. He looked at me with sympathy for the first time. "They're not going to make the call," he told me flatly. The burning in my gut and the spinning in my head returned as he explained that the officers believed their intelligence, insisted that this was a terrorist training camp, and would not accept the story I'd given them. My orders: go back and interrogate them until they break.

My response to Polk was short and sharp, and included liberal use of the words "fuck" and "bullshit," but I knew this wasn't his fault. He saw with his own eyes how wrong we'd been. Maybe he didn't argue forcefully enough, but he was far outranked here. I realized, as I walked away, that I might as well finish these interrogations, collect evidence, and put together a forceful argument on paper. The evidence was overwhelming. This shouldn't take too long.

I also made sure, as I checked out prisoners, to photograph the injuries these guys had shown up with. I put the photos into their medical files. These allegations of abuse were *definitely* going into a report.

The ministry guards were all kept together in a single tent, and they were still trying to figure out why they'd been arrested. I told them it was a mistake, without going into too much detail. And, one at a time, I interrogated all fifteen.

The family members still thought this was about Qaqaa, Ghanim's family in particular. Seems the arresting marines asked them a lot of questions about a small scope they found in the house, so they figured we must have assumed they got it at Qaqaa. They all told me the scope was something the youngest son had found and brought home, and they had no idea what it was—just a curiosity. I honestly couldn't identify it myself. It wasn't for a rifle or mortar, but probably had some military purpose. In any event, they knew this was not enough reason to stage such a major and violent raid on their house, and they were very curious to know what that reason was.

Ghanim himself wasn't directly connected to the Ministry of Oil, but he'd helped As'ad get the job as security director, and continued to help facilitate for them. He knew most everyone in town, and he knew who could be trusted and who not. Many of the guards got their jobs on Ghanim's recommendation.

It took me a couple days, but I finished these interrogations and submitted full reports on each prisoner, along with paperwork from the Ministry of Oil site, to Polk. I repeated that my report could be either confirmed or thrown into question with a single phone call to the Ministry of Oil. I found it inconceivable that someone could read this and continue to believe that these men and children needed to be kept in jail, but nevertheless, I braced myself for disappointment.

Inevitably, it came. I got no response to my report—nothing but a simple order to keep up the pressure and find out more about this scope they'd found. And they were particularly interested in Ghanim's houseguest, an Egyptian national. Any foreigner was immediately flagged as a jihadist, but this guy seemed unlikely to fit the bill. He was an old man who'd been in Iraq for thirty years. Ghanim had hired him to fix a tractor, and he'd traveled from the north to do the job. He was supposed to get a ride home the next day.

For two weeks I performed a series of absolutely useless interrogations on these two families and the fifteen guards. This case completely dominated my time, guaranteeing a backlog of cases that Wayne was left to plow through. That meant longer waits for other detainees picked up for absurd reasons at checkpoints. It also meant that I was steadily producing more useless paperwork that wasted the time of Polk, Jones, and the marines' analysts. Of course, this was all minor compared to what we were doing to these families.

I absolutely loved Ghanim's family. All his sons were incredibly smart and serious about education. They had wonderful, distinct, and idiosyncratic personalities. One was very interested in America, and wondered if he could ever go to college there. Another was not interested in America or American pop culture at all. Nor did he like Iraqi pop music, or Iraqi movies—he only watched those lavish Indian "Bollywood" musicals. I tried to pull Ghanim's sons out for questioning every day, because aside from their bathroom trips with guards, my interrogations were the only human contact they would get. Plus, I really enjoyed their company. Their father had, with limited means, done well for them, and instilled in them strong values, the same set of values any American middle-class family would be proud to uphold.

I was at the point where I was ready to call the Ministry of Oil myself, and let them bust me, court-martial me, whatever, but to use the phone I'd have to go through a marine sergeant, who'd ask me who I was calling and why. I didn't think I'd be able to pull it off. So instead, at the end of every day, I'd continue the fight with the officers, via Polk. I might as well have been banging my head against a wall. If they would just make one damn phone call . . . Their tenacity in the face of overwhelming evidence was amazing. Their initial intelligence reports were probably too convincing. The aerial photos of men with guns and the picture of Ghanim's house with a label "Insurgency HQ—Anbar Province" were very powerful images. But this had gone beyond the point of my story versus someone else's. There was no question here what had happened, and it would only take one phone call to confirm this once and for all.

I came to the sickening conclusion that someone with a lot of brass on his shoulder had already reported this operation as a success—"Hey, we smashed a terrorist training camp"—and now couldn't go back and admit he was wrong. And I had to face Ghanim.

I tried to reach out to him, with apologies and compliments about his sons. He didn't lash out at me, but he had a lot of anger stored up, and he had no one else to share that with. I asked him, for my abuse report, what happened during the raid. I was continually impressed with how dispassionately he spoke to me. He told me his interrogation, with beatings, went on for twenty to thirty minutes as other marines tossed his house. "It was terrible. They shot my refrigerator. They shot my television set. They broke all the windows on my cars. They punched and kicked my sons. They beat me in front of my family."

We talked for a long time, as he simmered. I could tell he was keeping a tight lid on a swirling set of emotions. "This is so very wrong. I've been attacked in my town because I work with the Americans. I've done nothing wrong. I've worked all my life to do good things for my family." I could tell Ghanim wasn't used to being helpless. Now, he knew that his sons were locked up, and he knew there was nothing he could do. He'd watched them get beaten by Americans, and there was nothing he could do. All the work he'd done to provide for his family and all the teaching he'd given them to make sure they walked a straight path, it all amounted to nothing because now there was nothing he could do.

The only time he cried was when he told me, *"Ana sharif.* I'm a noble man. This is not the treatment you should be giving a noble man." He obviously hated crying in front of me, and he quickly wiped his tears, pulled himself together, choked a little as he cleared his throat, and tried to sit up straight and look me in the eye. Ghanim had pushed and worked and fought to make something of himself in this screwed-up country, and he had a right to be proud. And then on one night, because of an arrogant mistake, we had robbed this man of his pride. Ripped it straight from his guts.

I left the booth in a blind rage. Someone up the chain of command was trying to royally screw Ghanim, all his sons, his houseguest, another family, and fifteen guards who fought insurgents almost as much as our side did. And whoever was trying to do this was trying to use me to do the screwing. I couldn't sit in front of Ghanim again, trying to apologize for the fact that he was abused and humiliated in his own home while he and his family rotted away in jail. I couldn't see clearly or think straight. I made it to our office strictly on autopilot, where I burst in on Sergeant Jones and Chief Polk in the middle of a conversation.

"Sergeant Jones! I'm finished! I'm sick of this shit, I quit, I'm done interrogating," I blurted out without really thinking this through, but it felt right. In fact, they could go ahead and court-martial me for this. I had every reason to not follow these orders. If we knew that these prisoners were picked up by mistake, but they kept ordering me to interrogate them, it was clear that those orders were intended to be interpreted as "Find something." I wasn't willing to do that.

"Okay, calm down. We'll talk about this." Jones was going to deal with this like he dealt with everything else. The man never lost his cool. Chief Polk took this opportunity to hustle out the door. I'll never know what he thought of my outburst, but he made the right decision in letting Jones handle it.

Jones and Wayne convinced me to stay on the job because I was in the best position to help these people get out of jail. Plus, if I left, Wayne would be doing this all on his own. We also resolved to make a formal complaint about this and everything else to our own command. We'd cc the marines, but we'd lodged complaints with them before that had gone nowhere. It was time to report this to our own people and start broadcasting our opinion of this situation.

Soon after, the pressure decreased somewhat. The command still wouldn't call the Ministry of Oil, and of course wouldn't let anyone go, but I got fewer ridiculous requests and direct orders for further interrogation. Except for Ghanim. They still wanted him because he had some kind of telescopic sight in his house, and because he owned a piece of property that had once been owned by someone who had a dealing with a known insurgent. Polk told me, carefully because he knew I wouldn't like it, that Ghanim was probably going to be sent to Abu Ghraib.

I broke the news. Ghanim took it well; he'd probably come to that conclusion already on his own, and told me, "Fine. Send me to jail, but please release my sons so they can go back and take care of my wife and daughter and my business, and so they can go back to school." I promised him I would do what I could.

Meanwhile, the Ministry of Oil had been trying to figure out what happened to their security detail. Their investigation finally pointed to our base, and an American working with the ministry placed a very angry call to our command, I heard. That should have been all it took to release everyone swept up in that raid, and it should have been automatic and on the same day. But after getting an earful from the American at the ministry, the command insisted on seeing a list of people they wanted released. The Ministry of Oil sent over a roster, and the command at North Babel sent me in to match names to the roster. If a prisoner wasn't on the list, he wasn't getting released. A few names didn't appear, and I had to work on this with As'ad, who suggested payrolls and other pieces of evidence I could find in the material we'd confiscated.

The one prisoner from this group I couldn't get released was the Egyptian. For the first time, I learned of a rule that any foreign national was placed on an automatic six-month military intelligence hold. So it was Abu Ghraib for him.

My rage slowly dissipated into a simmering anger and frustration. One thing was certain: I wasn't going to hold back on reporting any future abuse I saw or any problems I witnessed. This place was immoral and corrupt, and there were a lot of people here who clearly didn't give a damn about reconstructing Iraq. I asked Polk for the appropriate forms to file abuse. He should have taken a sworn statement, but instead just told me to send him a memo. I wrote up everything I had on the kid who had his foot smashed with an axe and on the beating taken by Ghanim. I referenced the photographic evidence in the prisoner's medical file. I didn't hear about these cases again until after I was discharged from the army.

I later wrote another report on a chicken farmer who'd been whaled on during his arrest. This was another case without evidence—no weapons, nothing. He'd only been arrested because he tried to leave an area that the marines were swarming. He ran, which is a totally reasonable reaction when a large group of men with sophisticated weapons show up in the middle of the night.

The final report I sent up in North Babel was on a man who had been detained for questioning. He was not a suspect. And yet, he told me, he'd been forced to sit on an exhaust pipe after his arrest. He had a blister on his leg larger than I thought was possible. It looked like a big water balloon hanging off the back of his upper thigh.

A lot of this abuse was detailed again in a memo from our unit to our company commander. Our team drew up a list of complaints, then winnowed it down to the four most serious problems: lack of documentation; unwillingness to take recommendations; volume of work (we'd been responsible for the screening and interrogation of over four hundred prisoners in just over eight weeks) and how it made us ineffective; and finally, we complained about the abuse of prisoners by arresting units. We cc'd the marines as a courtesy, they freaked out, and our memo went sailing up the chain of command. Word spread around base, and we were instant pariahs. Not long after, we were pulled.

We were in incredibly high spirits when we got word we were moving out of North Babel. We bummed a ride on a convoy back to Camp Slayer. Slayer was just a few miles away. It should have taken us fifteen minutes. But along our route, in three different locations, were three separate incidents involving roadside bombs. Each time our convoy spotted one, we had to wait for EOD to be called, then wait while they figured out how to safely detonate it. The trip took most of the day.

CHAPTER 23

The Dead

November 2004. Two months left on this tour, and then our battalion would ship out, unless we caught an extension like so many other units had and got trapped in Iraq for another six, eight, twelve months. I tried not to think about that possibility.

I was back at Camp Slayer, and it occurred to me that unless the Fallujah offensive opened up soon, I might rot here for the next eight weeks. The possibility was both attractive and depressing. I knew I'd get bored quickly, but on the other hand, if I got another mission, it could land me in another hellhole like North Babel.

The boat that Matt and I had surfaced from the man-made lake had returned to the muck, and we accepted it. Matt had also been on a mission at a forward operating base near Baghdad. He saw things that made him less laid-back than usual. There was a time his convoy stopped while waiting for EOD to clear an IED. Suddenly, without a word, a captain jumped from a Humvee in front of him, raised his rifle, settled into a firing position, and opened up on a white truck pulling out of a feeder road in front of them. He kept firing until the truck slowly coasted to a stop. No one got out. The captain returned to the Humvee and claimed he'd seen the truck in the vicinity of a previous attack, but to Matt it just looked like another nondescript white truck. No one ventured over to the shot-up truck, and the convoy left it and its occupants, their condition unknown, sitting on the side of the road.

Matt was disturbed enough to tell me this story, but he was also numbed.

It was just another shooting in Iraq, hardly remarkable anymore. I listened more out of concern for my friend than to add his story to my list of screwed-up shit in Iraq. The event itself was totally unsurprising.

George W. Bush won the election, and to me that was surprising. I couldn't believe that Americans could stand to elect the leader who sent us here under false pretexts and flimsy, cherry-picked intelligence. Friends back home were not surprised, and I realized how out of touch I was—the voters clearly weren't thinking about Iraq when they went into the voting booth, so what exactly were they thinking about?

With the election behind him, Bush could finally unleash the marines on Fallujah. For months, our troops had sat at a relatively safe distance from this town but were not allowed in. Everyone knew that retaking this city would be bloody, and everyone knew that we were putting it off so Bush wouldn't have that blood on his hands during the campaign. The delay allowed the insurgents to arm, recruit, dig in, and prepare to kill our troops. Many analysts believed that it was in Fallujah, during this delay, that al-Zarqawi and al-Qaeda established themselves firmly as players in this conflict. The delay was a clear-cut case of election-year politics dictating tactics, which always produces bad tactics and always sucks the most for the grunts who have to fight it out.

But still, the soldiers and marines in Iraq went off to vote for Bush—the pampered, Vietnam-avoiding Bush—in overwhelming numbers. It didn't make any sense.

Not long after I arrived in Fallujah, I heard about our battalion's first fatality. The young specialist had spent most of her entire year in relative safety on base at Abu Ghraib. Like most of us, she tried to get off base as much as possible, in spite of the dangers. A month before we were to go home, a roadside bomb blasted her truck while she was on a convoy. There was a lot of bitterness about this and a general opinion that it did not have to happen, that the convoy was not necessary. There was further bitterness over the fact that her truck wasn't armored up. Few of our vehicles were, and it was common for soldiers, throughout Iraq, to see their requests for armor denied. Why? We weren't allowed to take modified vehicles back home.

If this young woman's death was in fact unnecessary, I could understand the anger, but I was too overloaded with absurdities at that point to share it. Commanders everywhere in Iraq ordered unnecessary convoys and pointless "show the flag" patrols. The rule about armoring our vehicles was typical of a distant leadership who pushed men and equipment around like pieces in a board game, who seemed to care more about getting trucks back home than getting us back home. So was it surprising that maybe poor leadership got someone killed? Hardly surprising at all. As Donald Rumsfeld might have put it, we went to war with the leaders we had, not with the leaders we might wish to have at some future time.

The Fallujah mission called for, as my company commander said, "someone with a strong stomach." I accepted without knowing quite what that meant, just to get out of the enormous block of boredom and waste of taxpayer dollars that was Camp Slayer. I went with a sergeant, Marty, a corn-fed Ohio boy who was a good interrogator and a good leader, but a terrible Arabic speaker. Whenever he tried to talk to an Iraqi, I had to translate his bad Arabic into passable Arabic. But we worked well together and he was good company. I'd served with him on my second mission to al-Asad, and I knew he could handle rough conditions, which this assignment promised to provide.

A helicopter dropped us in the middle of a field in the middle of the night, with the battle of Fallujah raging at a fairly safe but still disorienting distance. After the chopper took off, we realized we had no idea where we were or how to find our camp. We were a hundred yards from a marine post, where we would be able to make a call to our point of contact, but we couldn't see it and it took us twenty-five minutes of stumbling around in the dark before we found it.

We learned about our mission in fragments. Apparently, there was a debate raging in the intelligence community about whether the people we were fighting in Fallujah were Iraqis or foreign jihadists. So our mission was to sort through the pockets and personal effects of people killed by our offensive and try to determine where they came from. At the same time, we would use some nifty new hardware to take the dead folks' biometrics—fingerprints, pictures, and retinal scans—and software to build a database to be used for future reference.

The bombardment of Fallujah was on a massive scale and we could hear it and see it all the time. To me, now, those were sounds of Iraqis dying by the thousands, and lying there waiting for me to pick their pockets. This assignment sounded ghoulish and disgusting, but in my state of mind at that time I could see one clear benefit: I wouldn't be interrogating living people. I wouldn't have to stand in judgment and struggle with trying to make a recommendation that had the potential to destroy their lives. No, the fates of these subjects would be sealed and their guilt or innocence would be irrelevant to my job.

We went into the city with marines and organized a small forward operating base at a compound we called the Potato Factory. The main building was an agricultural warehouse with high ceilings, moderate refrigeration, and small piles of potatoes scattered through its vast space. Smaller buildings were scattered around, and we moved quickly to clear them and envelop them in our perimeter. We found one that had a Red Crescent flag flying from the rooftop and a sign that clearly identified it as an aid station in English and Arabic. Inside were six Iraqis, whom we ushered into a spare room while we searched the house.

It looked like an aid station. The walls were covered with shelves and the shelves were covered with medical supplies, UN-packaged food, bottles of water clearly from America, and tons of soap. Way too much soap for the comfort of one of our marines, who looked at the soap, saw the pots that looked to me like someone had been rendering fat in them, and decided this was a bomb factory. Maybe, I thought, or maybe he had seen the bomb-making scene in the movie *Fight Club* and let his imagination run away with him. This is exactly the kind of situation I wanted to avoid, but I turned to the six men in the house and started my interrogations. Meanwhile, EOD got a call to come check this out.

I was so skeptical at this point in my tour that I still harbored doubts when EOD agreed that all this could well be used to make homemade C-4. They took the stuff out back and blew it up, shattering the windows in the house and covering the walls with debris.

The aid station's supervisor, whose brother owned the house, claimed that Americans came here all the time, and that's where he got the soap. I went pretty hard on him, but got nowhere. My interrogation wasn't important anyway. Once EOD delivered their judgment, these Iraqis were destined for Abu Ghraib, and there was nothing I could do, even if I wanted do. Honestly, if EOD said it was C-4, I was inclined to go along with that.

A few days later, the brother who ran the facility, Rasin, showed up, wearing a suit and leading a delegation from the Iraqi Ministry of Agriculture. We'd asked the ministry for permission to set up on this site, and they refused, not wanting a unique and essential way station for food to be used as a dumping point for dead Iraqis. Now they were here to protest. Rasin also wanted to know what we'd done with his brother and what had happened to the aid station. He was going to be a disappointed man.

After we arrested him and I interrogated him, he realized that no matter what he said he was going to prison. Still, he tried, asking me, "Think. If I were making bombs, and I knew Americans were here occupying these buildings, would I come back?" It was a good question, but not convincing enough to even generate a strong recommendation from me for his release. My report, such as it was, was handwritten and hasty. I did it mostly as a favor to my friends who I knew were at prison facilities in the rear, just so they'd have some paperwork with this prisoner.

The delegation went free, fuming at our occupation of their facility despite their refusal and over the arrest of Rasin. To them, the aid station would always be an aid station. To our command, it would always be an IED factory. In fact, the whole episode was condensed into a bullet point on a PowerPoint slide that I understand made the rounds at high levels. To me, it was just another unresolved case, another occasion for later doubt and uncomfortable reflection. For the time being, I let it go, and waited for the bodies to arrive.

I quickly learned that these marines were more like the ones I'd served with in al-Asad than the ones I'd served with in North Babel, and I soon learned why. Their commander, Lieutenant Colonel Franklin, was a humble, respectful, forceful leader who made smart decisions and hacked through red tape. Instead of setting himself up in a separate room, or taking the best room for himself and sending us outside, he put his cot next to those of his men and shared our close quarters.

After he saw me reading a Bible (you were never far from a copy of the Bible in Iraq—they were everywhere), I found that he was a devout Christian in the evangelical mold. We launched into a series of long conversations about his faith and his service, and I always left deeply impressed with his commitment to both, not to mention his patience with pointed questions from a committed agnostic. I needed this kind of conversation. I am not religious, or even "spiritual," but at the time I was struggling daily with how my duties often ran up against my morals. Franklin had thought deeply about how his service was in some ways incompatible with Christianity, and he was willing to talk openly about it. The chance to think about bigger questions for a while helped me prepare for what came next.

When the first body arrived, a small crowd of soldiers and marines gathered around to watch as someone unzipped the body bag. The dead man's skin was black, crawling with maggots, and wet with slime. Half his face was gone, and I peered into his skull. All his teeth were showing. Everyone in our small circle gagged.

We'd been briefed on what to expect by a chief warrant officer from Mortuary Affairs. She had the worst job in the military, reassembling dead marines and preparing their remains for the return home. She and her team were with us to help do the same for the dead of Fallujah. She told us we were going to gag, and that we'd never get fully used to the smell. Don't try to overcome it with Vicks VapoRub under the nostrils, she advised, because you will forever associate the smell of eucalyptus with the smell of the dead.

This first body didn't have much in the way of retina or fingerprints to scan, so we took a picture of his face—which not even his mother could recognize—cut off his clothes (I tried to make out the logo on his T-shirt, but it was in tatters), emptied his pockets, put all his belongings in a bag, tagged him with a number, labeled his stuff, and dragged his body bag off to the side.

A team of marines was out there in Fallujah, which was already more than half destroyed, grabbing bodies for us to examine. They were worried about booby traps, so they fashioned a grappling hook out of rebar and would drag each corpse down the street for a while behind their truck before bagging it. They had no trouble finding bodies, and the battle was still going on in parts of the city, so there was a steady stream of new customers for our examination. The first day we got ten, some days we got more. We tagged and bagged over five hundred over the course of four weeks.

At first, they were all old, rotten, and maggot-infested, barely recognizable as human. It was worse when they started bringing in fresh bodies that stared off into space. There was still a person there. If they were fresh, we could easily tell what killed them. We could count the bullet holes or see where an explosion had caved in their skulls. And if they were still more or less intact, I'd have to pull out the fingerprint scanner and try to twist their stiff hands over the screen.

Many of the dead carried ammo or other military gear. I told myself that they knew what they were getting into, but no one really knows what they're in for when they set themselves up to die.

The sight of women and children blown apart was heart-wrenching, and I never had time to prepare for it. When I unzipped the bag, I never knew what was going to be inside. If the bag felt light, it could be a partial torso, or it could be a kid.

One of the army sergeants working with us started to annoy me. He was making a big show of how he wasn't afraid to get gore all over his gloved hands, and he spoke loudly and disparagingly about the dead. He also saw "evidence" of foreign fighters everywhere. A dead guy whose Koran was printed in Algeria must be an Algerian. Another dead man must be Hezbollah because he wore khaki pants and a black T-shirt.

There were a few who were obviously foreign because they carried their passports. I wondered a lot about the dead man with the Russian passport. What was his story, and what did he hope to accomplish here?

Some of the bodies were mutilated. One very fresh corpse had his lips removed and a permanent smile cut into his face with what must have been a very sharp knife. He looked like the victims of the Joker villain in *Batman* comics. A few days later we got another one who'd received the same treatment.

I was collecting bits of gore and body grease on my uniform as I handled one dead man after another. The stink was with me all day, all night, while I ate, while I read, and while I slept. I could go outside and stand there and breathe deeply, and still smell it. We had no shower, no way to wash the dead off our living skin. I felt like I was drawing flies.

We had a satellite phone and a lot of minutes for personal calls. During most of my early tour, I'd rarely call people at home. During this mission, I reached out often, but it was always very strange. I always ended the calls thinking that I was no longer of the world.

Of course, it hardly bears mention that we were frequently taking incoming fire. I was on the phone with my closest friend during a particularly bad mortar storm, one of the times that they seemed to be marching ever closer, and I was listening to him prattle on about a girlfriend situation that to him must have been the most important thing in his world. I was trying to focus on his problem through a cloud of fear and an awareness of the hundreds of dead bodies piled up inside. He paused when a shell fell close.

"What was that?"

"A mortar, Dan. Look, they're really pounding us hard."

"Oh." He paused to consider this, and then seemed to decide that his problem really was more important. "Well, anyway, so then she said . . ." I resisted the temptation to hang up.

I understood my friend's inability to connect with me in that moment. I realized it that night while watching a DVD. On most bases, the most popular movies were—what else?—war movies. And not just the Reagan-era glorifications like *Top Gun, Red Dawn,* or *Rambo.* Our warriors liked antiwar films like *Platoon, Full Metal Jacket, Apocalypse Now,* and *Three Kings* even more. The irony wasn't lost on them, and in a way they felt they were getting one over on the directors by absorbing the violence and rejecting the message.

But, in this warehouse in Fallujah, war movies were not to be found, and I think it had to do with our daily look at the final end product of war. Here, we went for pure cinematic escapism. So I was sitting with a marine sergeant watching a saccharine romantic comedy staring Jennifer Garner, totally absorbed and fascinated, when he pointed out in his rich Kentucky accent, "We're two trained killers about a half mile from the hottest combat zone in the world and we're watching 13 Going on 30."

This was, for me, just a little beyond entertainment. I would soon be going back to the world depicted in this movie, where the most important things were shopping, looking good, getting the guy or girl, and completing your own pathetically short journey of self-discovery. It was a mirror image of Americans trying to peer into my world by watching war movies. What I saw was frightening, alien, and incomprehensible.

The days piled on and the weeks blurred into one another. I felt like the dead would never stop coming. We'd started this job will all due seriousness and solemnity, but we soon started to crack.

One of the Mortuary Affairs guys was trying to reassemble a body that had been ripped into maybe a dozen different pieces and left to rot. He picked up and pondered a shinbone that had lost all its flesh but still had a sneaker attached. He rooted around in the body bag and found another just like it, and entertained us with a little dance that recalled Charlie Chaplin's performance with two forks stuck in two potatoes.

Standing next to one of my army buddies, one who was very quiet and never made jokes, we unzipped a bag to find a torso that had been hollowed out. There was nothing there but a set of ribs speckled with pieces of charred flesh. We stood there in silence for a minute. I couldn't believe it when my buddy deadpanned, "Man, I can't wait to get home and go to Tony Roma's." At that moment, it was the funniest thing I'd ever heard in Iraq.

I laughed at the dead, and they took their revenge as I slept. I started having a recurring nightmare in which I was lying down next to the body bags and couldn't get up. I could feel maggots crawling on me. I knew, each and every time, that the longer I stayed, the greater the chance that I would never be able to leave. In my dream, I tried to wake myself up, but the dream kept lasting longer and longer. I tried to avoid sleeping as much as possible.

I thought the dream would stop once I left this place, then I thought the dream would stop once I left Iraq, then I thought it would stop once I left the army. But it followed me all the way back to Chicago.

PART V

MY RETURN AND LESSONS LEARNED

Let us set for ourselves a standard so high that it will be a glory to live up to it, and then let us live up to it and add a new laurel to the crown of America.

—President Woodrow Wilson

We also have to work, though, sort of the dark side, if you will.

—Vice President Dick Cheney

CHAPTER 24

Panic

After three flights and a five-hour delay in Atlanta, we got into Fort Gordon sometime between one and two in the morning, and still they wouldn't let us go. We had to stand in formation, wait, wait, and wait, until the motor pool was totally ready and we could march in to meet a crowd of officers and families and members of our battalion who didn't deploy with us. Then we had to listen to speeches.

I'd gotten myself really worked up about how the bars had by now already closed and how all this pomp was interfering with my idea of a homecoming, which involved not parades and flags and speeches, but cheap beer, tawdry sex, and rolling around in a dirty gutter. I'd have continued with my self-absorbed fuming, but someone pointed out to me two civilians standing quietly alone in a corner. The parents of the young woman killed in a convoy—our only fatality—had come here to welcome *us* home.

I'd not known this woman very well and the news of her death barely affected me in Iraq. Now, looking at her parents, I was devastated. They watched everyone except their daughter get off the plane, and they were now surrounded by everyone else's joyful reunions. How could they stand it? How could they be here, and how could they look at us? I wanted to talk to them, but what would I say? I suddenly felt hollow inside, and even though the sight of them pained me, I couldn't take my eyes off them.

We got one day off, and then we fell back into the typical army routine.

Physical training in the morning, followed by formation, followed by whatever mind-numbing tasks had to be done next.

As much as I tried to push memories of Iraq out of my mind, I could feel anxiety creeping over me. Most of us were jumpy. Most of us reacted badly when a car backfired or a Dumpster lid slammed too loudly. We all had our separate issues, but I was trying to figure out why I felt such an acute combination of anxiety and depression. As far as trauma, I'd gotten off fairly easy. I hadn't seen buddies killed, I hadn't done any killing myself. I should have been able to get over this soon. I put it off to just needing a vacation, and luckily I had one coming up.

Going back to Chicago, a couple weeks after returning to Fort Gordon, was much the same as going back from Iraq months before. I still felt that disconnect and still felt general anger toward my fellow Americans for their detachment from the war. I was so wound up I got into two near fights. One was with a cousin who was drunk at a family reunion, who asked me if I tortured anyone and made it clear that he hoped the answer was yes because he wanted those terrorists either in severe pain or dead. Our family separated us once he learned about my views on the subject and called me a traitor. Having just spent a year in Iraq, I wasn't going to take that.

The next near fight was with a total stranger who didn't deserve to be pulled into my private hell, but he was driving a Hummer with a yellow ribbon on the back. Something about seeing a luxury version of the same vehicles we'd risked our lives in really set me off, and the yellow ribbon was just too much. I couldn't even articulate to this poor fool why I was so mad, but he kept asking me if I was jealous that I didn't have one. That brought out the "I just got back from Iraq" part of my rant, and he hastened to explain to me how he supported the troops. I was an asshole, but I had his support anyway.

I was on a hair trigger and couldn't seem to calm down. In fact, it was getting worse. Late in my vacation, the anxiety tried to push its way out and I had my first full-blown panic attack, which hit me in the middle of the night. I was shaking and my mind was racing. There was a woman next to me asking if I was okay, and I said no, I was not. I felt like jumping out a window, out of the confines of my friend's small apartment. I spent a good part of the night standing naked in the middle of the kitchen, trying to breathe. It was intolerable to be in my own skin and I couldn't get ahold of my racing thoughts. The next night it was the same damn thing, the day after that I was back at Fort Gordon, and the same thing happened again my first night back.

At the emergency room on base the following day, they asked me if I wanted to hurt myself or others. No. Do you want to die? I told them I couldn't take another night of this and I'd rather be dead than go through another panic attack. That was partially true, probably just a little hyperbolic. More accurately, I continually felt like I was just about to die. I was put under observation and my first sergeant, P. Edgar, got a call. He came by and I tried to talk to him about what was happening, and couldn't get the words out of my throat. My breathing was shallow and my voice shaky. I tried to sign papers they thrust in front of me, and the pen flailed around madly in my hands.

The army started me up on two potent and (I found out later) extremely addictive drugs that took the edge off. I ate them like candies. These were just the first of the six different drugs I'd receive while under army psychiatric care. Next, I started sessions with a counselor and a psychiatrist, which were the first occasions I had to sit and talk at length about torture.

I liked my psychotherapist, Dr. Baum, but I had to argue with what she was trying to achieve. She wanted to cleanse the guilt I carried around with me, which would help give me a start on dealing with the depression, and remove some of the inner conflict that was causing the anxiety. The quickest way out was to get me to deny responsibility.

People do terrible things during war. I was acting under orders. Had I heard of the Milgram experiment? Yes, I told her, I had. (This surprised her.) This was the experiment where normal people were ordered to deliver shocks to someone behind a curtain. The shocks were not real, and the screams of agony were those of an actor, but the subject didn't know that. Nevertheless, they continued to follow orders. "People go into a state of agency and act not on their own volition," she explained to me. She made it sound like I didn't have a choice, and I knew that was wrong.

As we talked over several sessions, we discussed the circumstances surrounding the actions more than the actions themselves. I could see what lay ahead if I chose this direction, and it seemed to me like the worst kind of moral relativism. If I could legitimately absolve myself of responsibility, anyone could, in just about any situation.

Stanley Milgram himself wrote: "Even Eichmann was sickened when he toured the concentration camps, but to participate in mass murder he had only to sit at a desk and shuffle papers." Meanwhile, the man who did the killing "was able to justify his behavior on the grounds that he was only following orders from above. . . ." In this, or any organization, where everyone believes he is simply an agent, and believes he is acting not of his own volition, as Milgram concluded, "The person who assumes full responsibility for the act has evaporated."[1]

Dr. Baum offered me that escape hatch; I contemplated it, and refused. Looking at this problem of my guilt, it became clear that it was not in the realm of psychology, but morality. Finally, I told her, "If you don't include torturing helpless prisoners in your definition of evil, your definition of evil is meaningless." To that she simply nodded.

If the problem here was one of evil, though, the lasting effects on me were more than just guilt. I surfaced something very dark and unsettling that won't go away. I fed it and followed it, and although I was fully aware of what I was doing, I was only dimly aware of where it was leading me. In Iraq, against the backdrop of war and with like-minded soldiers, I could deal with that awareness, but back home with friends and family, it was unbearable. Being alone was even worse.

I have never owned a lot and have never identified myself with my job. I've drifted and looked for experiences, for walls to glimpse over and an abyss in which to swim. Because I could never identify myself with my possessions, how much money I made, what kind of profession I was in, or where I was living at that particular time, my identity became lashed tightly to my morality. I'd never been a perfect person, but I'd never failed as completely as I had in Mosul.

So now, if I was a moral failure, what was left? Dr. Baum, as helpful as she tried to be, never realized this wasn't just about me doing something wrong

---

[1] Stanley Milgram, quoted on John Conroy, *Unspeakable Acts, Ordinary People: The Dynamics of Torture*, p. 99.

and feeling bad about it. This was a full-blown crisis of self. I am not who I thought I was.

The army mandates regular training on various subjects, which usually involve a lot of PowerPoint presentations. One of the subjects in regular rotation was "The Seven Army Values." These values sound timeless, but as formal declarations of principle, they've only been around since 1998, when the army included them in basic training as a quick fix to a series of sexual harassment scandals. We had to carry them around on little wallet-sized cards; being caught without your card was almost as bad as being caught out of uniform. Officers or sergeants major would stop us at odd and random times and ask us to repeat them. Luckily, the army believes that any concept worth communicating must have an acronym, which makes things easier to remember. The Seven Army Values were contained in an acronym that would have been at home on the vanity license plate of any inspirational and motivational speaker, "LDRSHIP." That stands for Loyalty, Duty, Respect, Selfless service, Honor, Integrity, and Personal courage.

They were fine words, but the training around them always just went too far into the realm of pop psychology and self-esteem building, like Dr. Phil dressed in camouflage. But now, with all of us just back from Iraq, it seemed to me to be wildly inappropriate. I had not seen the army's values reflected in the army's conduct, or in my own conduct.

About halfway through the lecture, I lost it. "I can't believe you're teaching this class. This is hypocrisy. The mission was total bullshit. We didn't act on our values. We ruined the lives of thousands of Iraqis for no purpose. Is that honorable? Selfless? Respectful? Rumsfeld and Bush are war criminals and should be tried in international court." This was insubordination on a high level, but I didn't care anymore.

I went on like this for I don't know how long. I wasn't making a lot of sense. I was really on the verge of embarrassing myself, when our platoon sergeant and instructor of this class, Staff Sergeant Spencer, actually came to my rescue. Spencer really did embody these values, and on a much deeper level than what the army could reach through a PowerPoint slide. He never lost his cool. He engaged me with concerned questioning and turned my rant into a conversation. I still think of him as a kind of calm Buddha, a real prince. We talked one-on-one after the lecture, and I apologized for making a scene, but he was more concerned about my mental state. If I couldn't control my anxiety and rage, I would have real problems in the army. I knew he was right. Not only was I an affront to my leadership, I was a drain on morale, because when I lashed out like this, other soldiers secretly cheered me on and told me so later.

My friend Tomas started his application for conscientious objector status. As I mentioned before, this route was closed to me because I was merely opposed to "this war now" and not opposed to "all war ever," but I wished Tomas well and had no doubt he should have been released as a pacifist. Alas, he was turned down with extreme prejudice.

Tomas's leaders had learned to hate this newly minted left-winger for his sass, his rabble-rousing, and especially for his views, and set about to make his life miserable. I was a witness at his hearing and I was appalled when one after another of his leaders, including the company commander, testified that Tomas was not a moral human being. How could they make that judgment on Tomas's very soul? Because Tomas didn't have a religious basis for his claim, they didn't believe it was valid. If he had no religion, he had no morals, and therefore he had no moral basis for objecting to war. His objection was clearly political, the investigator decided, and not moral.

Just before Tomas's hearing, as if to make a point, the same group of knuckleheads had let another member of our company sail through CO status, but this man actually wanted to become a priest. So his decision was deemed moral, not just political. And as if to rub Tomas's face in it, they came to believe that Tomas was just copying this first guy who got out. Tomas had years to go. He was certain to be going back to Iraq.

Staff Sergeant Spencer encouraged me to follow up with CID, despite my two previous interviews and the multiple reports submitted to the marines at North Babel. I sat for an interview, talking for the third time to special agents who could not turn up any other sworn statements I'd made. I thought that providing more information to investigators would be therapeutic, maybe calm down my anxiety and anger, but when I learned that there was not only no apparent action from my previous statements, but no record of them, the interview proved to be a real setback.

After about a dozen meetings, Dr. Baum came to the conclusion I was suffering from adjustment disorder and being in the army directly caused this condition. If I were removed from the stressor, the army, I would fully recover, by the very definition of the disorder, within six months. If not, I would continue to be a discipline problem and a drain on morale and resources. In one of our sessions, she explained this to me, and told me that I basically had no business being in the army but that this was no reflection on my past service or on me as a person. With me constantly popping pills to avoid panic attacks, arguing with my superiors, suffering through a steady stream of nightmares, and coming to the conclusion that I was a moral failure, I was in no position to argue.

Nor was I inclined to: with a little less than a year on my contract, I could easily be sent back to Iraq, caught up in stop-loss, and denied the chance to leave the army when my contract expired. They had the power to trash my contract and keep me for years beyond my original departure date. It was happening all the time now, and my knowledge of Arabic made me an especially attractive target. I accepted Dr. Baum's diagnosis, not that I actually had a choice.

I received an honorable discharge in July 2005.

CHAPTER 25

Terror

I had a girlfriend now in Chicago, Amy, who was going to be a big help if she could stand my insanity.

My first night back, we shut off the lights, and I immediately jumped up. "There's a bat in here!" There was nothing. I could have sworn there was a bat. "Uh-oh," I said. We both realized there was something terribly wrong.

After I walked out of the gates of Fort Gordon for the last time, without my uniform, I felt incredible joy. I had a plan to house-sit in New Orleans, calm down, relax, then move back to Chicago and get a place and a job and maybe one day I'd wake up and realize this had all been just a dream.

Going to New Orleans was a mistake. The friends I house-sat for were very generous to put me up, but after Amy visited for a few days, I was totally alone. The anxiety attacks were back in full force and I was adjusting to new medications; the army had loaded me up with prescriptions before I left. I couldn't sleep and I couldn't shut down my racing mind, so I hit the booze, and hard. By drinking enough gin, I could achieve something that slightly resembled sleep each night, but gin also left my psychological defenses even weaker than before, which led to more drinking. I developed a vague idea that this was spinning out of control, but didn't have the strength to stop it. I was lucky that my friends returned to their home and got me moving again.

On the train ride to Chicago, I felt intensely sick, worse than I'd ever experienced. Waves of nausea were slamming into me and my hands wouldn't stop trembling. I grabbed one hand with the other, and they both started shaking. I started to worry.

Amy picked me up, left me at her apartment, and went to work. I couldn't sleep on account of the loud music her neighbors were playing, all day. It was driving me crazy, and who would play klezmer all day at top volume? When Amy returned home, I asked her about her neighbors and their music, and she couldn't hear a thing. Now it was bluegrass. "Can you hear it, the fiddles? It's Bill Monroe! 'Blue Moon of Kentucky'!" I walked over to the A/C window unit and turned it off so she could hear. The music stopped. I turned the A/C on, and it started again. Strange.

So we got out of the apartment and I felt better. When we returned, I just needed some rest, but then we had this problem with the bats in Amy's apartment. I kept pointing them out, and described them to her. Then the bat turned into a large purple jellyfish, and I tried to explain that to her too. As she pointed up at the ceiling, saying, "Is it there?" the jellyfish landed on her arm.

Amy fell asleep about the time the cockroaches came. They swarmed all over the ceiling in superfast swirling patterns. I wanted to shut my eyes, but the visions I had with my eyes closed were maddening: rapidly moving pictures, so very vivid, of nonsensical images mixed with scenes from Iraq interlaced with a surreal American dreamscape. I opened my eyes and the cockroaches were still there, and sometimes snakes poured out of the shadows on the walls. I wasn't afraid of these images, but the implication of them was worrisome and I couldn't sleep.

This went on for three days. Any white noise became talk radio or music. The air conditioner announced itself as a radio station, "one-oh-two point five, the K-bomb," and the refrigerator was singing German folk songs. I was losing my mind from sleep deprivation, and I was certain that whatever last vestiges of sanity I had left would soon be gone. I'd live my life in a small white cell, hearing things, seeing things, and never sleeping. I made the totally uninformed decision to stop all my meds. In the evening of the third night I was terrified of spending another night like that and called a cousin who was a psychiatrist. She convinced me to see someone the next day.

I went to the VA hospital, and, after I was stripped and searched by a policeman and given a prisoner's jumpsuit to wear, they locked me up. This was standard procedure but I didn't know it at the time. For those two hours I was under observation, I thought they were going to commit me right then and my new life in a nightmare fantasy world would begin.

But they let me go, and that night it all stopped. I turned on the window unit, and it was just a window unit. I turned off the lamp, and I saw shadows and streetlights, but no animals came up out of my id to haunt me. I finally got the most solid sleep I'd had in weeks.

I'll never know what caused this, but it was probably a combination of a bad reaction to the medication, lack of sleep, and an inordinate amount of gin, all piled on top of latent anxiety, crushing depression, guilt, fear, and the haunting moral questions. But it was mostly the medication. Months later, I tried to restart my meds and felt the same creepy anxiety come up on me within hours. I flushed the medications, and my sick mind was left to care for itself.

My last encounter with CID convinced me to go to the media. The army clearly had no interest in investigating itself, and the public still debated not just whether torture was acceptable but even whether it was actually going on in Iraq.

I went to the media fully admitting that I'd done terrible things, and the very last thing I wanted was to gain any kind of celebrity for my actions in Iraq. I hoped that if I made a few appearances, it could reframe the public debate, spur a more serious investigation, and let people know about some of the things that were being done in their names.

I gave my first interview to a public radio station in San Francisco, where a friend of mine produced a news show, and from there I made no other effort to "publicize" myself to TV or radio. Later, I met a lawyer who was bringing a civil suit against a defense contractor in Iraq. He gave my phone number to a *Frontline* producer and I made an appearance in a documentary. At the time, I was the only army interrogator willing to talk openly about abuses I had participated in, so I was very suddenly in high demand. I turned down many more interview requests than I accepted. It was still very difficult to discuss this, plus, some of the reporters and producers who called had that same creepy tone I got from people who asked if I'd killed anyone. They were looking for the brutality, not the morality.

The interviews I did do were always a chance to talk to someone who was very well informed about the torture debate in America, and that was consistently refreshing. All my interviewers were tough and demanding and took this stuff as seriously as I did. I think they saw that I was sincere in my motivations—they probably get a lot of people trying to simply promote themselves, so it might have been novel for them to interview someone who didn't want the limelight but felt compelled to stand in it briefly for a good cause.

The interviews always felt right while they were going on, but I always left feeling dirty, not at all cleansed, not the way confession is supposed to make you feel. I knew that my words would always be edited and cut, or at least packaged and promoted, to serve the purpose of the reporter or the show. I'd always feel like I'd lost control over what I was trying to say, and my terrible moral failings were now the property of someone else who would bend them for their purposes.

The producers and reporters always did a good job with my interviews, and I never felt totally betrayed. But larger forces were still sweeping me along. There were so many filters between myself and the viewer or reader, including the intense and polarized political climate that all my statements had to pass through.

With the reporters aching to get the best possible story, I found, they generally wanted to hear about the worst abuses. The problem was that the worst abuses I knew about always came to me secondhand. I saw the injuries, and I heard the stories, but I was not witness to those actual events. Nevertheless, any reporter doing his job is going to push on those more brutal tales, leaving behind the facts of what I actually did myself.

I was slow to realize this, but audiences were not. I took a lot of criticism for making accusations based on evidence that, while overwhelming, was also circumstantial. Because some of the reporters didn't want to dwell on my own actions, a number of ex-military and right-wing bloggers took that as an opening to call me a hypocrite. I took part in a number of online exchanges with ex-military who couldn't get past these problems inherent in the reporting, and who couldn't let go of their code of silence. To them, I was nothing more than a "buddy fucker," or a "shitbird."

I fully accept that I violated their code of silence, because I never agreed to it in the first place. "Duty" to some in the military means closing ranks and keeping quiet about the military's own failings and illegal activities, no matter what. It helps preserve the brotherhood and helps keep civilians out. "Duty," to me, means both owning up to what you have done and reporting the illegal activity of others. I took no joy in reporting abuse; I simply wanted it to stop.

Most of the folks who attacked me in the blogosphere did not want it to stop. They felt it was perfectly legal and, if not legal, then certainly justified. But either way, even though they were totally comfortable with it themselves and among other military types, they didn't want the rest of the nation, the people who "can't handle the truth," to openly debate the issues. I find this very telling.

After the *Frontline* documentary aired, I got a call from a CID special agent, who pointedly asked me why I didn't go to CID before I went to the media. Amazing. Still, after all this, none of my sworn statements had surfaced. As for the reports I put in to the marines at North Babel, the marines claimed they had only one of the three I formally submitted. A year later, eighteen months after I left North Babel, the Naval Criminal Investigative Service contacted me and wanted sworn statements, especially concerning the man who claimed his foot had been smashed with the back of an axe head. That report I had submitted was just beginning to be investigated. The marines' public affairs unit had previously denied the existence of my report on this episode.

As I mentioned, few interviewers wanted to address my own abuse directly. Maybe my own stories weren't sensational enough, or maybe their idea of a whistleblower didn't include someone who points to his own actions as evidence, or maybe they didn't want to confront me. One exception that stands out in my mind was a Danish filmmaker who caught me off guard. By the time he interviewed me, I'd gotten used to answering the same questions and had grown more confident in my presence before the camera. But I wasn't prepared when he asked me why I shouldn't be tried for war crimes. He didn't accept that I was in the clear because I was following orders. Everyone knows, he said, that the Nuremburg defense is morally bankrupt.

I was angry and defensive, but I couldn't deny what he was saying. I fumbled through that part of the interview, claiming that I was as careful as I could be to follow the law, and added that I wasn't as bad as many others. I've since learned that torturers invariably try to alleviate their guilt by pointing to worse cases, and no matter how bad torture gets, there always seems to be a worse case to point to. So my answer was following a classic pattern of shifting blame and comparing actions to worse cases. Obviously, I was trying a little moral relativism to escape a set of crushing and unavoidable conclusions.

It's not the answer I would give today. The more I come to terms with what I did in Mosul, the more it seems that I had simply no moral justification and tenuous legal justification. I knew, when I crossed into the abyss that is Iraq, that the year ahead would change me forever, and I knew I was in for an experience few could ever have. I knew this, but I couldn't even begin to fathom the full depth of the change or the experience. I didn't know I would discover and indulge my own evil. And now that it has surfaced, I fear that, even if I never act on it again, it will be my constant companion for the rest of my life.

CHAPTER 26

Torture

I was sitting in the backseat of a car, playing with my cousin's eight-month-old son while my cousin drove. He was playfully testing the limits of my tolerance, and annoying my cousin at the same time. She pleaded with him to stop, "You can't do that to Tony. You're torturing him. You can't torture . . ." And she trailed off. She realized she was going to call me "the torturer," And realized she was very uncomfortable vocalizing that thought. If that is what I am, I thought, should she be letting me play with her baby?

I've been very open in very public forums about what I did, and it's been strange watching my friends, and especially my family, try to adjust. Most people do a series of mental gymnastics and settle on the idea that the Tony they know is still a good guy, and in some way he was a different person in Iraq. Someone else did those things. Their discomfort reflects exactly what I see in this country at large. Despite the fact that we are seriously and openly talking about torture, I don't think we really want to confront, at all, what it really means.

I can't speak about the efficacy of torture with authority. I never got intelligence using torture, but it is possible that I was a bad torturer and perhaps a bad interrogator. But since every debate about torture involves the question of whether it works, I'll address the practicality of the issue as well as I can. A torturer can often get an innocent man to confess to murder. We know this from domestic cases of police interrogation. For example, in 2003, then Governor Ryan of Illinois exonerated four men on death row who had confessed under torture to crimes they did not commit.[1]

But a confession, valid or invalid, is not intelligence. A confession is backward-looking and not the forward-looking kind of information a commander wants in the field, nor the kind of information an investigator needs to thwart a terrorist attack. The military is not requesting permission to torture, nor is the FBI. Our civilian leadership in Washington, not the professionals, wanted to legalize torture.

I spoke with Joe Navarro, a retired FBI agent and an expert in the field of interrogation. Joe has had great success gathering intelligence during interrogations and interviews without the use of torture. He outlined four main reasons why torture is ineffective. First, talk can't be confused with truth. A torture victim will say anything, true or false, to get the pain to stop. Second, the stress pain creates confuses the subject and he simply can't remember details well enough to produce good intelligence. Third, the torture subject may die or go into shock, in which case no information can be obtained from him. Finally, and perhaps most compelling, the torture victim, if he tells the interrogator anything at all, is likely to give one piece of information, or very little information, whereas a cooperative source will talk and continue talking. Joe added that he believes that torture strengthens the resolve of the detainee, citing Senator John McCain, who, after having his shoulder torn from its socket by interrogators in Vietnam, was more determined than ever to keep his silence.

My experience tends to bear this out. But those who want to legalize torture can, and will, continue to come up with examples where torture "worked." I myself interrogated prisoners who, I heard secondhand, had been tortured, and limited information was supposedly gained. The bodyguard in Abu Ghraib and the suspected insurgent who had been waterboarded in North Babel are two main examples in this book. Jafar, whom I interrogated in Mosul, admitted to all kinds of insurgent activity, after he'd spent some time with the special ops interrogators. These are cases where torture may have

---

[1] Steve Mills and Maurice Possley, "Ryan to Pardon 4 on Death Row," *Chicago Tribune*, January 10, 2003, p. 1.

"worked" in that some limited information was gained. I don't like to admit the possibility that even scant pieces of information or intel can be gained from torture, but to be honest, the examples may be out there. If we always argue for or against torture on grounds of efficacy, however, we will always be stuck in the realm of "dueling anecdotes." We have to take this debate to another level.

My opposition to torture rests entirely on moral grounds. I'm opposed to its use in all circumstances. Americans should never use torture, and to this there should be no exceptions. Even if there were practical reasons to torture someone in particular situations, the consequences of torture go far beyond individuals and individual circumstances, so we can't let short-term gain or practical considerations decide this question for us. We have to look at a much larger picture before we decide. This is how, after my experiences in Mosul, the larger facts about torture appear to me.

Torture cannot be contained. It is not something you can do once and then go back to your regular routine, hoping you won't have to do it again, but keeping it in reserve just in case. As a method, as a human interaction, and as a moral choice, it is simply too large and too powerful to confine.

Rights advocates, from those who oppose gun control to those who oppose school prayer and everything in between, have used the slippery-slope argument so promiscuously that it's become unconvincing. So I want to make clear that my view of torture isn't exactly a slippery slope. When we start using torture, we don't just fall down a pit. There's a mechanism of many interlocking parts that pushes the thing forward. It grows like an ink stain and spreads like a disease, and along the way its face changes, so you end up in a place totally unlike where you started. But most important, unlike gun control or school prayer, you can't have just a little bit of tightly regulated torture. It can't help but expand.

One of the reasons lies in the interaction between the torturer and the victim. I learned in Mosul, while trying a set of techniques on prisoners, that torture cannot be effective, even for achieving the limited goal of domination over a prisoner, unless there is escalation and the continued threat of escalation. If a person is in pain, he is enduring that pain. It may be excruciating and he may wish for death, but he is still enduring it, and he knows that he is enduring it. He has no reason to give the torturer what he wants unless there is the threat of more pain and worse pain.

In Mosul, the silence of my prisoners illuminated this for me. I could cause fear, but it would plateau, and I found myself wanting to go further, push harder, and cause more pain. The fear told me I was on the "right track," so taking it to the next level seemed like the right thing to do. Once I got started, it seemed pointless to stop, and each escalation appeared seamless, natural, and justified.

It's not just me who's noticed that the "next level" is more serious to prisoners than the current situation. The CIA's "Human Resource Exploitation Training Manual" notes that "the threat of coercion usually weakens or destroys resistance more effectively than coercion itself. For example, the threat to inflict pain can trigger fears more damaging than the immediate sensation of pain." The same manual notes, ominously, that an interrogator should never make a threat he can't carry out.[2]

In the small and very personal interaction of torturer and prisoner, we can see an inevitable escalation that bleeds over into the world outside the interrogation booth. In the beginning of America's response to 9/11, interrogators in Afghanistan started using a set of enhancements, including sleep deprivation and stress positions, which they thought were quite mild. Before long, prisoners were dying during interrogations. The Bush administration approved a set of expanded techniques for a select set of prisoners at Guantánamo, and these techniques soon migrated to Iraq. In Mosul, the rumors and eyewitness accounts of what our special forces were doing migrated to us lowly army interrogators. The torture lite enhancements could not be confined by geography, nor could they be confined to a specific class of prisoners. In Mosul, once we found others were using these techniques, we saw no reason we should not do the same. We heard they were successful and we wanted to be successful also.

Among our small group of army interrogators, we escalated from stress positions and sleep deprivation to muzzled dogs, and our harsh tactics migrated

---

[2] Quoted in McCoy, A Question of Torture, p. 91.

from a particular pair of prisoners to all prisoners in a matter of weeks. I noted earlier how one interrogator would prepare for each and every interrogation by putting the detainee in a stress position for forty-five minutes before he ever asked a single question. This seemed logical. If he assumed these techniques worked and were legal (and because of the written rules we saw, we all certainly thought they were), why not use them every chance he got?

One other change happened in parallel with our increasing torture: we moved from seeking intelligence, our original justification, to seeking confessions. It was as if the domination we exercised over our prisoners was not complete until they admitted what they had done. This was the most frightening change that came over us, because it signaled a shift from torture for an intelligence purpose to torture for the sole purpose of controlling another. We all know from 1984 why Winston Smith wasn't simply killed when he was captured. The state could only consider itself dominant if it tortured this man until he confessed and renounced his crimes.

Once introduced into war, torture will inevitably spread because the ticking bombs are everywhere. Each and every prisoner, without exception, has the potential to be the one that provides the information that will save American lives. So if you accept the logic that we have to perform torture to prevent deaths, each and every prisoner is deserving of torture. In a situation like Iraq, it wasn't just a few abstract lives that might be saved somewhere, at some future time. The mortars came almost every day. The life in question was my very own.

Once we accepted that any prisoner might be holding information that could save lives, we gladly used everything in our toolbox on everyone. This resulted in an expansion of the class of people who could be tortured. Now it included people who had been picked up for questioning but were not suspected of being insurgents, and it included people who were picked up on hunches—people against whom we had no solid evidence—and it included relatives of our real targets. Again, I see the spread of torture to these groups as natural and inevitable. At the time, I barely noticed it happening.

We should be very concerned about this steady progression and where it will lead, because the essence of torture—tyrannical control over the will of another—is everything that a free and democratic society is supposed to stand against. We should be very skeptical of the idea that our use of torture overseas will never come home.

In watching my friends, family, and new acquaintances try to imagine that my acts of torture were committed not by Tony, but by Tony's evil twin, I've noticed something else, something very disturbing. People are absolutely fascinated by torture. As soon as someone learns that I was an interrogator, I can see him formulate the next question and look for an opening in which to spring it: "Did you torture anyone?" It comes from people all across the political spectrum, from people both disgusted by torture and from people who actually want troops to do it. Either way, it's a fascinating subject.

The United States participated in and propagated torture throughout the Cold War, but it was always something that the general public wanted to deny, and our secretive branches of government obliged. Since 9/11, however, the debate has been out in the open and a large majority of people is fully willing to support torture. Why? We never openly supported torture against agents of the Soviet Union, and it was a real threat to the very existence of our nation in a way the terrorists can never be. So isn't the act of putting torture on the table now a totally disproportionate response?

Those attacks, coming as they did from people who rejected the rules of civilization, made us want to respond in kind. Suddenly, their defeat was not enough. Standard military operations using high-tech weaponry and the utter obliteration of the enemy via cruise missiles and five-thousand-pound bombs was not enough. They should be made to feel the same pain we felt, and America, the mightiest power in history, should be able to dominate this enemy utterly and tyrannically. It came to be perceived as our right, due to us as a hegemonic power. So we suddenly had no problem putting absolute tyrannical power in the hands of army specialists. They would show each terrorist the face of America, and they would dominate the terrorists' very souls as much as our military dominates the battlefield. That's the kind of victory I believe many Americans want.

As I discovered in Mosul, this kind of dominance requires evil. The prisoner will not break unless he believes the potential for escalation is endless, and the only way to convince him of that is to be the embodiment of evil. For a truly evil person, the rules of civilization do not apply and any course of action is possible. The prisoner who faces an evil captor is transported to a totally alien world that makes no sense and that he finds impossible to fathom. This is where true terror and panic set in, for the prisoner can never know, or even imagine, what is next. If we want torture to "work," this is where we have to go. So we have to ask ourselves: Is this what we want?

This kind of evil is true of al-Qaeda. They have convinced us that they are evil people who ignore the rules of civilization, and their evil has an effect on us. All they lack is the absolute power over us that a torturer has over a captive. Many Americans, on the other hand, believe that we do have that power, and that using it is a perfectly legitimate response.

On the Senate floor, arguing for his antitorture amendment, Senator McCain made all the standard practical arguments about the inefficacy of torture that I think miss the point. But his most powerful argument was when he told an opponent, tersely, that this issue was "not about who they are," meaning the terrorists. "It's about who *we* are." This is what we have to decide. Torture might be an effective way to gather intelligence. It can be a very emotionally satisfying response to the vicious 9/11 attacks. But it also has the power to define what America is in ways that we cannot fully control.

In a survey taken around the time McCain's amendment was a matter of serious debate, almost two-thirds of Americans stated that they believed that torture against "*suspected* terrorists" (emphasis added) could be justified in order to gain "important information." Most of those who supported torture said it could only be justified "sometimes," while others said it should be used "rarely" or "often," but only a lonely third believe that it can *never* be justified.[3] Who are we? We are a nation that overwhelmingly supports torture. This is what we want.

This puts me beyond despair. I'd like to think that people don't understand what torture entails, but they've seen it done on TV, they saw the Abu Ghraib photographs, and they've heard about our string of detainee deaths. Maybe they believe that if we only do it "sometimes," it can be contained, but the worst

---

[3] The Pew Research Center for People and the Press, "Opinion Leaders Turn Cautious, Public Looks Homeward," released November 17, 2005; http://people-press.org/reports/display.php3?PageID=1016 (accessed July 20, 2006).

part of seeing this survey is the fact that torture was accepted even for "suspected terrorists," not just for proven terrorists, and not just to obtain lifesaving information, but "important information." The escalation and spread of these techniques is poised to happen. We're accepting some terrifying stuff.

Maybe people can accept torture because they don't know that it's evil? I wish I could believe that. I think we know. Richard Mouw, a Calvinist theologian, thought about why he was horrified by accounts of Americans torturing Afghanis and Iraqis, and discovered that it was not because what he saw was alien and strange: "it is not because I am witnessing an evil that is unfathomable to me. . . ." No, he realized that it was all too familiar, and that's why he was horrified. He saw that same evil, he said, "lurking inside me."[4] That's why he was repelled.

And what if we feel no revulsion, or feel torture is okay "sometimes"? I experienced this, and here is what happens. We see the evil, both outside and inside of us, and we accept it. We accept the evil, and it comes to us whole and fills our being. We accept this evil in us, and then we accept all that it is capable of doing.

---

[4] Quoted in Joyce S. Dubensky and Rachel Lavery, "Torture: An Interreligious Debate," in Karen Greenberg, ed., *The Torture Debate in America* (New York: Cambridge University Press, 2006), p. 164.

December 2006

The news and commentary this month has been all about change. The Democrats regained control of the House and Senate because they promised change; my bête noire, Donald Rumsfeld, resigned immediately after the midterm election; and the much-ballyhooed Iraq Study Group led by James A. Baker III unveiled their recommendations. Meanwhile, in Iraq, very little changed. By most accounts, it just kept getting worse. By the time this book comes out, we will see if our leaders were really ready to change course, or if a change in strategy was really possible.

A lot of people ask me what I think we should do in Iraq, and I have absolutely no idea. There are no options I've seen that will bring about peace, and I can't think of any new ideas myself. We're locked into a terrible set of limited options, and the only thing we can be sure of is that any course we choose will have long-standing implications for the security of the region and the security of the United States. In the short term, of course, the Iraqi people will just continue to suffer. Its hard to see any practical way to prevent that.

For months after I got back, it was too painful to pay any attention to the news. Now, it's slightly easier. The news from Iraq hits me harder because I can conjure up the sounds, the smells, and the voices. When I see an explosion on TV, I can easily remember how it felt to have a shock wave move through me. So I often feel like I'm still there, and I'm so personally invested in the events and the outcome that it's like I'm living in two places at once. And every time I see Iraq on the news, I want to go back, but since I'd never go back with the American occupation, my options are pretty limited. I want to be home, but at the same time I feel exiled from Iraq.

When I learned that over thirty-four hundred Iraqis were violently killed in July 2006, and how that was a 9 percent increase over the number killed in June and twice the number killed in January, I couldn't really fathom the numbers, but I could picture the faces of four hundred or so Iraqis I interrogated, and I wonder how many of them have been killed. Did the professor in Mosul manage to maintain his high profile without pissing off one sect or another? Did the Shia imam and his Sunni wife survive the sectarian bloodletting? Or the big, friendly nicotine addict who played us all for fools: how long did he survive once we let him go?

I think back on these Iraqis, and I sink further into despair. We're trapped, they're trapped, and the killing seems to have no end. The news coming out of Iraq seems to want to prove that the only reasonable response is hopelessness. We can't win, they can't win, and our leaders can't regain the confidence of either the Americans or the Iraqis. We just keep sliding into despair. In an August 2006 press conference, a reporter asked President Bush if he was frustrated. In his typical way, he fumbled through an answer, barely coherent. But I think his conflicting emotions were clear: "Frustrated? Sometimes I'm frustrated. Rarely surprised. Sometimes I'm happy. This is—but war is not a time of joy. These are not joyous times." I can't remember being happy about any news I heard coming out of Iraq since I've been back, but as far as these not being "joyous times," now this was something on which the president and I could agree.

In that same press conference, Bush took a question about strategy, and about whether he was going to keep the one he had. He took a lecturing tone with the reporter: "You know that the Pentagon is constantly adjusting tactics because they have the flexibility from the White House to do so." In that moment, he revealed a lot about the problems we've had over there—bad strategy, or no strategy. This is what we did in Vietnam, according to a special forces officer who'd been there: "When you're facing a counterinsurgency . . . [and] you get the strategy wrong and the tactics right at the start, you can refine the tactics forever and still lose the war."[1] Bush thought he was being helpful in letting the commanders constantly shift tactics, but what we all needed was a workable strategy.

"The strategy is to help the Iraqi people achieve their objectives and their dreams, which is a democratic society. That's the strategy," Bush said later in the same press conference. He was clearly confused about what the reporter (and most people) mean by "strategy." "Help the Iraqi people" is not a strategy.

It's become clear by now that confusion over strategy was our biggest problem in Iraq. We didn't have a clear set of objectives, and so didn't have an overall game plan. Everything we did was tactical and piecemeal, especially in the beginning. When it became clear that we needed intelligence, and that this would best come from human sources, we fell back on the tactic of using force to get it. We rounded Iraqis up by force, very often at random, and interrogators like myself tried to extract intelligence by force, using either Fear Up Harsh or, in my case and many others, varying types of torture. Getting massive quantities of intelligence, rather than getting quality intelligence, became an end in itself. So I interrogated as many prisoners as possible in a sixteen-hour day, instead of focusing on the prisoners we knew were most valuable.

This was totally self-defeating. Not only were our tactics not helpful, they were counterproductive, alienating and angering the very people we always said we were trying to help "achieve their objectives and dreams." What we did was bad for the Iraqis and bad for our troops. Our tactics were incompatible with our objectives.

But looking back, it came so naturally. Heavy-handed tactics in service of a humanitarian goal is absurd, but it is also so very American. It was like we wanted to be both feared *and* loved; to flex our military muscle and have people rush to join the winning team. Isn't that what we, as Americans, would do? Maybe we're wrong in saying that Arabs understand only force. Maybe it's actually we who have that fixation.

---

[1] Colonel Robert Killebrew, quoted in Thomas Ricks, *Fiasco: The American Military Adventure in Iraq* (New York: The Penguin Press, 2006), p. 195.

At the same time, we really want to believe that we're good guys. I certainly did. Back in Mosul, I'd routinely apologize to prisoners I'd abused, threatened, and tortured. They thought I was crazy, and I didn't understand it myself, but maybe I was acting on a very deep American compulsion to try and believe, and to make others believe, that we are incredibly strong, even brutal, and yet at the same time very compassionate and caring.

"It was the way we had over here of living with ourselves," the fictional Captain Willard remarked in *Apocalypse Now.* "We'd cut them in half with a machine gun and give them a Band-Aid." In Baghdad, a *New York Times* reporter talked to an Iraqi man who'd not only been beaten severely by American troops but had been pissed on as well. But when he got to the American-run hospital, he got the best care we could provide. "I'm really confused. At the base, they beat me and tortured me. Here they treat me like a human being."[2] This and other episodes caused *New Yorker* reporter George Packer to observe, I think very astutely, "Americans were both too soft and too hard. Niceness and nastiness seemed to be two conjoined sides of their personality: Love me or I'll kill you."[3]

"What do the Iraqis want?" Chris Matthews barked at me. "Breakfast in bed?" I'd gone on his show, *Hardball*, against the advice of good friends, but he actually gave me fair treatment. Though with this question, I don't think he was being fair to the Iraqis, and I don't think I gave him a good answer.

The Iraqis don't want Americans to solve all their problems for them, but they do want to feel secure in their homes and to not be killed as they go about their days. As hard as we Americans are, as strong and as well equipped, we could never provide basic security for the country we'd invaded. Once we removed the former regime, this was wholly our responsibility—and that responsibility was mine as well.

It's an awful feeling, knowing that there were so many mistakes and missed opportunities, and knowing that I contributed, in a small but significant way, to the utter failure of the American project to reconstruct Iraq.

[2] George Packer, *The Assassins' Gate: America in Iraq* (New York: Farrar, Straus and Giroux, 2005), p. 238.
[3] Ibid.

If stability returns to Iraq, and if a responsible government takes lasting power, it will be because of the efforts of Iraqis. It will have had little to do with our occupation. But if it's up to the Iraqis, I'm actually hopeful. I briefly got to know these people, and I believe they are incredibly strong and resilient. I know they have suffered through much worse, from the sack of Baghdad in 1258 to twenty-two years of rule by Saddam Hussein, and throughout this blood-splattered history, they have kept intact a very strong tribal structure and a very strong family structure. I think of Ghanim, who raised a set of honorable and thoughtful sons in the face of a dictator's terror and an occupation's chaos. As long as some of his family survives, his values will survive. Iraq has enough of these people to save itself, though this will take time.

It will be their own doing. America will not be able to take credit for this country's transformation, when it finally comes. It will be an Iraqi victory, from which we will be largely shut out. Iraq will never forget that America was the nation that toppled Saddam Hussein, but also Iraq will never be able to forgive America for what came next.

ACKNOWLEDGMENTS

Tony Lagouranis:
Of course I want to acknowledge Allen Mikaelian, who had to listen to all my war stories. My agent, Miriam Altshuler, deserves a big thanks for believing in this book from the beginning and being its staunchest advocate. I would also like to thank the people at Penguin and New American Library: first, my editor, Mark Chait, and also Claire Zion, Kara Welsh, and Craig Burke, all of whom voiced their support from our first meeting, and then helped me through the process of publishing a book. My lawyer, Cathryn Crawford, deserves my gratitude as well. I also couldn't publish this without recognizing Eiliesh Tuffy, who helped me through what I hope will be the worst time of my life.

Allen Mikaelian:
It would not be redundant to thank Miriam Altshuler once again for her steadfast support through this and other projects, nor to extend further thanks to the dedicated professionals at Penguin and NAL. Tony deserves my thanks for letting me work with him on this book, and letting me pester him with endless questions. Finally, to my wife, Beth, thanks for everything.